THE
THUNDER
AND THE
SUNSHINE

THE
THUNDER
AND THE
SUNSHINE

FOUR SEASONS IN A BURNISHED LIFE

GARY HART

FULCRUM
GOLDEN, COLORADO

Library of Congress Cataloging-in-Publication Data

Hart, Gary, 1936-

The thunder and the sunshine : four seasons in a burnished life / Gary Hart.

p. cm.

Includes bibliographical references and index.

ISBN 978-1-55591-739-5 (hardcover)

1. Hart, Gary, 1936- 2. Legislators--United States--Biography. 3. United States. Congress. Senate--Biography. 4. United States--Politics and government--1945-1989. 5. United States--Politics and government--1989- I. Title.

E840.8.H285A3 2010

328.73'092--dc22

[B]

2010014919

Printed in the United States of America by Malloy Inc.

0 9 8 7 6 5 4 3 2 1

Design: Jack Lenzo

Cover image: © Kevin Fleming/CORBIS

Fulcrum Publishing

4690 Table Mountain Drive, Suite 100

Golden, Colorado 80403

800-992-2908 • 303-277-1623

www.fulcrumbooks.com

For
Andrea Hart
and
John Hart

No great cause is ever lost or ever won. The battle must always be renewed and the creed restated, and the old formulas, once so potent a revelation, become only dim antiquarian echoes. But some things are universal, catholic, and undying—the souls of which such formulas are the broken gleams. These do not age or pass out of fashion, for they symbolize eternal things. They are the guardians of the freedom of the human spirit, the proof of what our mortal frailty can achieve.

— John Buchan, *Montrose: A History*

CONTENTS

PREFACE

Every life requires some kind of accounting. For those who are religious, there is an accounting to the Almighty. For the public servant, there is an accounting to the electorate and, to a greater or lesser degree, to history. In a way, we all owe an accounting of sorts to our children and future generations for what we have, or have not, left them.

Not everyone is required to produce a memoir. But we all have reminiscences and in some cases have learned lessons from the experiences those reminiscences represent. It is impossible to know whether one's own experiences are ever useful under future circumstances.

But few rewards in life exceed that of having encouraged idealism in others, and perhaps even stories of failure might encourage others to continue to try.

Certain things make some lives more extraordinary than others. Much depends upon the distance traveled between where one started and where one ended up. Though they shared many experiences, Harry Truman's life was more extraordinary than, say, Averell Harriman's or Dean Acheson's. By the same measure, Barack Obama's life is certainly more extraordinary than George W. Bush's.

Using the same scale, I have been privileged to see and do many things that many others have not. Though those privileges were never to include the presidency, nonetheless many of my experiences are rare enough to provide interest, and possibly even some guidance, to those who follow and are yet to lead.

I bracket my stories with an exploration of Alfred Lord Tennyson's poem "Ulysses." I do so because I identify with the poem's sentiments, not because I identify with the classical hero Ulysses. Age does bring reflection, a sense of things done as well as a sense of what remains to be done. And it is the latter that interested Tennyson. *The Odyssey*, Homer's story of everyone's search for home, ends with Odysseus/ Ulysses finally returning home. But then what happened?

Years passed and little happened. For most, home is more than enough. For some, there are still discoveries to be made, lessons to be learned, horizons to be sought, new ideas to be thought.

We all live history. Only a few—the historians—record it. They are trained to do so and recognized according to their various skills. But there are no permits required to write one's own history or one's observations regarding what one has seen and learned. I have observed, and in many cases experienced, much during the past four decades. A great deal of what I have seen is shared by many of my generation. Some experiences have been shared by only a few. And in a small number of cases, I alone know exactly what happened.

History ultimately is its own judge. Only history will determine whether this one man's recollections are worth noting or remembering. In the end, one does not record for history; one records for oneself. The only thing unique about this history is that only I could have recorded it.

The stoic says that very little matters, and the cynic responds that nothing matters very much. But some things do matter, and some stories deserve to be told.

ACKNOWLEDGMENTS

For a voyager on the turbulent political seas to acknowledge the family that both accompanied and intimately observed that voyage is perilous. That acknowledgment must avoid the Scylla of convention and the Charybdis of sentiment, greatly devalued currencies in today's world. We are all, to a greater or lesser degree, Ulysses in this world. But very few Ulysses have for their beloved companions Lee, Andrea, and John Hart. This voyager offered a complex and occasionally mysterious figure to his family. But its members never waivered, never complained, and always encouraged the search for knowledge and that newer world. By comparison, the estimable Penelope was fainthearted, for Lee stood steadfast near the prow of this ship through rough seas. The remaining journey toward that newer world could not and would not be made without them.

The Fulcrum Publishing house, represented by Robert Baron and Sam Scinta, offered a vessel to an aging voyager when others might not have. It is hoped that they, and the scrupulously professional editor Faith Marcovecchio, embody the future of publishing in the United States, for they are the best.

INTRODUCTION
AN ARCH WHERETHRO' GLEAMS THAT
UNTRAVELL'D WORLD...

We come upon our aging warrior-king—his hearth cold, his queen Penelope now old—sitting idle among barren rocks, administering justice to a barbaric people who can think of nothing more than to eat and sleep and accumulate the gadgets of the day and who cannot take the trouble to understand their monarch, a leader with experiences more spectacular than their wildest dreams can hope to encompass.

For this is no ordinary king. This warrior's story has given a name to every life journey from the most mundane to the most exotic. His life has, indeed, been an odyssey of almost unimaginable danger and delight, a master legend that would be used for ages to come as the enduring metaphor for human existence. And now he has been home for unknown years.

But home offers no appreciation for that which he has seen and known. His mind and memory are now a prison of that startling journey of his younger years, whose account those around him now find tedious. The scope and magnitude of the events that he has witnessed and that he has brought upon himself and others are beyond the comprehension of his family and his people. Some, in fact, secretly whisper that the monsters and seducers, the demons and the gods of his many tales, may have existed only in the aged adventurer's imagination.

We cannot help but wonder how Ulysses thought about home during that long odyssey. Was it always in the back of his mind? Or did he occasionally permit himself to think of never returning? The theme of return, even of resurrection, is powerful above all others. "Breathes there a man with soul so dead, Who never to himself hath said, 'This is my own, my native land!'"[1]

Robert Frost said that home is the place where, when you go there, they have to take you in.[2] With Calypso and the Lotus Eaters, Ulysses had some Dionysian times. But mostly, he had been a man on the run. And we never doubt that, somehow, like his fellow warrior Menelaus, "our man will make it home."

The fact that *The Odyssey* is epic and its hero iconic does not elevate them above the understanding of ordinary human beings. The reality is just the reverse. We may not be kings. We may not have fought in great battles. But we all see our lives through the prism of struggle, of surprises and detours, of more defeats than victories. We do not have to be Odysseus to consider our lives an odyssey of one dimension or another and an endeavor to find home.

We all seek to be known, but kings especially so. Those among whom our adventurer now lives, so focused on the routine of life, do not know him. To be known for some is perhaps to be loved, or feared, or even in some cases to be hated. But this warrior thinks that to be known is to be honored for what he has done and for who he is. To struggle to find home—sometimes not too relentlessly—against odds few others ever experience is a story for the ages. Yet now, years gone by, no one cares. No one knows him.

He is Odysseus. He is Ulysses. There is no other hero like him, at least none who has the immortal Homer as his chronicler. And to have a timeless biographer, a singer of one's life, is a guarantee of immortality. But age and boredom now surround and perplex him. He is restless and eager to be off again—somewhere—to rejoin those who do know him and share his wanderlust. "I cannot rest from travel."[3] There will be all eternity for resting.

Having seen a world that few can even imagine, his little kingdom of Ithaca has become too small. Indeed, it is small.

A modest island off the mainland of western Greece, it has boundaries and limits. Boundaries are meant to make us secure. This is mine; this I possess; this is where I live. But that is for everyday people, not heroes. And certainly not an epic adventurer who has seen more and larger and more mystifying worlds than all of Ithaca can begin to dream.

Despite the countless dangers and setbacks of his odyssey long ago, Ulysses has no choice but to resume the voyage.

PART I

SAILING INTO A REVOLUTION: AN ODYSSEY BEGINS (1968–1972)

Through the lens of traditional politics, the presidential campaign of George McGovern in 1972 was a disaster. In the social context of its time, though, that campaign was much more complex, and thus more interesting and important, than conventional political wisdom would suggest. To one who set sail from political youth on to a degree of political maturity through that period, the context, rather than the outcome, offered considerable instruction.

Unsuccessful political campaigns, like unsuccessful Broadway shows, business ventures, or advertising campaigns, are of importance only if they prove a point or teach a lesson. More often than not, any point or lesson is inseparable from the context, the times, in which a campaign takes place. There must have been something different about the unsuccessful McGovern campaign, or why else would Hunter S. Thompson have written such a colorful, and successful, book about it?

Let's consider the reasons. First of all, Richard Nixon was there in the villain's role. Not all presidential actors are so lucky. Then there was the suspense of a potential Act Two in the form of the Chicago convention, with riots, tear gas, and blood in the streets. The Democratic Party was tearing itself apart over the Vietnam War, civil rights, a feminist uprising, and urban riots, and its New Deal and Great Society programs were running out of steam. Most of all, though, the McGovern campaign rose out of a revolutionary time and, in almost every way, mirrored that time.

Despite their qualities as national candidates, it is impossible to imagine *Fear and Loathing on the Campaign Trail* being written about the Mondale, Dukakis, or Kerry campaigns, or even any of the winning Republican campaigns. Losing Democratic campaigns in any case are almost always more interesting than winning Republican ones. And despite the Bubba and Elvis aspects of the first Clinton campaign, it is difficult to find great drama in triangulation and centrism. Playing the saxophone on late-night television doesn't hold a candle to a candidate, McGovern, who said to his colleagues on the floor of the Senate, "This chamber reeks of blood."

An examination of the times is required to discover whether Hunter Thompson was on to something other than a wacky political tale, and to establish the fact that McGovern discovered Thompson—that is, provided him a ringside seat to a revolution—not the other way around. With all revolutions, the closer you come to their center, the less you understand what is really going on. The cultural and political revolutions of the 1960s were no different. You had to be there to understand them, but if you were there, and particularly anywhere near their center, the harder they were to understand. These revolutions were, on the one hand, less catastrophic than their many culturally conservative critics—those who viewed their turmoil with horror—claimed. But, on the other hand, they changed the direction of America, socially perhaps more than politically, in dramatic and permanent ways.

On the surface there was flower power, vivid experimentation, and erosion of traditional norms—sex, drugs, and rock and roll, as it was more vividly described. Beneath the Happy Days society, tense social tectonic plates, under great pressure, suddenly broke free. Women rose up to insist on dignity, respect, and equality. The demand for equal and full civil rights for African Americans moved center stage. Artificial taboos succumbed to ridicule. Political and military authority was challenged. Divorce rates soared. And presidents were laid low.

Of lotus eaters and assassins in every form, there were many.

One supposes that the Achaeans, returning after a decade spent before the walls of Troy, found a different world at home. This would be even more true of Ulysses, who would add another decade and more of sea-tossed wandering.

Vietnam was our Troy, at least in the metaphoric sense, though it is doubtful Pentagon planners ever conceived of the Trojan horse offense. Ironically, the Vietnamese Trojan horse was moving north to south. Half a million troops went a distance relatively comparable to the distance the Greeks traveled to meet the Trojans in the known world of their time, and half the nation, metaphorically, went with them. The other half of the nation not only did not go with them, it actively opposed them. Over fifty-eight thousand troops never returned alive. And of the hundreds of American prisoners of war, one would return to seek the presidency thirty years later. John McCain would be, in both real and symbolic ways, the last veteran of the war that tore America apart.[4]

It has been argued, with a degree of plausibility, that the broader domestic revolutions grew out of the Vietnam War, that the many fractures that occurred throughout society were the product of the one great national fracture over that conflict. But these many social fractures, these tectonic plates, were waiting to crash into one another, fueled by the heat and pressure underlying them, in any case and merely required a match to the fuse that underlay them. Once in the streets to oppose a war, why not oppose social constraints, gender repression, the casual industrial poisoning of the air and water, moralistic hypocrisy, and a host of other decrepit ghosts from the 1950s?

A revolution may start for one reason but then sweep up a host of other causes in its path. And then the revolutionary beast becomes unrecognizable, even to those who gave it birth.

There is little profit in rehearsing, yet again, "The Sixties." The histories of the era are voluminous, repetitive, and quaintly nostalgic to a modern generation that views the whole period as some kind of stoned comic opera or bell-bottom horror show, *Hair* on stilts. It is sufficient to note that, twenty years after the McGovern campaign, presidential candidates, including most notably one who worked on that campaign, would be required to confess whether they actually inhaled, whereas sixteen years after that, another successful presidential candidate would, with aplomb, say about inhaling: "That was the point."

The McGovern candidacy was an exercise in almost total implausibility. George McGovern was from a very small, conservative, upper midwestern state, South Dakota, that had produced few if any previous statesmen, let alone presidential candidates. He was, by profession, a university professor with a doctorate in history. His thesis had to do with the Ludlow Massacre of April 1914, which occurred when union-busting Colorado national guardsmen, sent into battle by a governor, Elias Ammons, owned by the Rockefeller mining interests, gunned down miners and their families on the theory that this would encourage the others to return to work, a theory of tyrants throughout the ages.

Though he, along with all but two of his Senate colleagues, had voted for the Gulf of Tonkin Resolution, authorizing President Lyndon Johnson to do pretty much whatever he wanted to do in Vietnam (the prototype of the Iraq war resolution roughly four decades later), McGovern soon saw the folly of the enterprise and understood earlier than most that the commander in chief may have had other cards up his sleeve. In the later Iraq project, that card became a deck dealt from the bottom by the vice president.

More important, for national visibility McGovern had been invited to stand in at the 1968 Democratic convention for the recently assassinated Robert Kennedy, and, when nominated by his courageous colleague Abraham Ribicoff in a finger-shaking speech aimed at Mayor Richard Daley and the Chicago police who patrolled the streets outside with mace and clubs, overnight George McGovern became a name, at least in antiwar, liberal Democratic circles.

The seeds of national ambition were sown, or possibly having already been sown, merely began to sprout. When I asked him a couple of years thereafter what persuaded him to run for president, McGovern said, "I knew all the others who were running, and I said to myself, If *they* can be president, *I* can be president." Curiously enough, this same theme would be repeated to me only four years later by then governor Jimmy Carter. Proximity to ambition has the effect of inspiring ambition.

The myth that Fate reaches out, and sometimes down, to touch a mere mortal with the wand that makes him or her presidential is no more than that. Ambition is self-generating, if not also somewhat genetic, and it touches even the most ordinary of people. Great ambition is no different. What makes the spark combust is acquaintance with others sharing the genetic strain. They eat and breathe and behave pretty much as I do, and, surprise, they are not nearly as clever as I am. If they can do it, I can do it.

Even if it does not breed contempt, familiarity does diminish awe.

Still, with only marginal name recognition, very little money, low standing in the opinion polls, and no Establishment support, a McGovern candidacy was, to say the least, a chancy vehicle to get to the White House or even to impact national policy. For a young Denver lawyer emotionally gutted by assassinations that seemed to represent some monstrously perverse plot to rid America of any semblance of idealism, it was nevertheless an odyssey worth taking. However remote winning, in the traditional political sense, might be, this venture contained its own rewards of purpose, nobility, and a small gesture toward national redemption. The effort justified itself.

But it was not a choice easily made. A divinity student in transit to law school handing out leaflets on New Haven street corners would see John Kennedy speak on the town green the Sunday morning before the 1960 election, and three years later would spend a summer and then a year working for Robert Kennedy at the Department of Justice, and five years after that would help organize Colorado for him, and then would hear, for the rest of his life, the raspy but hushed voice on the bedside clock radio early that June morning say that Robert Kennedy had died from the assassin's bullet. Under the circumstances of all that had gone before, if that voice did not break your heart, then nothing would.

In part what made the McGovern odyssey attractive enough to pursue was the extreme remoteness of the chance, at least at the beginning, that he would be the assassin's target. Stalking remaining Kennedy brothers seemed to have become a national pastime. But who would want to shoot a harmless South Dakota history professor?

The day-to-day details of the McGovern campaign, much of it tedious in rendition, would be set down elsewhere in sufficient detail that a successful presidential candidate from Georgia would reportedly use it as a campaign guidebook.[5] But the political education the McGovern campaign experience provided was beyond compare.

There would be very small living rooms in icy Iowa, not much larger town meetings in New Hampshire, and eventually huge outdoor rallies in California. There would be campaign train trips through the San Joachin Valley, propositions to ride on Hunter S. Thompson's giant Vincent Black Shadow motorcycle (pictured in *Fear and Loathing on the Campaign*

Trail, as was this hirsute odyssean), a turbulent national convention made even more turbulent by Nixonian machinations, a bizarre political train wreck involving a vice presidential running mate, and drama enough for most lifetimes.[6]

Presidential candidates came and went during a five-month nomination process that gyrated and ricocheted around the nation and seemed to be without end. The nominal front-runner, Senator Edmund Muskie, would be among the first to go. But before him, Senator Harold Hughes of Iowa, Senator Birch Bayh of Indiana, and an earlier candidate, Senator Fred Harris of Oklahoma, would enter and leave. Senator Henry "Scoop" Jackson campaigned for a period. And finally, and perhaps most notably, former vice president Hubert Humphrey entered the scene as the last in a series of "stop McGovern" candidates. All this was implausible on several levels. How had a seemingly harmless history professor from South Dakota, given little attention and virtually no respect by Establishment Washington, suddenly become the nemesis of the Democratic Party and a kind of virus threatening American democracy itself? And how could Humphrey, the archliberal of the day, attack McGovern, his longtime friend and neighbor, as being too far to the left? Much of this remains mysterious decades later and can be accounted for only by the twin expediencies of ambition and power, which always manage to trump principle and belief, not to say also friendship and loyalty.

Oddly enough, to prove that history does repeat itself, I would have an almost identical experience twelve years later as a national candidate.

Opprobrium, of which there was an excess during this era, would not be confined to the candidate alone. Joseph Alsop, a noted Washington columnist and centerpiece of all fashionable salons of the day, wrote that the nominal McGovern campaign manager, myself, was the "Baldur von Schirach of America." Being even weaker on history then than now,

I turned to a colleague, Rick Stearns, Rhodes scholar and now eminent federal judge, for interpretation. "Baldur von Schirach," he said with a wry smile, "organized the Hitler Youth." One senses the temper of the times when McGovern was Trotsky to Humphrey and Hitler to Alsop.

Figures of awe emerged from the past. Frank Mankiewicz, of renowned Hollywood lineage, the whispering voice on that June radio announcement only four years before, came on board to add weight, reputation, credentials, and humor, most of all humor, to a beleaguered campaign. And before him the legendary Pierre Salinger, likewise press secretary, in his case to President Kennedy. For a grassroots Kennedy follower, these were historic figures who made one feel amateurish by comparison. Likewise, before the kind of political breakthroughs that attract celebrities, the sister and brother combination of Shirley MacLaine and Warren Beatty arrived early and stayed throughout. Like Pierre, Shirley crisscrossed the villages and hamlets of New Hampshire, and Warren invented the political concert as fund-raiser.[7]

The Democratic National Convention in Miami in 1972 was characterized then and thereafter as a circus of sorts, featuring a kaleidoscope of races, genders, ages, hats and banners, endless vice-presidential nominations from the floor, first-time Democrats, a flamboyant speech by the young San Francisco state assemblyman Willie Brown, the Reverend Jesse Jackson, feminists Gloria Steinem and Bella Abzug, and a ragtag band of hundreds of "volunteers" occupying the Doral Hotel lobby late at night or the upstairs ballroom early in the morning, demanding assurances that McGovern had not abandoned his liberal instincts or credentials.[8]

This latter crowd, the Watergate exposés would later reveal, was the product of the organizational genius of the eponymous Donald Segretti, whose members agreed, for a little cash and all the dope they could smoke, to bedevil McGovern and those around him throughout convention week.[9] It is difficult to find political organizers as imaginative as Segretti anymore, especially if they have a reluctance to serve hard time.

But in the process of saving the party from self-destruction, experience was gained and lessons learned. The twists and turns of reformed party rules produced parliamentary situations at the Miami convention of such complexity that no more than four, and possibly fewer, people would comprehend.[10]

Of lessons, however, sorting through this maze produced its share. One drama in a side arena involved efforts to negotiate resolution of a conflict between two Illinois delegations, one headed by reformers Jesse Jackson and the young Chicago alderman Billy Singer, and the other headed by the original Mayor Richard Daley. I proposed a deal that would seat both delegations with half votes each; it was accepted, reluctantly, by the reformers who had followed the rules, but it was then rejected by the Daley party regulars. This same formula was briefly adopted for the Florida Democratic delegation in 2008, but later came not to be needed. If there was a Mr. Democrat in America, it was the original Mayor Daley, and by his own choice he would not be participating in this national convention. The omens for the fall were not good. But the real lesson from this experience would come twelve years later when, as a presidential candidate myself, I would seek the support of Daley's heirs.

In a somewhat larger ring, I found myself shuttling up and down Miami Beach in the hours before and after the convention began, meeting with a group of Democratic governors led by Marvin Mandel of Maryland and with various senators, including Abraham Ribicoff and Frank Church, and congressional leaders trying to resolve a host of delegation credential conflicts. What should be done with elected officials and party leaders who had refused to comply with the new delegate selection rules and therefore were barred from convention participation, yet who had been at every party convention since William Jennings Bryan was the nominee, and whose help and support would be needed in the coming general election? It was in each case a struggle between principle and pragmatism. Frank Mankiewicz and I bore most of this burden, Frank much more adroitly than I, and only rarely were we able to cobble together a resolution that permitted the party dignitaries to obtain credentials without driving angry reformers into the streets in protest.

The lessons learned from these intricate negotiations by a young Denver lawyer would serve him well in the halls of the Senate two short years later. Though, as will be surveyed further along in the odyssey, this would be complicated by the fact that many important party figures, who no doubt shared Alsop's assessment, were among those upon whom the convention doors would be closed and who would soon find themselves serving in the Senate with that same Baldur von Schirach.

Even a brief account of this convention period, and effort to mine it for meaning, must acknowledge the horrendous difficulties created by the launching of a campaign ticket on which one of the members, the late Senator Tom Eagleton, would not survive two weeks. As with any complicated human situation, there are as many versions of what did, and did not, happen in the vice-presidential fiasco as there were participants. Within hours after Eagleton's selection by McGovern, an anonymous informant left word at campaign headquarters in Washington that the vice-presidential candidate had been treated with shock therapy for depression on at least two occasions, both following his own election campaigns.

In this somewhat more enlightened era, this would be a matter for consideration, concern, and discussion. Then, during a Cold War whose most vivid image was a "finger on the button" of nuclear launch, the idea of a potential commander in chief with recurring depression, not to say a history of shock therapy, created political tidal waves of serious dimension.

It has never been ruled out, or in, that the Committee to Re-elect the President (CREEP) was behind the anonymous calls to the McGovern campaign regarding Eagleton, though the FBI spent considerable time denying it had any involvement. Given the dirty tricks of that time, virtually anything is possible.

After confirming his support for Eagleton, McGovern was forced by the ensuing controversy to backtrack and ask Eagleton to step aside. A new, underdog presidential campaign led by a controversial figure of a divided party had taken a large torpedo amidships before it got out of the harbor. From a purely practical political standpoint, thereafter there was no hope—except, perhaps, for a miracle in the form of the lid coming off the Watergate sewer. And that was not to be, at least in any manner timely enough to benefit McGovern.

It would have required the smile of Fortune beyond wild dreams to have unseated an incumbent president in wartime, especially when that president was promising—eventually—to win the war "with honor." Not only would McGovern not receive any lucky breaks, he would suffer endless setbacks from his own colleagues and party and, occasionally, his own campaign. He deserved better. But, a cynic might say, Don't we all?

Campaigns are always judged on the standard of success and failure, winning or losing. All well and good. They may have value otherwise, however, value such as elevation of the national dialogue, expansion of the political process, and attraction of new participants. On these counts, the failed 1972 McGovern campaign did not fail.

The Democratic Party came closer to schism if not total self-destruction in 1968 and thereafter than is usually understood. The chaotic Chicago convention was the tip of a very jagged iceberg. So many movements—the already mentioned tectonic plates—were at work on many different levels. The civil rights pot, simmering for a century, was on the boil. In Newark, Detroit, and other cities, whole neighborhoods and communities were ablaze, both figuratively and literally. Women had had enough of housekeeping as the only life option and of second-class political and economic citizenship. An exposed sewer called Love Canal later became a metaphor for a century of casual industrial poisonings, and environmental consciousness, focused on sickened children, was forming a movement. Most visibly, a war in Southeast Asia, premised on a deeply flawed domino theory, was going nowhere but down, casualties were in the tens of thousands, and the cost of guns was coming out of butter for family tables across the nation.

At the 1968 Chicago convention, the Democratic Party, with only token exception (most notably a young state legislator from Georgia named Julian Bond) looked white, male, upper middle class, older, and supportive of a war president...and vice president. To outsiders, this array resembled a Democratic politburo on a large scale. But one thing must be said for career politicians: either they are sensitive to political earthquakes, or they no longer have careers. To the delegates leaving Chicago, an earthquake of considerable dimension was taking place and attention had to be paid. After the election defeat that fall, attention was paid in the form of a commission created by the Democratic Party to reform the process by which delegates to the next national convention, four years hence, would be selected.

This commission, chaired by none other than the party's future nominee, George McGovern, was composed of activists and senior party figures, including Hubert Humphrey, astute enough to know that the political process had to be democratized or one of two things would happen: either the next convention would make the struggle between the

Trotskyites and the Leninists look mild, or there would be several Democratic parties as an outcome.

Reforms were adopted, and they required that future convention delegations more accurately reflect gender, generation, and racial proportions in the society, that there be more openness in party functions and processes, and that dissent be represented. Democratization of the Democratic Party was not without resistance, particularly from those whose traditional power was sacrificed in the process. As a result, the liberal party of Franklin Roosevelt became divided between a party of the conservative Democrats who still worshipped Roosevelt and were in reaction against reform, and a younger party of antiwar, feminist, civil rights, and environmental crusaders opposed to an unacceptable status quo. This division had precedent in both political parties when tradition encountered change, generations clashed, and forks were reached in ideological paths.

One of the truths to be extracted from this experience was that liberalism is not immune to reaction. When experimental methods in addressing social ills themselves become the object of worship, efforts to replace them with newer methods more appropriate for a newer age are resisted as heresy. Liberalism had become a cathedral in which old-time orthodox liberals worshipped. Its architect and archbishop, the pragmatic Franklin Roosevelt, would have been appalled and would himself have refused to worship there.

These two Democratic parties, orthodox and new age, met in Miami in 1972, with the new party in ascendance for the obvious reason that, in caucuses and primaries, activist outsiders turn out and inactive insiders do not. Open processes favor the motivated. And cause is more a motivation than tradition, at least for those who sense rising tides of change.

The "radicals" perceived by press and public in Miami contained some notable personalities. Most notable, of course, was a bushy haired law student named Bill Clinton tasked with

17

corralling southern delegates. His Rhodes scholar classmate responsible for recruiting him, Rick Stearns, then a walking encyclopedia of delegate selection procedures, rules, and calendars, would become a prominent, and notably conservative, federal judge. A small-town Nebraska prairie populist, Gene Pokorny, would become a legendary political organizer for future generations. An unknown Alabama lawyer and businessman called Morris Dees, who had made his first of several fortunes selling birthday cakes and padded tractor seats to Alabama college students, brilliantly raised funds through direct mail (this being well before the Internet) for an impoverished campaign, and then went on to found the Southern Poverty Law Center and single-handedly broke the back of the Ku Klux Klan. The campaign finance chair, the late Henry Kimelman, later became a successful ambassador. Of equal importance, out of the rank and file of campaign workers and delegates came two generations of future national officeholders, state and local elected and appointed officials, party officers, and distinguished citizens.

Young veterans of the much derided McGovern campaign became the backbone, and a responsible one at that, of the Democratic Party for the next two or three decades. Scarcely a week would pass thereafter that the former campaign manager would not pass an airline passenger, state legislator, or city mayor who did not say, "I worked with you in the McGovern campaign."

Forgotten in the political sport of winning and losing are those who play the game and play it so well they make it better. There should be a hall of fame of sorts for the very good players, republican citizens concerned enough to do their duty and do it very well, as well as for the stars.

Thus, a convention marked by its perceived chaos, subject to the unsolicited attentions of Nixonian operatives, and producing its own stars and citizen leaders achieved a notable, possibly its most significant, purpose. It kept the Democratic

Party together. It did not break into two, or several, political parties. Prostitutes in boats, thanks to the White House, there may have been, but there would be no riots in the streets. (See endnote 9.) For this, McGovern, in his mode as party reformer more than as presidential candidate, deserves the credit, credit generally not accorded in the wake of his defeat.

Attention will be paid throughout these reminiscences to the nature of defeat and victory in politics and in life. But in politics, at least, ultimate defeat should not overshadow successes along the way, and particularly successes that effect long-term outcomes. A Democratic Party of the late 1960s that did not reform itself, that did not open itself up to all those who would enter in regardless of gender, age, race, or opinions on divisive issues, would not today exist. That is what it did, with George McGovern's help, and today it is healthier and stronger for it. The man deserves some credit. Some presidential candidates come and go and leave little to remember. In addition to helping end the war in Vietnam and continuing to be the conscience of the nation on hunger at home and abroad, George McGovern, it can and should be argued, helped save the Democratic Party. How many others, including victims of less opprobrium, have that for their legacy?[11]

This voyage through this land of the lotus eaters offered much by way of instruction. From McGovern's point of view, he would have benefited greatly from having a seasoned political professional managing things, one with resources in wisdom and experience, not to say money, much greater than those of the one whom he had. One can only imagine how it might have helped to pull off the magic trick of maneuvering to the nomination without antagonizing a host of fellow candidates and party leaders. Of antagonisms, there were bushels. The trifecta awaited a candidate who could commit to ending the war in Vietnam without becoming vulnerable to the charge of being antimilitary, antidefense, and antisecurity. On this score, it all came tumbling down.

A decorated World War II B-29 bomber pilot with over two dozen combat missions in Europe, McGovern was one of those veterans who came to hate warfare and all its works. This is true of quite a number of veterans of combat, but less true of those who fought their wars, if at all, from the rear echelons. McGovern came early to oppose the Vietnam project, and his opposition grew as casualties rose, stakes were raised, and the supply of leadership candor diminished, then disappeared. During this period and beyond, too many Democrats, and a few Republicans, took out their anger at the Johnson, then Nixon, administrations by opposing new weapons systems and routine appropriations for military operations. The steps between being anti-Vietnam and anti-military shortened, and they shortened even further when senior military commanders testified to what the White House wanted them to say instead of to the truth (another precursor of Iraq), and permitted themselves and their services to become political chess pieces.

So the former combat bomber pilot lost to the former naval lieutenant who had not seen a shot fired in anger while perfecting his poker skills in the rear echelons. This pattern would repeat itself yet again in 2004 in the contest between a genuine warrior, John Kerry, and a nonwarrior, George W. Bush. In both cases the American voters permitted themselves to be mocked by candidates claiming to be stronger on defense than those who had risked their lives in combat in genuine defense of the nation. And this situation can confidently be predicted to continue in American politics so long as voters concerned for security permit themselves to accept catchall slogans instead of real understanding of the nature of conflict and warfare and when force should, and should not, be used.

The imbalance in the defense equation was exacerbated by the exhaustion of liberal economics. With the New Deal and thereafter, Democrats were associated with economic stimulation and economic justice, or fairer wealth distribution. This was so because of redistributionist tax polices over the years, but also because of the construction of the social safety net composed of Social Security and Medicare, and eventually Medicaid. To this had been added, during the Great Society era, housing, employment, community development, and nutrition programs, that is until this "butter" melted during the stagnant economic period of the late sixties and became hardened into guns in Vietnam.

In a word, the era of the New Deal had run its course. Within less than two decades it would give way to the age of Reagan (bracketed by Nixon and the Bushes). This cycle of American history, from liberal and reform era to conservative and consolidation era, might have occurred regardless. But any chance that it might have been slowed in the early 1970s was lost in the vacuum in liberal economics. The post–World War II growth, stimulated by the GI Bill, mortgage insurance, and industrial conversion to consumer production, was ending. Middle-class incomes were stagnant, and opportunity was confined. Moreover, taxes to pay for the social safety net and income redistribution programs continued to grow.

This odyssean has always believed, contrary to conservative dogma, that Americans (and most human beings) are to greater or lesser degrees charitable on a national, not merely individual, level. They don't like to see fellow citizens, human beings, left behind. Further, they had come to like the fact that grandparents were no longer living in their children's homes. But in the 1970s they wanted policies to stimulate continued growth and opportunity, and the Democrats had few, if any. Additionally, African Americans were increasingly competing for low-wage jobs, and women began to enter the workforce to make ends meet. Economics could not be separated from social and cultural revolutions.

The McGovern campaign, responsible now for representing the promise of the Democratic Party, had too little to suggest. The notable exception, a universal grant of $1,000 per person as a step toward welfare reform, was widely ridiculed as another liberal giveaway, "throwing money at the problem," particularly by those who, years later, would embrace the idea or one of several variations on it. Apart from this, new economic ideas were scarce. And they were not to be found in the mind of a young Denver lawyer who had been led to believe, or had led himself to believe, that somewhere in the upper reaches of the liberal academy great minds were preparing a grand second New Deal. If they were, they were doing so in hiding.

After the dust settled, in 1973 I wrote this:

> It was apparent throughout the campaign that the fount of specific proposals and programs was running dry. The traditional sources of invigorating, inspiring, and creative ideas were dissipated. The best thinkers of the 1930s, 40s, and 50s and even the 1960s were not producing. Whether this resulted from age, depression, frustration at the nation's ponderous rate of progress, or lassitude, the results were crystal clear: by 1972, American liberalism was near bankruptcy.[12]

As much as his perceived "weakness on defense," McGovern suffered from not being Roosevelt at a time requiring economic stimulation, and this failure resulted from not having a seventies version of Roosevelt's kitchen cabinet brimming with tools to create economic growth.

The primary lesson for a young, unseasoned odyssean in all this was forecast in the same campaign account: "New ideas must be found to solve old [economic and social] problems and those ideas must be related to ordinary working men and women."[13] An age of economic experimentation was required, experimentation taking account of and seeking to capitalize on an emerging set of new realities.

A few years later, in 1986, the historian Arthur Schlesinger Jr., borrowing a thesis from his historian father, wrote *The Cycles of American History*, in which he argued that our nation progressed through roughly thirty-year cycles of reform and progress followed by cycles of equal length of consolidation and conservatism. Based on that thesis, the reform age of Roosevelt begun in 1932 would have run its course in the 1960s. Lyndon Johnson's efforts to quell urban unrest through Great Society government activism maintained the cycle until it ran aground on the shoals of Vietnam.

Thus, McGovern inherited a party that had exhausted both its mandate and its intellectual energy and was drifting badly. That drift was exacerbated by cultural and social upheaval on many levels. Nixon offered "law and order," rejection of big government, and "peace with honor." In response, the Democratic Party establishment clung to the Vietnam War as a continuation of the struggle against communism, promised more New Deal programs, and sang "Happy Days Are Here Again." With little to construct a post–New Deal economic agenda, McGovern was left with his Vietnam opposition as a basis for his candidacy.

But a current even deeper than the closing of the New Deal was running. It had to do with the willingness of Americans to suspend our principles under the guidance of leaders who create conditions of fear. Looking back over more than three decades, the disparity between "Watergate," the catchall term used to encompass a massive cobweb of Nixonian paranoia, and even the most inflated dangers of the brief social turbulence in which the McGovern candidacy played only a small part, is striking and impossible to explain to later generations.

How could massive patterns of government wiretapping, mail opening, and citizen surveillance, carried out under an FBI umbrella code-program called COINTELPRO (for Counterintelligence Program), have been justified as a response to student protests, civil rights demonstrations, and anti-war activism, all specifically protected by the United States Constitution? How could break-ins at the Democratic Party headquarters and a psychiatrist's office have contributed to the defense of the republic in any meaningful way? Why send federal agents around to the humble apartment of the McGovern campaign manager, a harmless young lawyer from Denver, to collect what? Evidence of his disloyalty, simply because he worked for an opposition party candidate? What kind of twisted mentality could connive and scheme to such a demented extent, especially when that mentality belonged to the president of the United States?

Stuff happens, would be a latter-day dismissal of an invasion gone awry. And if one finds that response to be acceptable accounting for mismanagement on an international scale, then it surely works for subversion of the Constitution in home waters. Others find it less than reassuring, particularly when the same pattern reemerges three decades later. What extraconstitutional excesses the threat of communism would justify in one era, the global war on terrorism would be used to justify in another.

To pass through an extraordinary period of extraconstitutional government is one thing. To see it repeated with so little resistance relatively few years later, by many of the same people, now older, is troubling in the extreme. Is there a pattern here? Is simple fear the instrument? If so, primitive intelligence alone would tell a mendacious or megalomaniac president or presidential coterie to scare the hell out of American citizens, and they'll give you whatever powers you want. Surely we are better than this. If not, then George Orwell has written the most persuasive scenario.

For the understanding of democratic government, more important than deranged or misguided presidents is the study of those who either follow or misguide them. How could dozens of men (and they were men) in high places, and hundreds if not thousands of others who would obey them, carry out Richard Nixon's orders, which they knew to fall somewhere between ludicrous and demented, without a nay being uttered? Indeed, endless White House tape recordings reveal that high-level presidential staff members, a number of whom ultimately became convicted felons, actively encouraged this mad King Lear behavior. But so did figures such as Henry Kissinger, who would go on to positions of distinction, renown, respect, and esteem (not also to say great wealth) and be applauded in the courts and salons of official Washington for his cleverness in having adroitly escaped the attention of the prosecutor and the clutches of the warden. What lessons are offered here for students of our democracy at home and abroad?

What lessons particularly are offered for wayward nations such as Iraq that capture the attention of an American administration seeking to bring "democracy" to its culture and that watch more carefully than most Americans can imagine how we manage our political affairs? Let's see: the Americans are bringing democracy to us by wiretapping their citizens, suspending the writ of habeas corpus, fudging intelligence reports, crushing their critics, ridiculing their opponents, and scaring their people at every turn. This is their gift to us?

As if to prove that the American attention span and recollection of the lessons of history last no longer than a generation, a perverse reversal of the Nixon equation would occur thirty years later with a compliant president being consciously and willfully misled by a vice president, cabinet officers, and key advisors who were economical with both truth and constitutional principles. Whether the president involved is either puppet or puppet master, the practices are eerily similar: massive wiretapping and surveillance, punishment of objectors, outing of intelligence agents, intimidation of the opposition, accusations of disloyalty, and suspension of constitutional protections, including most vividly the latter administration's suspension of the Great Writ, the constitutional guarantee of habeas corpus.[14]

The instruction offered here is not encouraging. Rather than a view of history that says we profit by our mistakes, learn from our errors, and become a better and stronger people, this recycling of political excess strongly suggests that we forget all too soon, learn little from abuse of political power, and casually sacrifice our freedom to manipulative leaders willing to frighten us into obeisance. The truth of this proposition requires exploration further down this odyssey's road.

George McGovern and all those who supported him lost and lost badly. Contrary to later, superficial analysis, he did not lose solely because of his opposition to the Vietnam War. Both candidates promised to end the war, and the victorious Richard Nixon and his enabler Kissinger went to the negotiating table a few, ineffective million tons of bombs later. The election got down to "not changing horses in the middle of the stream," the colorful description of the incumbent's advantage, and the perception of competence. Nixon was competent, all right. But, as with other valued leadership qualities, the question is always competence to do *what*. If you wanted orders obeyed and trains to run on time, then Nixon was your man. Others had somewhat higher expectations for American democracy and the more noble competence its leaders were expected to possess.

We Americans do not much favor overly reflective politicians. Introspection is often seen at best as weakness and at worst as deep emotional instability. Some think there is such a thing as being too smart in American politics. In any case, even when it is uncomfortable, it is worthwhile to think about how and why we choose our leaders, if for no other reason than to avoid further King Lears and Prince Hals. Experience, wisdom, and judgment are all worthy, and one might say obvious, qualities. But so are decency, humility, intelligence, and a sense of history. We shy away from professorial Stevensons and McGoverns, Woodrow Wilson being an exception. Yet we are attracted, at least on occasion, to the Kennedys who read books. The value of this practice in John Kennedy's case was proved by his reliance on the lessons of the historian Barbara Tuchman's study of the causes of World War I in *The Proud Tower*, thereby avoiding catastrophic miscalculations and resolving the Cuban Missile Crisis.

Those born with natural qualities of national and international leadership, whose genetic origins are mysterious, are rare. There is ambition in abundance, but it seldom guarantees the qualities that mark true leaders, those able to look over the horizon, fashion innovative solutions to challenging new realities, and convince the nation to leave past comforts behind and pursue a new and better path. The halls of power are full of men and women who can imagine themselves behind the great desk in the Oval Office, but very few possess the elusive combination of personal qualities and skills required to occupy a pedestal in history. There is evidence aplenty that becoming president is open to quite a few, but becoming a great president, a historic national leader, is possible all too rarely.

The troublesome excursions collected under the category called Watergate are to some an inconsequential distraction and to others a kind of national descent into Hades, as unaccountable today as then. If you are willing to believe it was all an aberration carried out under a man about whom the nation was—twice—badly mistaken, then you can dust off your hands, write the whole thing off, and move on. Stuff happens. If, however, you are inclined to wonder whether we saw in Richard Nixon something of ourselves, some qualities we needed at the time, whether you choose to call them (as he did) "toughness" and "strength," and that, given enough fear, whether of communists, terrorists, or simply Martin Luther

King, we would call on a Nixon again, either in the Oval Office or the office of the vice president, then it wouldn't hurt to think a good deal more about ourselves as a nation.

This entire experience, cast in the form of a national political campaign, offered two important lessons. One had to do with the often gigantic gap between perception and reality. The other had to do with the existence of a de facto virtual Establishment. As to the first, the distance between perception and reality requires the illumination of the media. Perception is the media's interpretation of reality. Well before the advent of the Internet, the Web, and every-person-a-reporter (if of nothing else than his or her own reactions and biases), "news," that is to say the reporting and interpretation of events both public and private, was the business of "the media," journalists, reporters, editors, and publishers of newspapers and magazines and owners of radio and television networks. What they produce is their perception of reality, in the current case of political reality. By the latter half of the twentieth century, journalism had gone well beyond the who, where, why, when, and how of traditional journalism and had ventured well into the realm of impressionism. By the latter quarter of the twentieth century, under the historic drama of Watergate and impeachment, journalists had become heroes and self-appointed tribunes of the people.

Our republic has experienced worse guardians. But if Woodward and Bernstein could become rich and famous, who is to say Suzy and Ricky couldn't become rich and famous simply by calling out any errant politician or public figure? Rewards for exposé were great and highly attractive to a generation. Thus "reality" came to be more subjective and career motivated. There is perhaps no greater vantage point from which to view the gap between that increasingly subjective reality and authentic reality than an upstart insurgency campaign. Countless were the times when I would experience firsthand an event, a conversation, a speech, or any one of hundreds of kinds of developments and then read about it or view it as totally different from what I saw and knew.

The camera does not lie, it might be said. Well, yes, sometimes the camera does lie. It provides no context, and it has a finite frame. And even the moving picture is subject to editing and splicing, and thus manipulation. All this is to say that journalism is a human endeavor and thus subject to all the human failings, mostly those of selection and interpretation. Americans are congenitally, and healthily, skeptical people, and thus capable of weighing and balancing what they are told. But the more of them who experience the gap between perception and reality—"that story in the paper isn't what happened"—the more skeptical they become of the purveyors of perceptions.

For many years after the McGovern days, I would puzzle over this gap and whether it could or would be closed. I ultimately concluded it could not and would not, if for no other reason than that the late twentieth century witnessed the rise of a new era of advocacy journalism driven as much by the voracious Rupert Murdoch (a foreigner, it must be noted, not a homegrown William Randolph Hearst) as by anyone. Any hope of closing the perception–reality gap promptly evaporated.

The Establishment held the other lesson. Contrary to black-helicopter mythology, this is not a secret society holding meetings in Bilderberg, wherever that is, and deciding the fate of the world, including the selection of presidents and treasury secretaries, interest rates, and oil prices. However, are newspaper editors and publishers, powerful lawyer-lobbyists, elected officials, corporate CEOs, and investment bankers part of a well-acquainted network? Of course. Do they share connections, ideas, and agendas? Naturally. Is it better and more rewarding to be inside this network rather than outside? Surely, you jest. This basic truth made the emergence of a place called Davos all but inevitable as it would, in a way, make the catastrophic financial meltdown of 2008 and beyond inevitable.

If you wish to disarm the watchman, first make him your good friend.

Though he knew and had socialized with many of the figures in this virtual Establishment over the years, George McGovern was never of it. No single attribute or action accounts for this. The ways of power are mysterious. He simply didn't make the cut. Not everyone can belong to Skull and Bones. Even if he had made the waiting list of member-acolytes, however, his stance on the Vietnam War, and particularly his increasingly inflammatory rhetoric, would have invited the blackball of Fate from which there is no recovery. Even worse, he upset the odds and the oddsmakers. In horse racing and politics, the smart money follows the odds. The odds were heavily against McGovern. And, at least for the nomination of his party, he beat them. That meant he beat those who had bet the odds, followed the polls, and comforted the front-runners. It is considered a form of treachery to defeat the Establishment. Dark horses are meant to stay that way or risk charges of treason for their audacity. Just bring Joseph Alsop back and ask him.

This was a lesson not lost on a young Denver lawyer. But learning it was one thing and following it, given a strong streak of independence, was quite another. The virtual Establishment, whose structure and makeup shift and change with time and generations, strongly dislikes surprise and insurgency, and most of all being proven fallible.[15]

There is no doubt that George McGovern would have been a "good" president in the ethical and moral sense. Whether he would have been an effective one is more difficult to determine and, in any event, unknowable. But which is more important to us, ethics or effectiveness? How much are we willing to sacrifice the former to obtain the latter? We tend toward the effective over the good, especially in troubled times. That presidents so rarely combine goodness of character and effectiveness in statecraft is evidenced by the fact that a temple on the Potomac was built to honor one of the few who did.

Even more to the point, which is more important to us, our constitutional principles or our security? How you answer this question determines what kind of president—or senator or congressperson—you will vote for. For me and others, this is the true "Watergate" question, and it is less a question about our politicians than it is about ourselves.

Dostoevsky's Grand Inquisitor reduced the question to its dramatic essence: bread or freedom? *Bread* in this case means security. Authority can provide security, but it rarely pauses to respect freedom in the process. We saw this under Richard Nixon (and J. Edgar Hoover) as well as under George W. Bush (and Richard Cheney). In 1972, as well as in 2004, we chose security, and our Constitution paid the price.

History has proved the United States Constitution to be resilient. But does that mean it can be casually suspended, overlooked, or violated without some cost? I think not. The deeper and more savage the wound to the Constitution, the longer the recovery period and the more long-lasting the scar. No scar will last longer than the violation of its condition that only in time of rebellion or invasion can the article 1, section 9 guarantee of the writ of habeas corpus be suspended or the Fourth Amendment protection against unwarranted searches and seizures be ignored. Somehow George W. Bush missed this central thesis of democracy while traversing through both Yale and Harvard. But members of Congress of both parties, some of whom at least knew better, enabled him.

And of rebellion or invasion there was none.

In an ideal world we would have both security and freedom. But until we Americans become astute enough to find leaders who can help us achieve both, we will probably continue to go for the authoritarian when we are afraid. One could write this off as basic human nature were it not for its obvious lesson for the political marketplace: frighten people enough, and they'll elect you to protect them. This is not a new idea. It is the essence of authoritarianism and it is both Homeric and biblical, and long predated Karl Rove.

Being men of inner nobility, republican heritage, and high principle, our founders thought the best hedge against the fear ploy and human vulnerability was our Constitution. That elected administrations would casually suspend or brush aside the Constitution seemed, to them, a possibility, though a remote one. By locating sovereignty, power, in the people themselves, they exhibited their abiding belief that Americans would hold their leaders accountable and not surrender their freedom so lightly. In at least two remarkable instances in recent years, they were wrong. Watergate's end was a form of restoration of national sanity and judgment. Rightly or wrongly, the latter Bush would leave office without the prosecutor in pursuit.

Instead of a judge called Sirica, however, George W. Bush will stand before a judge called History.

The odyssey called modern life has held many surprises, not least the surprise of how casually the Constitution can be suspended without political resistance and massive public protest and, at least up to now, how resilient it eventually proves itself to be when faced with assault. If Ithaca had had a constitution, and particularly one as subject to assault as ours, one wonders if Ulysses could have sailed off without more concern for its resilience and for the vigilance of his son Telemachus and his generation. It does all get back to the oft-quoted response of Benjamin Franklin to the citizen question of the kind of government being created by the founders in Philadelphia: "A republic," he said, "if you can keep it."

After the turbulent election of 1972 was all over, there was time for observation and reflection. And this reflection would heavily condition the next leg of one man's odyssey. Observation revealed that turbulence at home was partly connected with tidal historic turbulence in the world. Two epic revolutions were under way, globalization and the information revolution, and they were changing and would continue to change the face of America. While tied down by Lilliputian nationalists in Vietnam, the American Gulliver was neglecting the steps necessary to adapt to this revolutionary world. America's mighty industrial base, its auto and steel industries, was cooling down and rusting under the barrage of cheaper foreign competition. But as steelworkers entered the unemployment lines, their children were picking up new devices called computers.

Nineteen-seventy-two was arguably too soon to mount a national campaign based on the promise of international trade and high technology, and transition to a new economic base requiring training in new skills, investment in technological invention and research, and leading the world in information. But there were better ideas then and later than the protectionist proposals, such as the so-called domestic content legislation promoted by traditional Democrats and their union allies, that represented a desperate effort to shovel back, like doomed King Canute, a massive tide, this one of trade and international competition.

The struggle between the Democratic Party's past and its future would dominate my life and represent its own odyssey of sorts. This boat's sails were filling in the port as early as 1972, and the filling sails and the running tide would carry a generation of new Democratic odysseans out onto the turbulent political seas of the remainder of the 1970s and the 1980s and into the twenty-first century.

In 2008, the audacity of hope would carry an improbable candidate into the White House. More than three decades before, that same audacity would carry me at an early age into the "world's greatest deliberative body," the Senate. Like Barack Obama, I trusted that the power of principles and the belief in ideals were greater than political connections, money, and networks. Democratic republicanism was my secular religion, the Constitution of the United States was my Bible, our government was its church.

The odyssey from small-town Kansas to Colorado and on to Washington was one motivated by the simplest desire, that of service to the nation. It seemed more honorable than any alternative I could think of. But the hope of a more perfect Union had already become clouded by a web of secrecy the Cold War had cast across that nation. Would Ulysses have continued his struggle to return home if Ithaca was becoming a different country than the one he sought?

PART II

GOVERNING IN A DARKENING GROVE
(1975–1981)

This warrior-king, Tennyson's Ulysses in old age, wants to see and hear and sense it all, to discover those few remaining worlds and mysteries yet undiscovered: "I will drink life to the lees…" Joy and suffering, spitting in the face of risk, companionship and loneliness, on land and sea, living is what it's all about. And for this old hero, sitting on this barren rock amidst those who do not know him is not living.

It is a mystery that the poet would reduce the magnificent Penelope to "an aged wife." She who kept a raft of slavering suitors at bay, weaving a shroud that would never be finished, who climbed the watchtower night after night and year after year, yearning for that distant sail. It is less than seemly that this adventurer, the slayer of the Cyclops and the survivor of Scylla and Charybdis, who overcame the seductive charms of Circe to make it home, would find the object of it all a tedious distraction from the experience of life. Ah, Penelope. What a story she has to tell. Where is her Homer? Or did he think to spin a complete epic about her and have it somehow lost to the ages? Were there justice in the world, there would be a *Penelope* as companion to *The Odyssey*.[16] For Penelope has earned her tribute. Of course she has added a pound or two. But so has that old man out there on that rock. Sitting there day after day, looking out to sea. Doesn't he realize what that does to her? She thinks he is pining for that Calypso woman. She sees only an old man, lost in his own memories. But from time to time she does remember that thrilling young warrior who captured her heart, who sailed away to war and almost never came back.

As is true for warriors throughout the ages, the man who goes away to war is rarely the man who returns. The thousand-yard stare, it is called. That stare to which she has become so accustomed sees not Calypso or even Cyclops, it sees the heavens black with arrows, the Trojan lance whose wind can be felt as it passes near his head, the cacophony of clashing shields, grunting warriors, and agonizing screams. That stare sees the great Achilles and the most legendary fighters of his or any other age.

For this king, this Ulysses, has "become a name." Throughout the known world he is now an early celebrity of sorts whose exploits would be talked about and kept alive and even would become the stuff of myth for the wandering heirs of Homer. He has seen the cities of men and been honored by their councils. It is the rare king or noble adventurer who has seen virtually all there is to see and who would not miss that turmoil and that triumph—the thunder and the sunshine—in later life. This king, this odyssean, is not content to live out his remaining life locked in his own memories.

It all began with a war, the greatest war of his or any other age, a war that would compel him and his mariners all the way across the Aegean to the "ringing plains of windy Troy." There he would meet and struggle with, and raise his sword with and against, the greatest warriors of the age, the great Achilles not least among them.

Only the rare few favored by the gods have packed up and sailed off to rescue the beauteous Helen, heard the raging Achilles pacing outside his tent at night even after dragging Hector's body round the camp, formed up beside Agamemnon and the mighty Achaean armies, and hammered together the broken slats of battle with warriors of worldwide renown to construct a giant horse to harbor two or three platoons of men like Ulysses. Together they will breech the impenetrable walls of Troy by stealth and then rout the Trojans, slay their great king Priam and all those around him, take back the gray-eyed Helen (perhaps wondering, once she was finally paraded through the Greek ranks, what all the fuss was about), and then set sail for home triumphant and without a clue about the epic odyssey that lies ahead.

What if Ulysses had decided to refuse his commission to sail for Troy? What if he had chosen not to muster in favor of the charms of the estimable Penelope? For most, inaction is the default position. We take for granted that Ulysses would not have been absent without leave from the greatest conflict in the known world. But, of course, Ulysses would not have been Ulysses had he chosen to stay home.

This king was front and center of the war to end all wars, and that was just the start of it. "I am become a name," he would much later reflect, for having experienced that colossal combat enshrined forever in human memory, but even more for having wandered the utmost boundaries of the known world in his struggle to return home. All of this became him, and he became all of it: "I am part of all that I have met." He and his odyssey are forever inseparable. He cannot now know himself or be known, as a name, apart from the majestic song of Homer.

This aging king understands that the circle of life and human existence closes only for those who wish it to or who permit the arthritic pains of age to which all are subject to crush out the desire for knowledge. Except, for him and the rare few like him, all that has gone before is but an archway, an archway "wherethro' gleams that untravell'd world," the world whose boundaries recede every time he advances toward them.

The past, even the illustrious past, must always be prologue. And the search for ways to penetrate secrecy's veil must continue.

"Gary, I'd like you to be on this committee with Frank Church," he said, "the one looking into the CIA." The speaker was Senator Mike Mansfield, then the majority leader of the Senate. It was early in 1975 on the floor of the Senate. "It's important. Do a good job." Then he walked off.

This was a long speech for the leader for whom terseness and laconism were major attributes. He was notoriously spartan with words and economical with language. I hadn't a clue what he was talking about. I had taken the oath of office only days before and was only vaguely aware that the Senate had enacted a potentially explosive resolution. That resolution authorized the creation of a select committee, an uncommon event in itself, to investigate the activities of the intelligence agencies of the US government, an unprecedented undertaking.

Though tasked with the constitutional responsibility of overseeing the performance of the executive branch of government, serial Congresses had theretofore assiduously avoided peering behind the veil of secrecy sewn together following the creation of the Central Intelligence Agency by the National Security Act of 1947. Even before this, little if any effort had been made by previous Congresses to oversee the activities of the Federal Bureau of Investigation.

Any mystery regarding the reasons for this congressional reluctance fled during an early organizational meeting of the select committee, soon to be known as the Church Committee after its chairman. Our eleven members, almost all distinguished by seniority and sobriety, were pondering how and where to begin. The subjects of our investigation were not about to open their books and operations willingly. After a good deal of hemming, hawing, and foot shuffling, I, the most junior member, suggested this: "Why don't we all ask the CIA and the FBI for our own files...the files they have on each of us?"

Silence overwhelmed the room. Barry Goldwater looked at Howard Baker. John Tower studied the ceiling. Frank Church looked at Walter Mondale. Philip Hart and Charles Mathias smiled wanly. Senators were deep in thought as to the personal implications of this suggestion. I suddenly began to feel very small. The spell was broken by Senator Goldwater: "I don't want to know what they've got on me!" he blurted. Laughter dispelled contemplation.

I had more than an abstract interest in viewing my own security files. Roughly forty-eight hours before my election in November 1974, only three months before, the Denver Police Department notified us that they had been informed of a threat against my life. Further, on election night a high-powered rifle had been discovered in a heating vent in the Democratic Party's celebration hotel. Two days after the election, after I had joined family and friends for a brief holiday in Mexico, Idaho law enforcement authorities apprehended a drug hit man, one Thomas Eugene Creech, who fit the description of the man identified with the threat, and he admitted to having been hired to shoot me. Once apprehended, Creech confessed to forty-two contract murders in thirteen different states. In 1981, he killed a fellow inmate and now, thirty-five years later, remains on death row.[17]

Senator Mansfield must have known that the following two years on the Church Committee and much that followed thereafter would be an education of sorts for a very young senator, especially one who had never before sought, let alone held, public office. It would be an education in many things: the constitutional responsibilities of Congress; the courage or lack thereof of the members of the Senate; the role of secrecy in US foreign policy and its relations with other nations; the nature of covert operations; government intrusion into the lives and activities of American citizens; what is and is not legitimate for a constitutional democracy to do in defending itself; the abuse of executive power; the multimirrored world of espionage; the embrace of evil in furtherance of the national interest; a war being carried on in the back alleys of the world; and lurking beneath it all, the dark side of power.

Once the cover began to be pulled back from a long-secret cesspool of misdeeds, past ghosts emerged, assassination plots unfolded, and key Mafia figures were brutally murdered during our investigation.

All this began to transpire even as a young senator would seek to make his mark on economic issues, environmental and energy crises, the continuing arms race, the collapse of the Vietnam War, and almost the entire smorgasbord of national and international issues of the day. For a wonkish type, it was a delicatessen of delights.

But the times were out of sorts. In the mid-1970s, America was locked in what appeared to be an endless Cold War. Our economy had stagnated; indeed very soon a combination of economic stagnation combined with inflation would cause a new word, stagflation, to be coined. We had just suffered the first OPEC oil embargo shock and would soon be pounded by another. Foreign competitors were undercutting our vital industrial base, especially autos and steel. A place called Love Canal in New York forced us to peer into the abyss holding the hidden and sinister costs of the industrial age. Urban ghettoes were smoldering. Long-haired flag burners were being chased down the streets by long-haired blue collar workers.

The land was not at ease.

But hopeful signs were on the horizon. A new economy based on globalization, the internationalization of commerce, finance, and markets, was emerging. American airplane manufacturers, telecommunications companies, and software designers were beginning to flourish in worldwide markets. The information revolution was replacing the industrial age. Let the Japanese and Germans compete in our automobile markets. We would build their telecommunications systems.

Helicopters lifting off the Saigon embassy signaled that America, or at least her troops, was coming home. Earth Day announced the dawn of the environmental age. Self-liberated women were entering the workforce, albeit for unequal pay.

A transformation was under way, one that would require decades to complete.

From an economic point of view, the United States found itself at a crossroads. And, of course, all economics are political. One road led to the rescue of the cooling steel mills and auto plants. That road was called protectionism. The other road led to the new information economy. It was called competition. If you were younger, college educated, and looking to the future, you would seek the computer wizard down that yellow-brick road. If you were older, skilled in manufacturing, and burdened with a mortgage, you tried desperately to hold onto the old assembly line. The industrial Northeast was rusting. The new West was rolling in gold. In economic terms, the nation was dividing economically, generationally, and demographically, not to say also along racial and gender lines, and it would continue to do so for some time.

Worse still, even as Richard Nixon, leader of the party of free enterprise and limited government, declared that "now we are all Keynesians," Keynesian economic tools used by governments to stimulate economic recovery and growth were either working less well or not working at all. Fiscal measures, tax cuts and government spending, were not producing economic expansion as they had in previous decades. Monetary policy, the expansion of the money supply by the central bank leading to interest rate reductions and more corporate investment and consumer spending, also was not producing the traditional results. These twin failures of traditional economic policies led to controversial and mostly unprecedented experiments in the Nixon years of abandonment of the gold standard for the US dollar and wage and price controls. Economic rules and long-established doctrines were being retooled or abandoned all over the place to counter the new phenomena of stagflation, oil producing cartels (OPEC), international competition, and the silicon chip.

Conventional economics was not supposed to work this way. Inflation, increases in wages and prices, led to bubbles if not booms. Stagnation, reduced investment and spending, was supposed to bring down inflation. How could the two coexist? The answer rested in large part in globalization. The price of energy, literally the fuel of any modern economy, was now dictated by foreign oligarchies that had formed a producers' cartel. By permitting ourselves to gradually but steadily increase our addiction to what had before been both a reliable and relatively cheap source of energy, Persian Gulf oil, the great United States had become as helpless and dependent as any addict, obvious to some of us as early as the 1970s but to George W. Bush only in 2008. And a global market in manufactured goods had made foreign cars, steel, appliances, and textiles more attractive to American consumers than our own products.

The full impact of international economic integration would be demonstrated some thirty-five years later when the highly leveraged, high-risk securitized mortgage bubble burst in the United States and abroad, shocking and fracturing highly integrated international financial structures.

But in the 1970s, the political process, including previously reliable economic advisors, was slow to respond to this new economic world and to accept the hugely consequential new reality that we were no longer self-sufficient and thus no longer controlled our own destiny. We had reached a historic turning point in our national history, and too few recognized it or were willing to accept it if they did.

A handful of new, younger members of Congress, mostly Democrats, arrived at this crossroads and began to experiment with ways to structure a transition. We proposed measures to train and retrain workers for new technology jobs. We proposed investments in innovative technologies and laboratory inventions. We offered new incentives for education in math, sciences, and technical skills. We suggested tax incentives to companies that would install automated equipment. We opposed permanent protection for old industry so that our new industries could flourish in international markets. For our efforts, we were quickly labeled "Atari Democrats." More than three decades later even this label is an anachronism, because Atari computers disappeared long ago.[18]

Needless to say, the new Democratic Party met great resistance from the traditional Democratic Party, which sought to maintain its old political base in the manufacturing economy.

For their part, newer Republicans responded with a simplistic idea called supply-side economics. Its premise was that huge tax cuts would lead to investment, more investment would produce economic growth, businesses would grow and hire more workers, and consequent revenues produced by this growth would pay for the tax cuts. Oddly enough, the only time this theory worked was during the Clinton years, in the 1990s, when the technology sector, the new information economy, took off (so successfully that it created a bubble of excess speculative investment that burst in the early twenty-first century) and the United States moved into leadership in technology, especially information and communications technologies, in the new world economy. This was not a triumph of the dubious supply-side theory, but rather the signal that the transition from manufacturing to information had finally occurred and America had moved to the forefront.

Having no other economic doctrine to espouse, Republican economists and politicians would continue through the second-Bush years to promote huge tax cuts, principally for the wealthy, and when they failed to produce the revenues promised by the theory, account for the predictable federal deficits by a second dumbfounding, anticonservative statement by then vice president Richard Cheney: "Deficits don't matter." It was a monumental lesson in the triumph of rhetoric over reality, politics over principle, and hope over memory.

Many of us knew this gambit and its hyper supply-side rhetoric was merely a smoke screen to reduce federal revenues in order to starve New Deal and Great Society social programs while at the same time further enriching the supply-siders' wealthy political contributors. The gilded yachts launched in the manipulative supply-side heyday sank in the Bermuda triangle of the 2008 meltdown.

In the old manufacturing versus new information contest, though older industrial states would still be divided on trade issues as late as the 2008 Democratic primaries, the nation at large was too far down the computerized yellow-brick road to turn back.

But a century and a half of industrialization had left a very large bill to pay. Industries large and small that had poured millions of tons of chemicals into the air, water, and land were not to be found to pay these bills. Instead, they were left to the American taxpayers. There was a salient lesson here in "free markets." Air, water, and land were not free goods inexhaustibly capable of absorbing poison. The mid-1970s and beyond saw new clean air and clean water laws, toxic waste cleanup and so-called Superfund site laws, long-delayed attention to the burgeoning nuclear waste problem conveniently neglected by both industry and government, and the urgency of preventing the harvest of industrialization from poisoning one or several generations of young Americans.

Those of us elected during this period, especially from the West, came with ardent environmental credentials and marching orders from our constituents to "do something" about these problems. We were held to account, rightly or wrongly, for the sins of the fathers.

Our army was returning from Southeast Asia, depressed in spirit though not defeated in battle. In political and military terms the war was lost. This is not an easy thing for a proud army to bear, especially when its homecoming was less than hospitable. For inexplicable reasons, too many Americans held ordinary soldiers responsible for a war begun in haste and error and for the sins of the politicians whose responsibility it was. Ever after this would be a cause for wonder. These men and women did their job. They obeyed their orders. They kept faith with their oath. What kind of mindlessness takes out its anger on those in uniform for the stupidity of the nation's political leaders, civilian defense officials, and a small handful of generals?

Arsenals were depleted. But more important, morale was seriously eroded. It was not merely a matter of buying more weapons. The perceived communist threat would take care of that. But morale is a more complicated proposition. Ways had to be found to reverse the damage done by a hostile segment of the population and to incorporate the lessons of the Vietnam experience into the process of devising our future national security.

This was the backdrop for a Senate campaign in Colorado in 1974 under unusual, and highly improbable, circumstances. I had not only never held public office, I had never sought public office. Too much motivated by Watergate-fueled anger, with no money, little identity, and no elective experience, nevertheless the times called for action. With the volunteered time and small dollar contributions of hundreds (probably even a few thousand) people, I won the Democratic nomination out of a field of six candidates and then defeated a wealthy two-term incumbent Republican. The entire campaign cost $350,000, and the average contribution was $17.

Then as now there was a general assumption that senators were wealthy or at least comfortably well-off. Such was not the case with us. The 1974 elections to Congress brought in what came to be called the Watergate class. Some of us were of pretty ordinary economic circumstances. Political volcanoes, of which Watergate certainly was one, have the consequence of bringing new ores to the surface. The value of these ores is determined by a later assay process called political performance. For better or worse, a new generation was introduced on the political stage.

My family's story illustrates the point. Heading to Washington in the family Oldsmobile (well over 150,000 miles on the odometer) and an ancient sports car whose motor seized up in western Kansas, adventures abounded. With the small car temporarily abandoned on I-70, Lee and I, Andrea, ten, John, eight, the aged dog Duffy, two hamsters, and luggage to supply us until movers arrived in Washington were apprehended by a Kansas highway patrolman. Anxious to get this exotic collection to the home of Lee's sister Martha, who herself had just been elected to Congress in Manhattan, Kansas, I was exceeding the speed limit. In response to the usual "What's the hurry, buddy?" question, I explained our mission. Dubiousness would not begin to describe his response to my claim of senatorship. The patrolman demanded proof. There I was, in a snowstorm on the interstate in western Kansas, searching through a maze of suitcases for a small card that, happily, I had received before departure that certified my election. Kansas's finest studied the card in disbelief, shifting his gaze from the card to me and back, praying, I am sure, that it was a forgery.

He finally sent us on our way, studying the hamsters spinning endlessly on their wheel in the car's back window as we headed eastward. The scene would be repeated several nights later near midnight outside Columbus, Ohio, with the antagonist this time being an Ohio state patrolman and the complaint being, "Do you know there's not a light on the back of any of these cars?" (The Oldsmobile was now towing the frozen-up sports car, soon to end its life on a junk pile.) I surrendered the certification card only as a last resort when the patrolman (a profession driven to permanent dubiousness by the bizarre tales of woeful travelers) refused to accept my assurance that this traveling menagerie was headed to the nation's capital so that I, a still-fluffy-haired thirty-some-thing-year-old, could join the ranks of the world's greatest deliberative body.

In the end, I suppose, we were rescued by the American creed: Anything is possible in this great nation. The patrol-man provided escort to the nearest motel.

Just two years after managing the McGovern cam-paign, widely and simplistically characterized as an exclu-sively antiwar, and therefore antimilitary, undertaking, I was awarded membership on the Senate's Armed Services Com-mittee, tasked with authorizing all things, from shoelaces to nuclear missiles, required by the United States Depart-ment of Defense and all of its uniformed services. My party, labeled by Senator Robert Dole as late as 1976 as the "war party," clearly had to regain its standing on defense and national security matters.

This was more easily understood than accomplished. Too many Democrats simply did not want to concern them-selves with military matters. The Vietnam experience, as well as a misunderstanding of the "come home, America" rhetoric, had diminished the ranks of engaged internationalists in the party. Conservative Democrats still supported most military requests, but they were largely southerners, and on racial and social issues, among other things, their geographic base was eroding under them. A few years of liberals voting against and conservatives voting for a wide variety of weapons sys-tems yielded to an unrewarding political cul-de-sac. This was not a thoughtful way to study national defense.

Fortune in the form of a small group of military reform-ers led by a retired air force colonel John Boyd offered a more creative option. Soon I was studying military history, why wars were won or lost, and in some case how some victories were achieved, following Sun Tzu, without firing a shot. The mantra of the reformers was weapons don't win wars; people win wars. That being the case, why spend all of our time in Congress debating the relative merits of weapons systems, which many congressmen and congresswomen didn't understand in any case? Instead, reformers argued, we should study people, how they are trained, how they are led and motivated, and what qualities make good battlefield commanders. These same people who win wars, and their families, needed to be better trained and well-cared for. Battlefield commanders, those seasoned in leadership, not desk officers, should get the first promotions. Then we must look to our strategy, tactics, and doctrines. The best people cannot win wars if they are pursuing the wrong strategy and using the wrong tactics and doctrines, a lesson painfully learned in Vietnam and then, years later, in Iraq. Only after the people and the strategy are in place do we think about what weapons are required to win what kinds of conflicts, and these conflicts were becoming increasingly varied and unconventional.

Military reform became a movement whose formation I led in 1980 and '81, with over a hundred members of Congress from both parties and both houses, largely from the new generation. We also sought to profit from the lessons learned by battlefield commanders, lieutenants, captains, and colonels in Vietnam, and incorporate those lessons in the positions we urged upon our colleagues in the House and the Senate.

As with the historic economic transition, however, moving from the old "more is better" defense mentality to one based on maneuver and innovation met great resistance from traditional political and military thinkers. Bigger weapon systems and military budgets appealed to those who claimed to care most about national security.

Given two oil-price shocks by this time, it was becoming clear to a very few of us that our increasing reliance on foreign oil, especially from the Persian Gulf, was a source of hazard for the nation. Our entire economy and well-being were dependent on a handful of fragile and undemocratic nations in the most unstable region of the world. The options were minimal. Either we reduced our dependence on that particular supply or we would have to fight for it. Though not clearly understood by most Americans then or now, that is not *our* oil under *their* sand. And with the overthrow of one or two oligarchies, that is to say undemocratic governments, our dependence made us incredibly vulnerable.

On repeated occasions in the late 1970s and 1980s, I wrote and said that we must take every measure of conservation and alternative-energy development to eliminate our dependence on Persian Gulf oil. Otherwise, we would have to go to war for it.[19] We have since fought two Gulf wars where oil was a clear, though unadmitted, factor, and we face more to come. The fact that we were unwilling to be honest about the role oil played in two Persian Gulf wars tells us all we need to know about the integrity of our energy policies. The historian Barbara Tuchman defined folly on a national scale as pursuing an admittedly flawed policy knowing that a better alternative exists. By this definition, our oil dependency was then and is now folly on a massive scale.

Even as economic transformation, environmental cleanup, military reform, and energy independence were being pursued in the mid-1970s, the lid was slowly coming off a breathtaking history of intelligence mysteries at home and abroad. The Church Committee operated from a remote Senate committee room kept constantly "swept" (cleared of listening devices). It was not beyond possibility that the very intelligence agencies we were investigating might find means to listen to our discussions about them. The US "intelligence community" included not just the Central Intelligence Agency and the Federal Bureau of Investigation, but also the National Security Agency, operating highly sophisticated eyes and ears worldwide including in space; the Defense Intelligence Agency, whose budget far exceeded the CIA's; and a dozen or more clandestine services scattered here and there throughout the government.

The existence of this "community" raised interesting if not profound ideological questions. Conservatives, notable for resisting government intrusion into the lives of individual citizens, by and large endorsed and supported its activities. Liberals, generally thought to favor governmental activism, demonstrated most concern for privacy and civil liberties. Even within the Church Committee, Republicans generally sought to protect the intelligence agencies from too much inspection, whereas Democrats were much more willing to question their excessive activities, bring them to light, and prevent future abuses.

The politics of intelligence are complex, and they become even more complex when intelligence activities run amok. Expecting little from flawed human nature, and only trouble when flawed humans collect to form governments, conservatives are less surprised to find perfidy in high places. Believing the human condition to be improvable, if not perfectible, liberals are distraught when even minor utopian aspirations are brought to nothing by treachery. Norman Mailer once compared rocket scientists to plumbers in that both are tasked with preventing treachery in closed systems. He would also have much to say about spies, whose very purpose is to insert treachery *into* closed systems.

As this exercise of laymen roaming at large in the fields of treachery evolved, it would become more intricately layered and multimirrored. Although the earlier genteel British proscription against gentlemen reading other gentlemen's mail had long since become anachronistic, almost cozy arrangements had evolved between CIA and KGB operators in certain local venues.

Politically, however, the fact that Frank Church and Barry Goldwater could sit across from each other in this committee was a testament to the sense that things had gotten way out of hand during the Nixon Watergate years, and even before.

It soon became apparent that the excesses of Watergate were abuses of power dating back at least to the Eisenhower years. So the committee's central question was, How did all this happen? Some, most notably Frank Church, concluded that the CIA was a "rogue elephant" and the intelligence agencies were virtually out of control. Others, including myself, concluded that an unbroken series of administrations, both Democratic and Republican, had abused power and used the intelligence agencies to achieve their own political and ideological agendas.

In the late spring of 1975, after several months of probing and poking, William Colby, then director of the CIA, appeared before our committee. The staff was removed, and the room was swept yet again. For almost three hours he revealed "the family jewels," a summary of a lengthy report prepared by the CIA's inspector general of many, though not all, of the agency's questionable ventures. These included plots to overthrow foreign governments, some known and some theretofore unknown; subornation of foreign political leaders, parties, and media; employment of a bewildering array of clandestine "fronts"; experimentation with drugs, in one case leading to the suicide of an intelligence officer; use of "false flag" officers in Chile and elsewhere; and, most startlingly, plots to assassinate at least five foreign leaders, including, with almost demented insistence, Fidel Castro.

The Senate of that day contained no more seasoned man of the world than Barry Goldwater. He had, or at least thought he had, seen it all. From across the table, I saw his jaw drop. Colby, an interesting figure who resembled nothing so much as a staid Presbyterian minister with eyeglasses that always seemed to reflect light and whose even-keeled demeanor almost never changed, continued on. The plots to assassinate Castro, begun under Eisenhower and continued under Kennedy, had been pursued by the CIA with the aid of the Mafia. A young senator from Colorado, now only months into his first term, wondered what planet he had landed on—and what country he had been living in.

Assassination as an instrument of foreign policy carried out by the democracy of Jefferson, Washington, Madison, Hamilton, and Adams was difficult enough to grasp. But plots to assassinate Fidel Castro carried out with the help of the Mafia up to and including 1962 and 1963 suddenly carried the implications of blowing the Warren Commission Report on the assassination of John Kennedy sky high. That commission knew nothing about the CIA-Mafia coalition for the simple reason that one of its members, Allen Dulles, then CIA director, chose not to tell his colleagues.

Suddenly the world, and conventional reality, looked stunningly different. Everything one had learned and had thought about America and its government was suddenly subject to question. Seemingly anything, not just for good but also for evil, was now possible. If the government of the United States could use its chief intelligence agency to assassinate a Caribbean communist and that agency could employ the Mafia in conducting the enterprise, what could not be done? Was anything now off limits? The world of ideals and principles, of democratic theory and standards, of nobility and national honor, was now cast in a new, and much less wholesome light.

Life in the United States Senate, simply because the Senate is what it is, is never routine. But to live that life on a daily basis while carrying around in one's mind the knowledge that a sewer of some dimension underlay the American city on a hill, and to find oneself proscribed from discussing this unsettling discovery with family or even other Senate colleagues, was an invitation to a kind of schizophrenia. Things would only get worse.

In the meantime, ordinary life, if it could still be called that, did not stand still. Indeed, all this was carried out against the larger backdrop of the Cold War, which, at least during this period, frosted more than it thawed. By the mid-1970s, the United States and the Soviet Union made an effort at rapprochement at the parliamentary level. The first exchange would be the visit of a Senate delegation to Moscow followed by a Duma visit to the States. Once again the thoughtful mentor, Mansfield saw to it that my wife, Lee, and I were appointed to this eleven-member delegation, headed by Senators Hubert Humphrey and Hugh Scott. Once again I was most junior. We flew to Moscow in late June 1975 for three days of meetings with Soviet officials. There was much dining and toasting, but the two consequential meetings were with Mikhail Suslov, variously described as the Kremlin's chief theoretician or principal ideologue, and then general secretary Leonid Brezhnev. Suslov lived up to his reputation. A stern, funereal figure with a face from a Goya painting, he lectured us severely for quite a long time about the evils of rampant capitalism, United States aggressions, and Western imperialism. Since up to that time most of the contact between the countries, such as it was, had been carried out at the ministerial or diplomatic levels, this was a sobering experience for parliamentarians and not one to encourage hope. The Brezhnev meeting was slightly more cordial, perhaps due in part to the fact that he was rumored to be suffering from a mysterious ailment.

In our meeting with Secretary Brezhnev, we sat according to seniority at the conference table, following senatorial custom. This placed me at the far end and, unaccountably, next to a small end table upon which sat a dozen or so small bottles of prescription medicine. It is necessary to keep in mind that this trip took place concurrently with my indoctrination into the murky world of espionage high and low. I had been given permission to take my camera into the meeting and, while seated, dutifully snapped off several pictures of our delegation and the Soviet leader.

Then, overtaken by an impulse to help supply a small but possibly important piece to the puzzle of Brezhnev's illness and its implications for the process of change in Soviet leadership, I set the camera's distance focus at three or four feet, turned it in the direction of the end table, placed my arm over it, and snapped off a half-dozen shots timed to be muffled by one speech or another. One could suppose that the Soviet leader's staff assumed none of us could read the Russian inscriptions on the bottles. But they should also have supposed that there might be people in Langley, Virginia, who could.

We ended our trip on July 4, 1975, in Leningrad, less than sixteen short years later to be renamed St. Petersburg, where at a luncheon hosted by the mayor, each of us gave a little speech in the form of a toast that we might give were we at home in our states on our national holiday. Being eleventh, all I can remember saying is something to the effect that Thomas Jefferson was our ideal of a true revolutionary. Under the considerable influence of their own vodka, the Russians laughed and cheered.

But intelligence adventures were only beginning. Before leaving on this trip I had asked Bill Colby to try to put me together with a dark figure known only to the Church Committee by his CIA code name, QJWIN. He had become a figure of interest because the CIA had contracted with him to participate in more than one assassination plot against foreign leaders. He was not an American, but was generally understood to be of some European heritage, and his code name briefly surfaced in connection with one or more of the several plots against Castro. That being the case, it is readily understandable that, even a decade or more later, he might have picked up a thread of information from the exile Cuban community or who knows where regarding the assassination of John Kennedy, particularly given the proximity of events and the newly mushrooming motives for that act.

Colby understood that our group would be transiting through Amsterdam on our way home and promised to contact me there if he was able to locate QJWIN. "We have not had contact with him for some time," Colby had said. At a press conference as we were preparing to depart Moscow, I was surprised to be approached by a youngish man who simply said, "I'm from the US Embassy and have this message for you." He handed me a sealed, unmarked white envelope. On the single sheet of paper inside was this: "You will be contacted regarding your requested meeting when you arrive in Amsterdam." It was unsigned, but I knew where it came from.

Our delegation checked into the Amstel Hotel in Amsterdam two days later in the afternoon, and plans were made to have rijsttafel at a leading Indonesian restaurant. I left my name and the restaurant number with the hotel concierge when we set out, and notified the restaurant maître d' that I was expecting a call. Halfway through the evening I received a call in the manager's office, and it was Colby's man. He gave me instructions as to how we were to meet very much later that evening, after all members of our party were tucked away.[20] Sometime after midnight, according to instructions, I made two passes through a dim, smoky bar and, on the second pass, was contacted by the CIA man. After retreating to a very dark corner table, he stated that the agency had located QJWIN and convinced him to come to Amsterdam to meet "a friend of ours." Two hours earlier the assassin had arrived as promised and the rendezvous was made. The assassin, who had been employed by a variety of intelligence services over the years and who considered himself a prime target of retaliation from more sources than one can imagine, immediately wanted to know if the "friend" had anything to do with the intelligence investigation under way in the United States at the time. Colby's man, one of his top agents, according to Colby and later a senior official of the agency, told me that he decided to tell QJWIN the truth. Whereupon

QJWIN left and returned to his then hideout, which I came to deduce was possibly somewhere in Belgium.

Three things are possible. One is that QJWIN was never contacted and never there and the whole episode was constructed to convince me that the agency had tried to cooperate in an exercise it wished to fail. Another is that Colby's man knew that the assassin would bolt if told the truth and therefore managed to have it both ways. The third is that Colby's man simply miscalculated and innocently told the truth, not expecting the result. To this day, I do not know which to believe, though the third seems the least plausible.

(Message: QJWIN, if you are out there, I would still like to talk to you. Anyplace, anytime. Contact me through this publisher.)

The emergence of Cuba as the nexus of an increasing number of troubling events and people should not have been totally surprising. Cuba could not be mentioned then or later without "a communist dictatorship ninety miles off our shores" being affixed. Cuba had always been trouble waiting to happen. A conquest of the early Spanish explorers, a way station on the slave trade routes, an occasional stopping point for various waves of pirates early and late, the locus for the launch of both the Spanish-American War and the political career of the ever colorful Teddy Roosevelt, by the mid-twentieth century it had become the dream venue of a very high-level Mafia cabal led by Meyer Lansky and Lucky Luciano.

These two collected every Mafia figure who counted in 1946 in Havana, including most importantly for purpose of this narrative one Santo Trafficante Jr. (who would later be joined by Johnny Roselli and Sam Giancana as investors in the Cuban operations) and Carlos Marcello of New Orleans, to solidify and considerably expand Cuba as the base for the mob's gambling, prostitution, liquor, and narcotics operations in the Western Hemisphere. It was Las Vegas before Las Vegas, and would become these gentlemen's Disneyland with a flair. Long before twenty-first-century advertising slogans, what happened in Cuba, stayed in Cuba. To make it all work, politicians at various levels had to be owned, including most importantly a handsome general named Fulgencio Batista who, for certain considerations, the Mafia made president of Cuba.

Repeated description of corruption as a cancer does not make it less true. Even fun-loving Caribbean climates can accommodate this cancer only so long before resort to political surgery is demanded. This arrived in 1956 in the form of the Castro brothers and a small band including Che Guevara, who landed their rusting tub, the *Granma*, on the southern shores of the island to work a revolution.

On New Year's Day 1959, the bearded ones (*los barbudos*), the advanced guard of the 26th of July Movement, arrived in Havana to take over the country. One kind of fun ended and another began. In either case, the murder rate stayed about the same. Coincidences of timing, place, and personnel compounded. Frank Sinatra was a favorite of both the Havana nightclub set and the Mafia starting in the late 1940s. The young John Kennedy was among the many who traveled there for recreation and relaxation. A very wide assortment of other figures who would come to play large or small roles in the events that began in this era and culminated in Dallas in November 1963 moved in and out of Havana over the years, at least until Castro took over.

To connect all the dots somehow associated with Cuba, Castro, the CIA, the Mafia, Kennedy, and the Cold War is the work of a lifetime. Libraries of books on these connections and these times continue to expand. As was said of Europe in an earlier time, this place was producing more history than it could ever possibly consume. Much of this might have lain dormant, as many still alive at that time would have wished, had William Colby not chosen to reveal the family jewels (or at least some part of them) and the CIA-Mafia-Castro plots to the Church Committee. Some years later, while canoeing alone in the tidewater near his rural Maryland home, Bill Colby would die what some considered, given the circumstances, a mysterious death. In sound health and at home on the water, he drowned. His death was ruled an accident.

The story of how the United States found Castro's brand of socialism no more to its liking than it did Moscow's or Beijing's is too well known even to require summarization. But Cuba's proximity and its more manageable dimensions brought disproportionate US attention to it.

The seriousness of what we were up to was underscored on Christmas Eve 1975. Bill Colby called my house to ask if I would be willing to seek a presidential order to have Richard Welch, the CIA station chief in Athens, buried at the national cemetery at Arlington. Welch had been assassinated the night before by three gunmen outside his house. He and dozens of other senior agency station chiefs and officials had been outed by a renegade former employee of the agency, Philip Agee, and a new magazine called *CounterSpy*. Their identities and private addresses were disclosed, and a long-time Greek terrorist group called November 17 took credit for killing Welch as his wife looked on.

This would not be the only murder that occurred during, or might be associated directly or indirectly with, the Church Committee's investigation.

Though it may have been the case, my understanding was that no CIA agent had ever been buried at Arlington. Regardless, a presidential order was required in this instance to do so. Though puzzled as to why Colby had contacted me, the youngest member of the Church Committee and a Democrat rather than senior Republicans such as Goldwater, Tower, or Baker with President Ford in the White House, I placed a call from my home to the president's chief of staff. He called back momentarily and I relayed Colby's request. The chief of staff said he would speak to the president and call me back. About two hours later, the call came through that President Ford had signed the order, and I relayed this information to Bill Colby. And Richard Welch received an honorable burial at Arlington for having died in the service of his country.

This incident is significant in two regards. It illustrates the highly precarious nature of intelligence activities during this period and the treacherous minefield those of us involved in investigating those activities were seeking to traverse. It also had historic implications. Largely as a result of the Welch assassination and the danger in which agency officials now found themselves, one of the Church Committee's recommendations was to enact legislation making it a felony to identify a covert CIA officer. It took until 1982 to pass the Intelligence Identities Protection Act.[21]

This is significant primarily because the White House chief of staff I called that Christmas Eve in 1975 was Richard Cheney. Three decades later he and his office of the vice presidency, along with his successor in the chief of staff position Karl Rove, would be implicated in the outing, and therefore serious endangerment, of the covert agent Valerie Plame, for no other purpose than political retaliation for her husband, Ambassador Joe Wilson's, honest report undercutting the Bush administration's false argument that Iraq was seeking uranium in Niger.

Earlier that year, at the end of April, I received a call from Dick Cheney asking if I would like to join President Ford and a delegation of Yale Law graduates from the Congress and Supreme Court to attend the 150th anniversary of the law school, where the president was to speak. I was honored to do so, and during the dinner Cheney came to my seat and whispered an invitation to fly with the president from Andrews Air Force Base back to the White House upon our return to Washington later that night. Once aboard *Marine One* helicopter at Andrews, President Ford, Cheney, and I were joined by Yale president Kingman Brewster (*Mayflower* descendent and later ambassador to the Court of Saint James under President Carter). During the twelve-minute helicopter ride, I expected weighty conversation between the presidents of the United States and Yale on matters of state.

Instead, Brewster asked Ford about his days as assistant football coach at Yale while he was also attending the law school. President Ford obliged by reminding us of how football had changed in the days since he played center for Michigan still using the ancient single-wing formation. He bent over in the center of the helicopter cabin and gave a demonstration of the difficulty of snapping the ball back to the halfback and even greater difficulty of the long snap to the punter.

There was, needless to say, a slight air of unreality about all this, at least for a first-year senator. Laid aside for the moment between two lofty leaders—and sports fans—were concerns for the Cold War, higher education in America, foreign policy, and economic distress. Gerald Ford, I came to believe, was among the most human and unassuming men ever to occupy the White House. And in 1984, nine short years later, Kingman Brewster, known to students in the 1960s and '70s as "the King," would ask to be named a Hart delegate from Connecticut to the Democratic convention. Even now, I can still remember looking down from the podium and seeing him waving his Hart banner.

The Castro-CIA-Mafia puzzle, however, continued to deepen. With Frank Church's approval, I approached Cyrus Vance, by then secretary of state in the Carter administration, about going to Havana to talk to Fidel Castro. The theory was that Castro had agents throughout the exile Cuban community based in Miami, agents who kept him thoroughly informed of assassination plots against him (and thus helped keep him alive), and through them he might have picked up information about plots against Kennedy by those angry at his administration's decision to suspend efforts to kill Castro as part of a Cuban Missile Crisis settlement with the Soviet Union.

Secretary Vance said he had no authority to approve such travel. Only one person could do so, Frances Knight, head of the Passport Office, and she was close with J. Edgar Hoover and his successors at the FBI. The concern was that Knight would inform the FBI, and the bureau would scuttle the trip by leaking it to the media. No one involved, particularly a first-year senator, wanted a clandestine trip to Cuba to view the Kennedy assassination through the other side of a one-way mirror to become front-page news.

Cy Vance did say that he had heard of people making the trip by private plane with Cuban approval. My assistant, Tom Moore, a former investigative journalist for the *Chicago Sun-Times*, went to New York and relayed to the Cuban representative to the United Nations my desire to see Castro and the purpose for the visit. After the Cubans at the UN checked with Havana, Tom was called back to New York and given approval. Castro knew why I wanted to see him and personally approved the trip. Tom made arrangements for a private charter flight from Key West, we relayed its tail number and the time of arrival to Havana, and we prepared to go the following evening.

Hours before leaving, I received a call from the acting director of the FBI, who solemnly informed me that the bureau had discovered a serious security breach in the Church Committee, and my office was involved. Consternation would not begin to describe my reaction. Resistance to congressional oversight of intelligence activities had always been premised on the inability of politicians to keep secrets. Only one leak from the Church Committee, particularly if it jeopardized national security, would end our investigation, crush the prospect of serious oversight, and bring disrepute on the Senate. Two senior bureau officials were on their way to my office with damning evidence.

In solemn tones they informed me of the security breach and said it involved my staff. They laid eight-by-ten photos on my desk of Tom Moore entering and leaving the Cuban office at the UN on two occasions. There would be no trip to Havana. I simply said, "Gentlemen, Mr. Moore was operating under my instructions with the approval of our committee chairman, Senator Church, and that is all I'm going to tell you." It would take more than twenty years before I got to Havana to discuss the Kennedy assassination with Fidel Castro.

Much of the work of the Church Committee during late 1975 and early 1976 involved following up on the family jewels, and particularly the question of assassination of foreign leaders. Our effort was focused more on how this happened and less on who was to blame. If we were to contribute to reform of a system, with the goal of intelligence services under control of elected and appointed officials but not abused by those same officials, up to and including presidents, we had to know how the current system worked. For prime example, who ordered Fidel Castro killed? After much confused investigation and interrogation of dozens of witnesses from previous administrations and agencies, the simple answer was no one.

The equally simple explanation of this conundrum is a doctrine called plausible deniability. Presidents or those under presidential command and speaking for them might tell the CIA, FBI, or others to achieve a certain objective but to do so in a vague enough manner, and without specific instructions as to methods, so that that president or those officials could, under circumstances of disclosure, deny responsibility, culpability, or even knowledge of the operation. Some denials were white lies and some were black as sin.

Neither John Kennedy nor Robert Kennedy, to the best of our knowledge, ever told Richard Helms, CIA's deputy director of operations, or any of his predecessors, "We want you to kill Castro." Rather, they and others around them, continuing and expanding efforts to overthrow Castro begun in the Eisenhower era, could and did say things like, "How do we get rid of this guy?," leaving it to the agency to fill in the blanks. It was policy by euphemism.

The major problem with this neat political arrangement was that presidents were not held responsible at the time, or later, when plans and actions got botched; the more or less defenseless CIA was. Thus, the "rogue elephant" theory.

The Castro plots were under way during the period that President Kennedy was making Ian Fleming famous, and wealthy. After a White House briefing session, the president asked Richard Helms, the CIA's director of operations, to stay behind. The president wanted to know if we had a James Bond. Helms thought it over and came up with the name of one of his principal operatives. Kennedy asked for him to be brought around. In due course, Helms brought the man, William Harvey, to see the president. Physically, Harvey was about as far from Sean Connery as one could imagine. The two sat outside the Oval Office, whose door was guarded by the Secret Service. After some minutes, and operating on a well-informed hunch, Helms approached Harvey across the waiting room and asked in a whisper whether he was armed. Harvey assured him that he was *always* armed. Taken aback, Helms identified himself to the Secret Service agent and told him Mr. Harvey, a top CIA agent, was armed. Stunned, the Secret Service man removed the .45 under Harvey's arm. Minutes passed, and Helms had a horrible thought. He crossed to Harvey one more time and, again in a whisper, asked whether he had any other arms. Harvey reached for the Derringer strapped to his ankle and said, "Of course, Dick, I *always* carry a backup weapon." These were yeasty times.

The Castro plots offered the most dramatic case of the plausible deniability doctrine. Eisenhower and Kennedy wanted Castro gone, they made clear to the agency. How you do it is up to you. Who knew Havana? Who knew the country?

Who still had contacts there relatively few months after the revolution? The list was short. Enter the Mafia, this time in the form of Santo Trafficante Jr., an original member of the 1946 Lansky-Luciano syndicate and longtime head of the mob in Tampa; Johnny Roselli, seeking relief from a lingering deportation order and semiretired head of the mob in Miami; and Sam Giancana from Chicago, as important a Mafia figure as there was at this time. All were now in their seventies.

Our committee and a similar one begun in the House of Representatives then set out to track down Giancana in 1975. It wasn't difficult. At that time he was under more or less round-the-clock surveillance by both the FBI and the Chicago Police Department. He was accustomed to their cars being parked outside his house and the places he visited. Occasionally he would mock them. On one occasion, when Giancana was helping the CIA with its Castro assassination plots, he emerged from a favorite restaurant with friends and proceeded across the street to the FBI's customary surveillance car and said to the startled and confused driver, "Why don't you guys ask the chief [Hoover] to ask the super-chief [Robert Kennedy] to ask the super-super chief [the president] what we're doing to help." The evening after, his attorney was contacted and demanded a subpoena for Giancana to appear before a congressional committee. June 19, 1975, Giancana, now well into his seventies, was cooking his dinner alone in his basement kitchen in Oak Park, Illinois, and was killed by six .22 caliber bullet holes in his throat. Giancana would never have the honor of testifying before a congressional committee concerning the Mafia's cooperation with the CIA in an effort to kill Castro. The method of his murder was signature Mafia and a graphic warning against talking.

Giancana's murder has never been solved.

Five days after Giancana's murder, the Church Committee summoned Roselli to come to Washington and, in secret, tell us what he remembered. He was a dapper, well-turned-out man with a gravely voice. In previous years he would have been played by an actor called George Raft, who coincidentally ended up as part owner of one of the mob's casino's in Havana. Roselli's memory was vague, except he recalled being asked to help and "because I'm a patriot and wanted to help my country," he did what he could, attended some clandestine meetings, and offered suggestions here and there. Roselli's self-proclaimed patriotism may also have had something to do with the federal deportation order he had been fighting for years. Thereafter, he made another appearance before the committee on September 22, 1975, again in secret.

We ran in circles until a committee staff researcher going through President Kennedy's phone logs at the Kennedy Library in Boston in an effort to find out who the president was talking to during the period of 1961 to 1963 turned up about seventy-five calls between the White House and a number in Los Angeles. AT&T helpfully identified the holder of this number as a Ms. Judith Campbell. Who might she be? In 1975 she was Judith Campbell Exner, the wife of a golf pro in Las Vegas. During the 1960 presidential campaign she had been introduced to John Kennedy by Frank Sinatra. This was now complicated but not unmanageable. But shortly thereafter we discovered Sinatra had also introduced her to his friend Sam Giancana around the same time.

Ms. Campbell had some kind of friendship with the president of the United States and the head of the Mafia in Chicago at the same time the CIA was using Giancana to carry out what it perceived to be Kennedy's orders to get rid of (i.e., assassinate) Fidel Castro. Now the complications were quickly becoming unmanageable, and the many dots surrounding Cuba were beginning to connect themselves in bizarre ways even as new, unimagined dots were popping up.

On April 23, 1976, we called Roselli back to testify about this new information, though this time, somehow, his appearance ended up in *The Miami Herald*. Roselli confirmed the Kennedy-Campbell-Giancana connections, and then on July 28, he disappeared. On August 9, Roselli's body floated to the surface in a fifty-five-gallon steel drum in the appropriately named Dumfounding Bay. It seemed more than appropriate for someone from our committee to find out what we could about the coincidence of his testimony and his murder, and I volunteered. Together with three staff members, I went to meet with Dade County sheriff's officers and, though traveling incognito, our presence was announced in *The Miami Herald* the following morning. Whoever wanted Roselli dead also wanted the world to know *why* he died.[22]

Neither the sheriff nor the Miami Police Department had any suspects other than their clear conclusion that, given all the evidence, this was a Mafia hit. After laying out the facts, we then were treated to pictures of Roselli in the barrel as he was hauled in. In the state of nature, people, even dead people, do not fit readily into barrels. To overcome this obstacle, Roselli's arms and legs had been severed and stuffed into the barrel alongside his torso. He had been garroted and, as I recall, shot. The detectives assume this considerable damage had been done, according to custom, in a remote garage while the victim was strung up on a hook. He had been in the barrel almost two weeks. Someone wanted this semiretired, golf-playing seventy-something-year-old dead. Consequently, they had killed him every way they could think of. Had they wanted him to stay sunk, he would have stayed sunk. (The Dade County coroner disputed this and held that his killers had miscalculated. My own view is that the Mafia has some experience with how to keep bodies in barrels sunk.) So they also wanted the world to know what had happened to him. And, according to his family, the only thing he had done out of the ordinary in months was to go to Washington.

The FBI wanted nothing to do with investigating Roselli's death, claiming lack of jurisdiction. And the director of

Central Intelligence at the time, George H. W. Bush, strenuously denied that his agency had anything to do with Roselli's murder, as some at the time claimed.

Roselli's murder has never been solved.

A search began for Santo Trafficante. Mysteriously, yet conveniently, Trafficante had managed to be out of the country on the very dates his longtime friends Johnny Roselli and Sam Giancana were murdered. He never testified before our committee and died a somewhat more natural death in 1987. For all practical purposes, case closed. To my knowledge, no investigation continued into these very high-profile murders thereafter.

After giving at least three different and almost totally contradictory stories about her friendships with Kennedy and Giancana, Judith Exner died of cancer in 1999. Richard Helms believed that during a White House meeting in the early sixties he had received a "marshal's baton" to dispel Castro. He died in 2002. And then, of course, William Colby, who uncovered this still-seething snake pit, also died.

Why, twelve or thirteen years after the assassination of John Kennedy, did two senior Mafia figures with ties to pre-Castro Cuba, who cooperated with the CIA in an effort to kill Castro, die during the first effort of Congress to look into these plots? A final small-world footnote that reveals the bizarre nature of all this was the fact that, during their collaboration to assassinate Castro, the American James Bond, Bill Harvey, and Johnny Roselli became fast friends and, before Roselli's murder, they and their families vacationed together.

Searching for harlots high and low, to use Norman Mailer's title, I took it upon myself to organize dinner with Mr. Counterspy himself, James Jesus Angleton, head of counterintelligence at the CIA. Known throughout the intelligence world as a walking conundrum and veritable human maze, he lived up to his billing. Throughout the evening at a small restaurant in Georgetown, the eponymous Angleton circled and dodged, tracked and then backtracked. Using every lawyerly skill I possessed, I tried to phrase questions that could only yield direct answers. He eluded them all. Finally, over coffee and his tenth or twelfth cigarette, I said, "Mr. Angleton, do you believe others besides Lee Harvey Oswald were involved in President Kennedy's assassination?" Eyes glittering in his deeply lined face and with only the faint trace of a smile, Angleton said, "In my father's house are many mansions."

As always, during this intense period of mayhem in high places, other duties continued. In December 1975 I made the first of several trips in the capacity of a member of the Armed Services Committee. Together with my chief of staff, Tom Hoog, I visited the commander, US Naval Forces Europe, in London, then proceeded down to Barcelona for briefings, dinner, and an overnight stay on board the flagship of Admiral Harry Train, then commanding the Sixth Fleet in the Mediterranean, and finally on board the USS *Nimitz* which, with its carrier task group, was on station in the Med. At dinner, I asked Admiral Train, a distinguished officer with whom almost a quarter of a century later I would serve on the US Commission on National Security for the 21st Century, how many vessels he had under his command. He gestured at the silver gravy boat on the linen tablecloth and said, "That's a vessel. I have fifteen (or some such) ships in this fleet."

The *Nimitz* was the first in its class of ninety-seven-thousand-ton nuclear aircraft carriers with a complement of almost one hundred combat and support aircraft on board and a crew, including the air wing, of about six thousand. By way of preparation, I had gone through a pretty thorough physical, including G-pressure tests, before leaving Washington and was offered the chance to fly in the backseat, the radar operator's seat, in an F-4 fighter aircraft. The second day on board, I went through the preflight brief with the squadron commander, Gene Tucker, and squadron aircraft crews and went on deck, suited up in the G suit, climbed into the cramped backseat, and rolled out onto the catapult launch. Commander Tucker saluted, the deck flight ops thrust his arm forward, the catapult operator punched us out, and off we went with both burners lit, from 0 to about 120 knots in just over two hundred feet.

Life holds few experiences more exciting.

I was told later that pilots who had experienced a certain number of catapult launches quite frequently developed hairline spinal cracks and, given the nature of the slingshot thrust, it was easily believable. As we left the deck, the F-4 fully loaded with fuel and armaments (weighing upward of seventy-five thousand pounds) sank before gaining full thrust from its twin engines, and I glanced over my shoulder to see the edge of the deck *above* us. We were out for well over an hour flying against *Nimitz* planes that had launched before us. Two combat aircraft with combined speeds well exceeding a thousand miles per hour close with each other in what seemed like a heartbeat. The incoming is five miles out and then, blink, and he's gone right past.

Landing was quite another matter. At ten thousand feet or so, the carrier looked the size of a postage stamp. This plane is never going to land on that deck, my layman's brain told me. And then in the approach a half mile out, the deck, even in a reasonable sea, seemed to pitch, roll, and toss as if daring the pilot to try it. In we came, and, though strapped in so tightly I could not move, my helmeted head hit the instrument panel when we caught the wire.

On the preflight aircraft inspection, Tucker showed me the cracks in the fuselage of the F-4. It had flown a large number of missions in Vietnam and was aging. Whether calculated or not, this had the effect of increasing my interest in supporting replacement aircraft procurement upon returning to Washington. Though often criticized by the press and public for "boondoggling," not enough members of Congress spend time with the troops deployed at bases or on board ships overseas. It is not possible otherwise to fully appreciate the day-to-day stresses and strains of military operations, including in peacetime, and the skill and dedication of the men and women committed to our defense.

The same theory led me to undertake an eventful trip in 1977. By this time, a permanent Senate Intelligence Oversight Committee had been formed as a result of Church Committee recommendation, and I was among its founding members. On very rare occasions in past years, a visiting member of Congress or delegation might have been briefed by a CIA officer during a foreign trip. But to my knowledge, no member of Congress had ever, up to this time, undertaken a full oversight trip through a series of CIA stations overseas for the express purpose of determining how they were doing their jobs.

Accompanied only by a staff member, Karl Frederick "Rick" Inderfurth (later an Emmy-award-winning correspondent for ABC News in Moscow during the consequential transition years of the late eighties early nineties and then assistant secretary of state for south Asian affairs), we made stops in Paris, Rome, Athens, Tehran, Tel Aviv, and Lisbon. At each stop we spent a day or two with station chiefs and their senior operatives learning about day-to-day and longer-term operations; their relationships with our embassies and host governments; whether they were "declared" (acknowledged as CIA) to the host intelligence services or totally clandestine and under full embassy cover; what their principal rivals, the Soviets, were up to, how they viewed political and military developments in their countries; how they got along with representatives of other US intelligence services such as the DIA (Defense Intelligence Agency); and occasionally the dangers they encountered in developing sources and information.

By and large, intelligence life is routine, occasionally boring, given over to the difficult and usually unrewarding efforts to recruit well-placed sources, either in host governments or other foreign services—or on very rare occasions in foreign intelligence services—and filled with frustrations, duplications, and undramatic daily life. For reasons never made quite clear, CIA officers, much like their diplomatic counterparts, are rotated to new assignments about the time they have put down roots, established networks, and learned local languages and cultures. The rotation rate is usually justified as preventing their identification as well as too much coziness, comfort, and ease. In many cases it seems to be a dubious trade-off.

We did not meet "our man in Havana," the paid agent in the local economy without embassy cover, acknowledged relationship with the US government, or intelligence credentials of any kind—in other words, the Valerie Plames of the world. These individuals may work for a CIA front, a wholly owned private subsidiary of the agency, or simply be operating under their own private cover as a businessperson, journalist, or academic researcher. On a couple of occasions, Rick and I met an American or two at a lunch or dinner who may have been in this category, but in no case were they declared to us. Unlike their agency counterparts, these agents have no embassy protection and understand they are on their own if detected by the host government or another intelligence service.

In almost every respect and in all venues this trip required innovation on the part of all parties. Local station chiefs and personnel did not know whether we were the forerunners of a hoard of noisy, headline-seeking members of Congress. There was no protocol based on precedent. We did not know whether we would be treated seriously, with disdain, and even whether we would be told the truth. No one was familiar with how Congress was going to exercise its newly discovered oversight responsibilities. Were we there to chastise, to probe for misdeeds, to showboat? Wariness would characterize demeanor on both sides, but once we had made a stop or two, and certainly the jungle drums were sending messages ahead, word got out that we were not calling press conferences, that we asked sensible and responsible questions, and that we knew how to use knives and forks. Things loosened up a bit, and among a number of notable developments two stand out in memory.

Rick Inderfurth and I were taken to lunch by the CIA station chief in Paris and, during a discussion of his operation's relations to his KGB counterparts, he nodded to a table against the far wall and said, "There they are. We stay out of each other's way and generally get along fine."

Tehran under Shah Mohammad Pahlavi had the surface calm that only a notoriously savage security apparatus called SAVAK could provide. Some time before we arrived, however, three US Air Force colonels there to provide assistance with weapons procurement and training were gunned down on a downtown street. Despite this, after our first day of briefings by our host, the station chief (name withheld), and a dinner at the US Embassy hosted by Ambassador, and former CIA director, Richard Helms with a couple of dozen Iranian government and community leaders and intellectuals, a couple of whom took the occasion to take us each aside and mutter that we should not believe what we were told or our lying eyes about the peacefulness of Iran, we were deposited at our hotel for that and the following night.

Entering the lobby of about a one-and-a-half star Iranian hotel, most of the shabby furniture was occupied by distinctly unattractive and unfriendly men who watched our progress to the desk, to the elevator, and thence to our rooms. Something was not right here. We were visiting a seemingly allied country by ourselves where every sign was that a seething cauldron of anger and hostility was just below the surface, where even a cursory reading of modern Iranian history would reveal that resentment over the US overthrow of the reformer prime minister Mohammad Mosaddegh in 1953 was as deeply remembered as if it were yesterday, and where the ruling shah, whose family we had more or less imposed on the country, was squandering national revenues in spectacular fashion, and we had been deposited in a hotel with a sieve for security.

By now I had become so accustomed to second and third thoughts, the forerunners of clinical paranoia, that a setup of some proportions suggested itself right away. What better excuse for a national crackdown on all dissidents, harmless or otherwise, could be offered than the slaughter of a visiting American senator and his aide? Would the CIA be so desperate to undercut congressional oversight and justify return to hard-line tactics that it would willingly collaborate in such a scheme? Things promptly got worse. Rick was on one floor of the hotel and I another. The place seemed abandoned. Why not adjoining rooms at least?

I opened the door to my suite, a long narrow affair with an entrance hallway, then a sitting-dining room, and eventually, way at the back, a bath and bed, neither of which looked especially sanitary but were in keeping with the run-down furnishings in the rest of the quarters. Under the circumstances, the distance from bed to door seemed about a hundred yards and the liberating light of dawn about a month away. This was going to be a very long night.

If the heavy-browed, unshaven, dark-eyed men with weapons almost certainly under their armpits downstairs were truly up to something, the desk clerk would be the first to abandon ship. I tried the phone system and a thickly accented voice answered. I requested connection to Mr. Inderfurth's room. This conversation ensued:

Me: "What do you think?"
Rick: "I don't like this at all."
Me: "Do we have any options?"
Rick: "We could check out and try to find someplace else. But who knows who owns the cab company, and I

don't have (name withheld)'s phone number. He's picking us up at 5:30 in the morning."
Me, after some silence: "How would you like to be a senator for tonight?"
Rick: "No thanks."

The night was endless. Though I'm not entirely fearless,
concern for personal safety has never been my major preoccupation. This night would be a monumental exception. Instinct
had served me well up to now, and this night it was not telling
me good things. I propped the biggest chair I could find under
the doorknob, scattered various objects that might make noise
in the long hallway, hunkered down, and waited for the assault.
Like most men of finite physical strength, I was determined not
to go down without a fight. There may or may not have been
a scattered half hour of sleep here and there, but eventually
predawn did come. The wake-up call was unnecessary. I met
Rick in the lobby of the hotel well before the 5:30 AM pick-up
time, and there the same men or their near surrogates were still
there. While time passed and (name withheld) did not appear,
Rick and I consoled ourselves with the conclusion that these
were SAVAK agents deputized to protect us from harm.

Eventually, after 6 AM, the station chief and driver
screeched to a halt at the hotel entrance and we piled in.
He apologized for oversleeping. "Almost never happens," he
assured us. "Good night's sleep?" he cheerfully inquired.
"Not quite," we told him. After recounting all the ways this
seemed less-than-secure procedure, we did thank him for
arranging the overnight security detail. He seemed puzzled.
"Those weren't our guys," he said, scratching his head.

We took an unmarked aircraft up-country, northwest to
a point north of Tabriz, very near the Soviet border. Code-
named Tachsman, the station's principal responsibility, after
helping secure the shah's shaky regime, was to operate a very
sophisticated listening station on Soviet missile launches

from a base a few hundred kilometers away, downrange to Siberia. Members of the operating crew at the station, accompanied by their faithful dog Airport, met us and took us on a tour, mostly of unfathomable radars and listening devises, even then being rapidly replaced by even more sophisticated overhead systems, and we received briefings organized around very detailed maps of the region. These were clearly dedicated people possessing highly sophisticated skills, and they operated in isolation on rotations of a month or so. They were direct about what they could learn, which was considerable, and what they couldn't.

On the way back to Tehran, Rick and I raised the issue of accommodations with (name withheld) and strongly suggested something a little less dicey. My guess is he thought us fraidy cats, but offered his home as accommodations for the last night in town. We ended up there, a walled compound that had previously belonged to some local grandee or long-dispossessed diplomat. The following morning he took us to the Tehran airport to pick up our ongoing flight. We loaded in the car with our host and his driver in front. At the end of a very long driveway, an employee stood poised. The station chief explained that he got a run at the gate every morning so the car could hit the street at speed, even though an immediate sharp right was required.

He turned to assure us: "The only thing we're really concerned about these days are car bombs." I noticed that the battered, boxy briefcase that seemed always to be in his lap was open and contained two semiautomatic firearms of at least .9 mm caliber. The timing was good, and we hit the street through the just-opened gate with a screeching turn to the right. There on the right, my side of the car, was an empty automobile. Through gritted teeth I struggled to keep my cringe from showing.

The following day in Lisbon we were the guests of Ambassador Frank Carlucci who, we discovered that evening in a briefing in a closed gazebo in a remote corner of his back lawn, was also de facto station chief. Not only was he conducting traditional diplomatic chores, he was also principal intelligence collector and agent manager, and he was playing possibly the key role in stabilizing what was perceived to be the fragile government of Prime Minister Mário Soares. In those days, despite the failed strategy in Vietnam, we were still pursuing various variations of the domino theory. Accordingly, it was believed that the emergence of a procommunist government in Portugal, especially one unfriendly to the United States, was a consequence devoutly to be avoided. Whether political reality justified our government's concerns in this occasion, as it had not in others, Carlucci proved himself to be a consummate and sophisticated diplomat then and later.

To my knowledge, little harm came of this novel expedition and, at least from my own perspective on and understanding of the operations of our nation's principal intelligence service in the field, much good. From all I can gather, very few trips like this by those responsible for intelligence oversight took place thereafter.

Some time later, in the early hours of March 28, 1979, as chairman of a subcommittee on nuclear energy, I would be among the first to learn that a nuclear power plant called Three Mile Island near the southeastern Pennsylvania border had suddenly experienced a nuclear "incident." A combination of reactor design flaws and increasingly disastrous operator responses, dismissed as virtually impossible by the nuclear industry, led to a severe meltdown of reactor Unit 2 and, later, the development of a hydrogen "bubble" in the reactor containment. If the reactor had breached (dropped through) the containment, either due to its own intense heat or the explosion of the hydrogen, the reactor core would have dropped into the water table just below (thus the "Island"), and a highly radioactive cloud of steam would have gone several thousand feet into the atmosphere and, within hours, would have drifted with the prevailing winds over Manhattan Island. The implications were beyond catastrophic. The casualties from intense radiation over New York City could have been in the hundreds of thousands.

While all this was beginning to transpire, I invited my new colleague Alan Simpson of Wyoming to join me, in his capacity as ranking minority member of the subcommittee, in an army helicopter trip to Three Mile Island. We made several passes over the melting reactor and then landed on the plant grounds to be briefed by officials of the operator, Metropolitan Edison, and the Nuclear Regulatory Commission (NRC). We were assured that all was under control, though during the entire visit, we later discovered, the reactor was releasing radiation.

It took more than seventy-two hours to bring the reactor under some control, and weeks before the full extent of the damage, and the potential for catastrophe, would be known.

When the radioactive dust finally settled and the plant was genuinely under control, our subcommittee undertook an investigation on behalf of the Senate into the accident and, after weeks of hearings and study, issued a report that led to substantial reforms of nuclear construction licensing and operator licensing, as well as more intense oversight by the NRC of all nuclear reactors. By this time communities across the country were having intense second thoughts about the benefits of nuclear power, and the number of reactor licenses requested and granted, even under self-proclaimed pronuclear administrations, fell off virtually to zero. But our investigation and recommendations for reform helped contribute to the prevention of nuclear incidents anywhere nearly as serious as Three Mile Island in the thirty years since then.

As an eerie coincidence, the movie *The China Syndrome*, involving a reactor meltdown, came out that month, and my wife and I went to see it on the same Friday night that I was notified that the Three Mile Island reactor was critical and melting and the governor of Pennsylvania ordered the evacuation of everyone within several miles of the plant.

Experiences as vivid as Three Mile Island, not to say immersion in the world of CIA, Mafia, and assassinations, had helped mightily to overcome any first-term hesitation about being up to the Senate job. For complex reasons, and for better or for worse, my indoctrination into highly eventful Senate experiences was remarkable by any measure. It was intense, to say the least, but produced an education few could equal.

By this time I had been in the Senate long enough to appreciate the legendary wisdom passed on to me by a senior senator shortly after my arrival. "You'll spend the first six months wondering how *you* got here," he confidently predicted, "and the next six years wondering how *everyone else* got here." This would be true of a few of my colleagues, but certainly not the majority. Even decades later, respect for a number of my colleagues remains undiminished, and with increasing frequency I thank the political fates for the extraordinary opportunity I had in those years to serve with them.

There was Mike Mansfield himself, an orphan taken west to Montana by relatives to be raised. During World War I, beginning at the age of fourteen, he enlisted in the army, navy, and Marine Corps in an effort to serve. When he met his wife, Maureen, he was an uneducated miner. A schoolteacher, Maureen insisted that Mike go back to school, and, with her encouragement, he eventually earned a doctorate degree and was a college professor when he was elected to the House of Representatives. Mike believed it was an aspect of leadership to promote the next generation of leaders, and I benefited greatly from that conviction.

There was Abraham "Abe" Ribicoff, former governor of Connecticut and cabinet officer under President Kennedy, and the son of Russian immigrants. The only time I saw him raise his voice was during the chaotic 1968 Democratic convention in Chicago when, in nominating George McGovern, he wagged his finger virtually under the nose of the powerful Mayor Richard Daley.

There was Stuart Symington from Missouri, former secretary of the air force, unlike Ribicoff from an old and patrician family. And Charles Mathias, a Republican from Maryland, like the others a man of stature. The gracious, humane, and much-loved Philip Hart of Michigan was in this mold. Daniel Patrick Moynihan was a scholar and one of the few in the Senate of that day or since with a sense of history. That sense permitted him to place current events in context and to judge them against the backdrop of decades and centuries. This historical sense alone made him, unlike many others, worth listening to when he spoke, and it enhanced his influence proportionately.

The senior senator from Louisiana, Russell Long, was a link between the present and the past. He was the son of Huey Long, and he occasionally told stories of his uncle Earl Long, though rarely of his father, in the senators' private dining room. The "Uncle Earl stories," as they were known, were bizarre, so much so that they became the basis of a Paul Newman movie called *Blaze*.[23] Blaze Starr, a famous New Orleans stripper, was a favorite of Uncle Earl's when, after Huey went to Washington as senator and was later assassinated, he became governor. Russell told the story of Earl ordering his state trooper, assigned after Huey was assassinated, to shoot down a fancy chandelier at Blaze's nightclub. The trooper reluctantly did so as tourists scattered for safety. The tourists regularly filled up the place because Blaze kept a sign in the window: "Governor Earl Long's favorite nightclub."

Regardless of the Uncle Earl stories, Russell Long was a serious legislator who, as chairman of the Senate Finance Committee, understood the canonical tax laws better than anyone and used his superior knowledge to the great advantage of his constituents and legislative friends. Almost anyone can be corrupt. Not everyone can be smart.

As a student volunteer for John Kennedy and a young lawyer in Robert Kennedy's Justice Department, I was a little in awe of Edward Kennedy when I met him, following my first election. And, without calculation, I ended up sitting next to him on the back row of the Democratic side of the Senate throughout my years there.

There were a few occasions for socializing at home and abroad, but our friendship was largely based on shared legislative efforts and the advice he had to offer, only when solicited, when he saw special-interest wolves in legislative sheep's clothing. Senator Kennedy and I cosponsored a measure in the 1970s to impose an escalating tax on tobacco and, for our efforts, received the derision of Ernest "Fritz" Hollings of South Carolina who, in the Senate debate, contrasted his "poor little tobacca fahmers, resting with an evening cigarette on their little pohches," with the elegant elitists sailing their yachts at "Mahtha's Vinyahd" and skiing at "fancy resohts in Aaaspin."

Lionized in his later years, Ted Kennedy made it a point to learn about virtually every serious measure brought to the Senate floor. His diligence and persistence, his unflagging dedication through times good and bad to favorite causes such as health care, and his superior legislative skills, courtship of his colleagues, and understanding of human nature went largely unnoted in earlier years.

Senator Kennedy would be the first to laugh at those who, having trivialized him in his earlier years, converted him to sainthood in his later years. For it is his laughter, boisterous, genuine, and immensely human, that I will continue always to remember.

Looking now at a generation or two of Republican senators elected only after passing through the rigid filter of the Religious Right and the convoluted prism of the neoconservative view of the world, those of us who served with their predecessors can only long for restoration of a Republican

Party that will once again open its doors to those who see the world as it is and not as a fantasy of our imagination, who believe in justice and fairness at home, who understand the need for well-managed regulation of economic activities and respect for the environment, and who do not insist on demonization of Democrats.

This breed of moderate Republicans is dormant but hopefully not extinct. When a restored Republican Party reemerges, its younger leaders could do much worse than to read the records of senators like Jacob "Jack" Javits (New York), Charles "Mac" Mathias (Maryland), John Chafee (Rhode Island), Charles "Chuck" Percy (Illinois), Mark Hatfield (Oregon), and a number of others. It will be a cause for wonder among historians why mainstream Republicans permitted their party to be hijacked by an unholy alliance of radical tax-cutters, neoconservative imperialists, and religious Torquemadas who drove a great party off its traditional rails and into a great ditch.

It all began with a purge of these moderates. If you have in mind to accomplish ridiculous and sometimes treacherous things, it is first necessary to get rid of thoughtful people.

In thinking why these many years later the memory of these large-scale figures lingers indelibly, certain shared qualities quickly arise. Despite dramatically different backgrounds and economic circumstances, they were all men (given the political realities of that era) of dignity, of practical wisdom, of dedication to constitutional principles, and of commitment to the national interest. I never heard one of them comment on how his party could get even with or undercut the other. I never heard one of them, or quite a number of others like them, put the interest of party or ideology ahead of the interest of the nation. They were statesmen.

Many others were in that pantheon. Edmund Muskie of Maine, Clifford Case of New Jersey, Hubert Humphrey himself, Howard Baker of Tennessee, Gaylord Nelson of

Wisconsin, Lloyd Bentsen of Texas; the list is lengthy. They had dignity. They were respected, not because they were given respect but because they had *earned* it. One kind of respect is provided by the office. The more profound kind is earned. They were and are men of honor.

In too many cases and in both parties, figures such as these were replaced by more ordinary, and in too many cases, less statesmanlike individuals. Why this began to occur in the late 1970s and 1980s remains unexplained. Some attribute this political and cultural leveling downward to media intrusiveness, the role of money in politics, the social fragmentation into a nation of special interests, to the passing of the World War II generation and the loss of national purpose, or to the introduction of an overall meanness in politics brought by bitter-minded consultants whose mission is "winning" at the expense of all else, including the interests of the nation, and who would invent and capitalize on so-called wedge issues to do so.

And in fairness, it must be noted that great figures are less and less apparent in other walks of life. Corporate executives are notable for extravagant salaries, not productivity and long-term investment strategies. Religious figures are known for narrow judgmentalism, not healing. Few university presidents of the age will be remembered for their elevation of the education system. Dignity, honor, earned respect, and statesmanship are not the hallmarks of our age.

At least as seen through the spectrum of the United States Senate, this fact more than any other marks for me the transition from the 1970s to the 1980s. In that unique forum, senators began to seem smaller. Perhaps this was simply the carrying out of the prophecy years before about wondering how everyone else got there. But there seemed an observable and almost quantifiable change. Certainly the level of partisanship, bitterness, and rancor rose perceptibly. The mood and atmosphere on the floor of the Senate and in its halls and committee chambers was altered. Motives began to be questioned on all sides. Blame became the name of the game. The interests of party and ideology transcended the national interest.

In late 1978, a small delegation of four senators, actually three sitting senators and one senator-elect, was designated to visit Asia and the Far East to consider US security interests and challenges in the region and the overall state of our relations. Sam Nunn of Georgia, John Glenn of Ohio, Bill Cohen of Maine, just elected to the Senate that fall, and I visited Bangkok, Beijing, Tokyo, and Seoul. Our military escort officer was the navy liaison to the Senate, the former Vietnam prisoner of war Captain John McCain, who held that position in the late 1970s.

Captain McCain had escorted me to visit our Indian Ocean fleet a year or so before, and we had become acquainted in a way that long-range foreign travel permits and office visits do not. Sam, who later became chairman of the Senate's Armed Services Committee and a recognized national security expert, and John, a famous astronaut and former Marine Corps pilot, also knew McCain, but perhaps not as well as I. On this trip Bill Cohen and I solidified a friendship with Captain McCain sufficiently to be invited to be McCain's groomsmen when he married Cindy Hensley in May 1980 in Scottsdale, Arizona.

We observed and participated in the annual meeting of more than a dozen US ambassadors from throughout Asia, including our nominal host and former colleague, Mike Mansfield, named American ambassador to Japan following his retirement from the Senate in 1977. Later, on at least two occasions, I visited Mike in Tokyo, where he continued to serve through most of the Reagan presidency, in large part because he was revered by the Japanese. As he was a great senator, he was also a great statesman. Though a skilled politician, neither I nor anyone else ever knew him to compromise his very keen principles.

After our evening with the ambassadors, and as comprehensive a diplomatic tour of the entire Far East as it was possible to get, Bill Cohen, John McCain, and I were given a late-night tour of downtown Bangkok, including its dark-side quarter, by an impressive and intense young foreign service officer and career humanitarian named Lionel Rosenblatt, who founded the refugee section of the US Embassy in Thailand and later became president of Refugees International. We saw where the wealthiest families in the region wined and dined, and we saw storefront "shops" where early-teen prostitutes recruited from impoverished families in the countryside wore schoolgirl pinafores and sat on tiered benches with numbers around their necks until summoned by a customer. For normally protected American senators, though perhaps not for a hardened combat pilot, it was cause for shock and disgust.

During our stop in Tokyo, McCain and I visited US military installations but also took the occasion to visit Japanese naval facilities outside the city. The Japanese military of that day and after was still very much a defensive force and officially designated as such. Its coastal patrol ships were small, and the submarine we toured, tiny by comparison to our giant subsurface cities, seemed quaint. We were told that I was the first American elected official to have this privilege granted, especially by a nation that kept its military forces very much in the background.

Though unable to continue to the final stop, in South Korea, due to schedule conflicts, I participated with the others in the delegation in preparing a report of our trip for the Senate and supported the most controversial recommendation in the report: that we maintain our forces in South Korea. Though contrary to the strong position of our own Defense Department and national security experts, President Carter was then proposing withdrawal of all but token US forces in Korea. He later wrote, with some heat, that our delegation's report signaled that the Senate would never ratify his position.

For reasons even I do not fully understand, I was reelected in November 1980 in a conservative western state that wholeheartedly joined the Reagan landslide. A dozen or so mostly senior Democratic senators dropped like flies all across the nation. A generation of Democratic leaders was dismissed in one of those periodic cathartic elections, even more lopsided than the one in 2008.

Even while learning of my reelection, my reaction was curiously somber. I sensed a sea change in American politics, and not one for the good. It was not just the loss on a large scale of Democratic colleagues, it was a foreboding of the meanness infecting the body politic. The campaigns that overthrew my Democratic colleagues, and in some cases required the primary defeat of moderate Republicans, featured bitter partisanship and divisive social and cultural appeals that were calculated to demonize opponents and even call into question their patriotism.

On the occasion of John Kennedy's assassination, the story was told that Mary McGrory, a gracious, well-loved columnist, mourned with her equally Irish friend Daniel Patrick Moynihan. "Pat," she said, "we'll never laugh again." "No, Mary," he responded, "we'll laugh again. We'll just never be young again."

And by young I believe he meant not just joyful and carefree, but also idealistic and hopeful. Being by nature skeptical and expecting little from flawed human nature, conservatives accept that life is just one damn thing after another, that we are on our own, and it is up to us to make the most of it. But for those with a sense of commonwealth and common good, the shattering of dreams and hopes is always viewed more tragically.

That feeling, in a minor chord, descended that election night. Perhaps it was the loss of the ideal of inevitable progress, that somehow we would find leaders and ways to improve the lot of our nation and all those in it. John Kennedy had been killed, and with him the New Frontier. Robert Kennedy had been killed, and with him the hope of its restoration. Martin Luther King's murder seemed a penalty for insisting on simple equality. We had had Pentagon Papers and Watergate. The post-Watergate tides of reform had risen and now fallen in six short years. The American people had chosen an actor to lead them. Perhaps this was appropriate. Perhaps life had in fact become a carefully scripted movie, and a not particularly good one at that.

Once begun, though, the odyssey had to continue, the search for home be revived. In a way, the labyrinth of intelligence was the odyssey. Perhaps the secrets, however dark they might be and if only they could be unlocked, contained answers concerning the American soul. Labyrinths and halls of mirrors were apt images for this exercise because once inside, there was no simple or obvious way out. There were more blind alleys than openings, more baffles than windows, more retreats and retries than success.

In the midst of all this, with stories mounting in my head, I happened on a late evening dinner in the Senate dining room in the early 1980s with new colleague Bill Cohen, who was by then a published poet. I sought to amuse him with legends from the Church Committee days, most of them true, and many of them still mysteries. He immediately grasped the theme and started outlining a novel. It later became *The Double Man*, one of the few novels ever written by any senator and the only one in history, perhaps, the result of a senatorial collaboration. It was the story of a senator caught in the intelligence labyrinth who unwittingly uncovers a complex Cold War plot and finds it necessary to fake his defection to the Soviet Union to discover the identity of a highly placed mole in the US government. He had to seem to betray in order to protect his country. The collaboration, all but impossible these days, led to a long and valued friendship.

During a congressional delegation participation in a conference in Venice in the early 1980s, this fledgling novel-writing career got me into trouble. A scene in the novel involved a CIA agent and a KGB agent chasing each other through the narrow streets and over and around the many canals in Venice, with one of the characters being apprehended and later killed in the Venice jail. On a Sunday morning when the rest of the delegation was touring, I asked a confused concierge at the Hotel Danieli where I might find the Venice jail. He showed me on the map, and I set out across the city on foot with a small camera and notebook to make sure I got an accurate description for use in the novel. After many twists and turns, I suddenly came upon the fortresslike prison and, standing on a nearby footbridge over a small canal, began to take pictures and make notes.

Within minutes, out came a platoon of carabinieri who apprehended me. Even though language was a problem, I was not about to identify myself and have to account to my delegation colleagues, called to bail me out, what I was doing there. After an hour or so, I was escorted into the presence of the chief of police, a modest-sized man who resembled Mussolini. Through a less than competent translator, I gave an unpersuasive story about traveling Europe while conducting a study of prisons. Though I don't think the chief of police believed me for a minute, in exchange for exposing the film in the camera he gave me a tour of the place, and I got vital details for the novel. I believe myself to be the only US senator in history to have been detained, incognito or otherwise, in the Venice jail.

In my case, and in Bill Cohen's, *The Double Man* was the forerunner of other fiction to follow. Whether for a presidential candidate or future secretary of defense, in the eyes of analysts and pundits fiction writing was a conundrum, a confusion, and for some a matter for concern. Never mind, it served its purpose, and confusion was a small price to pay. Fiction was a way of probing extraordinary experiences and raising various explanations for them. A few astute readers of two 1980s spy novels and two 1990s Cuban novels (written under the pseudonym John Blackthorn) got it and connected the odyssean dots therein.

When reality exceeds our grasp, we can seek to outsmart it by telling stories. Would that have been Homer's purpose? Were the Circes and Cyclops in his mind the images of realities of his day that would bear no scientific analysis or even rational explanation? Was our Ulysses to become the agent of a genius intelligence telling us that life is a journey with many unexpected adventures as we try to make it home? And had the political arena become for me the Mediterranean Sea of my time?

In political terms my odyssey shifted substantially. From Democratic to Republican majorities in the Senate, from a Democratic to a Republican president, the 1980s were to bring both a second Senate term and an uncalculated step onto the national stage. In later life, the miraculousness of the first Senate election was superseded only by reelection against even greater odds and then by the fortuitous chance to seek national leadership.

As Odysseus himself proved, what makes odysseys what they are is the element of miracle. Sitting on his rocky ledge overlooking his Ithacan harbor, Ulysses must have thought of those many miraculous adventures and the wonder and stunned awareness and instruction they provided. Late in life, all odysseans wonder whether they will know those experiences ever again.

Campaigning on horseback in 1974.

With Governor Dick Lamm at the 1975 Colorado Democratic State Convention.

On board *Air Force One* with President Jimmy Carter, headed for Colorado.

The Hart family en route to Moscow.

Meeting with President Leonid Brezhnev in Moscow, 1975.

Senator Frank Church seeking Senator John Stennis's support to be chair of the intelligence investigation.

With Senator Alan Cranston, President Jimmy Carter, Speaker Tip O'Neill, and Majority Leader Robert C. Byrd.

On board Admiral Harry Train's flagship.

With Chinese premier Deng Xiaoping.

On board the USS *America*.

Ready for takeoff, USS *America*.

My escort officer, Captain John McCain.

My mentor, Ambassador Mike Mansfield, with Andrea.

Heading to work.

With Vice President George H. W. Bush.

At Lee's birthday party with Senator Ted Kennedy.

With Henry Kissinger.

Campaigning in New Hampshire.

It stuck: the ax throw that won the New Hampshire primary.

New Hampshire primary night.

PART III

AMBITION IN THE COUNTERREFORMATION
(1981–1988)

Why not just take it easy, accept retirement, fish in the harbor down there, Ulysses? we can imagine his friends and family asking. To which his response is, To be idle is to be dull. Like the best tools of our labor, we shine when we are used. And becoming dull is an invitation to rust, indeed "to rust unburnished." So, for Ulysses the choices are to be idle and unused, to be dull, or to struggle to be useful and thus to shine. You've got your health, Ulysses, his critics say; after all you've been through, you're lucky to still be breathing. And the graying warrior responds, with majestic disdain, "As tho' to breathe were life."

Multiple lives, "life pil'd on life," are too little for this storm-tossed wanderer, and the close of the one life he has is approaching. Every hour he rescues from "that eternal silence" offers a chance for something new, not only some new adventure, but some new knowledge. And that—knowledge—is what all this is about. Any adventurer foolhardy enough to take risks can have experiences. What this life-explorer is about is learning, knowledge, understanding of this one life and what we are doing in it.

This king Ulysses, his gray spirit yearning in desire, demands "to follow knowledge like a sinking star, beyond the utmost bound of human thought."

And there we have the secret code for understanding, and caring about, this ancient spirit. He doesn't miss travel, or adventure, or new experience, or new honors, or more celebrity, or even fame itself. He has had all that, and we suppose he understands its limits and even its superficiality.

What this restless, idle leader wants is knowledge. And knowledge is rarely to be had sitting on the barren rocks of one's own kingdom among those who may, or may not, share that same insatiable desire for knowledge or the risks required to achieve it.

The hermit may gain wisdom through isolation. The academic may learn through books and study. But for him, this king, the odyssey in search of knowledge requires action and movement and even daring, the wish to sail beyond the sinking star, and this sinking star represents the ends of the earth, the utmost bounds.

Ulysses sees his beloved son and notices the differences between them. His son's destiny is to tame his savage people, to make them mild, and to convert them to "the useful and the good." In kindness and in love he wishes his son well. He knows this to be a noble duty, one to which his son is suited much more than he. "He works his work, I mine."

This ruler does not denigrate his son's talents or destiny. Nor does he suggest disappointment that the son does not share his restlessness. He is content to leave to his son "the sceptre and the isle," not something a king would do for an heir he felt unworthy.

Having passed his kingdom to his son, the aging king now turns his eyes outward once again toward the port. There a ship—"the vessel"—fills its sails. And it is to that ship that the king summons his mariners, those who had wrought and toiled with him, all now also old and gray. But they had also thought with him, and what better crew than those who had thought with him to go in search of knowledge "beyond the utmost bound of human thought." These companions, this band of brothers, are mariners all right, but mariners on the turbulent seas of man's most important voyage, that in search of wisdom and understanding.

These mariners had opposed their free hearts and free minds against whatever fate, both "the thunder and the sunshine," their destiny might bring. Acknowledging that "you and I are old," whether to the mariners gathering around him or gathering once more within his mind and spirit, this seasoned mariner admonishes them that before "death closes all" some notable deeds of honor lay still undone. And the nobility of those deeds would and should be worthy of "men that strove with Gods."

Like much of Ulysses' story, this is a universal theme. Do we not all seek honor, especially honor achieved through noble deeds?

And, in the twilight of this life, our king takes note that "the long day wanes." The slow moon rises and the deep, dark sea moans itself to sleep. He means to set off, "to seek a newer world," even as the sun sets on the world in which his idleness is no longer tolerable. As the sun sets on his life, this warrior is not afraid to venture forth in one last voyage out onto a darkening sea to find that newer, and hopefully better, world that had so long eluded him.

This king, Ulysses, seeks a newer world. He does not seek a younger world or a better world. He seeks a newer world. He does not argue that newer is necessarily better. But somehow he believes that a newer world offers a better chance to gain the knowledge for which he yearns. The newer world cannot be reached by observing political conventions or the traditional limits of age, geography, and boundaries. Dangers must, once again, be faced. Uncertainty characterizes every voyage into the unknown. And the ultimate unknown is death itself.

With the failed Iranian hostage rescue mission, the Carter administration's days were numbered and, in November 1980, the election of Ronald Reagan was virtually assured. What came to be called the Reagan revolution actually began in 1968 with the election of Richard Nixon. Others date the shift to conservatism in American politics to the Goldwater candidacy in 1964 and the emergence of a conservative intelligencia. Why it happened is less important than the fact that it happened. With the exception of one Carter term and two Clinton terms, 1968 marked the beginning of a four-decade dominance of the political culture by Republican conservatives of increasingly disparate stripes.

I only had two opportunities to see President Ronald Reagan in person. The first occurred at a dinner in December 1980 hosted by Katharine Graham, then publisher of *The Washington Post*, at her Georgetown house to welcome the president-elect and Mrs. Reagan to Washington, an occasion that had become something of a ritual for newly elected presidents. Lee and I were among only four or five Democrats invited. After a very pleasant dinner with welcoming remarks by Mrs. Graham and a Reaganesque response, I was digging our coats out of the closet when around the corner came the president-elect. I introduced myself, and he responded vaguely and seemed somewhat lost and confused. What struck me were the two distinct round red circles on his cheeks. I have no doubt they gave the impression of good health at stage distance but, at close range, they seemed like not very well put on makeup.

Then, sometime in 1985, the Armed Services Committee was invited to the White House for a presentation urging support for further development of the B-2 bomber (which ultimately cost $2.1 billion per copy). Being in the majority, the Republicans on the committee had the votes, so the purpose of the enterprise was unclear. There had been some criticism of the president for not being in command and being out of touch in those days, so this may have been a staged demonstration of leadership. After remarks by Secretary of Defense Caspar Weinberger and Vice President George H. W. Bush, essentially arguing that the fate of the free world depended on this bomber, whose costs were soaring daily, in came the president to stand at the podium and, against the customary multiflag backdrop, encourage us onward. Surprisingly, he read from note cards remarks that were, to be polite, obvious to all. Starting to leave, he suddenly turned and asked if there were questions. His cabinet paled, and my Republican colleagues studied their feet. To break the awkward silence, I raised my hand and stood to introduce myself. John Warner (Republican of Virginia) and others nearby snickered. Disconcerted, I came up with a more or less obvious question, which the president managed not to answer. He then grinned, waved, and excused himself, saying that he had to call a newsboy in Detroit who that morning had saved a family from a house fire.

Walking on the circular drive at the White House's north entrance moments later, I asked Warner why they had giggled. He said, "If you hadn't told him who you were, he wouldn't have known." That's all well and good, except I had just run for the president's job a few months before.

Before the so-called Reagan revolution, there were other, more moderate brands of Republicanism, as evidenced by the leading Republicans already mentioned. Another of my moderate Republican colleagues was Jack Danforth of Missouri, with whom I had studied at both the divinity school and law school at Yale. By comparison with what was to follow in the 1980s and beyond, however, even Nixon came to be seen as moderate. The Reagan revolution introduced a brand of conservatism that even Goldwater did not recognize. It resulted from an alliance among the Religious Right, which dominated social and cultural issues; neoconservatives, who espoused an aggressive unilateralist foreign policy in the name of promoting democracy; and libertarian tax-cutters, who took the supply-side theory beyond any logical extreme.

This odd political amalgam was characterized by intolerance, arrogance, sectarianism, and often vindictiveness. It was notoriously unwilling to compromise even with others in the Republican Party, let alone with Democrats. One of the first acts of the neoreactionaries was to purge the old Republican Party of any moderate or accommodationist elements, often taking over the grassroots party organization at the local and state level and running starboard-side candidates who had passed elaborate purity tests on such issues as prayer in schools, gay marriage, and abortion against incumbent moderate Republicans in primary contests. In the second Bush presidency, the new Republicans were also so suspicious of scientific inquiry that they seemed intent on returning the nation to a pre-Darwin and even pre-Enlightenment theocracy. Political payday finally came in 2008 when, collectively, the American people returned to their common senses.

In my own case, the virtual occupation of the traditional Republican Party by a certain branch of evangelical conservatives pursuing an all-or-nothing strategy that sought to drive deep wedges into the body politic was confusing. The product of an evangelical household, which dutifully made its way to the Ottawa, Kansas, Church of the Nazarene on Seventh Street for Sunday morning, Sunday evening, and Wednesday evening prayer meeting, I followed almost without question that church's guidance toward its regional college in Oklahoma, then called Bethany Nazarene College (now Southern Nazarene University). Under the persuasive counsel of Professor Prescott Johnson, I studied philosophy and formed a career trajectory toward college teaching.

The principal purpose of the church was to convert sinners, but it also harbored, mostly deeply concealed, the subversive social gospel of John Wesley, who with his brother Charles invented "field preaching" from their base in Oxford, inspired historic social reformations in eighteenth-century England, and brought their social gospel and antislavery, abolitionist message to the American colonies. Perhaps unlike most fellow Bethany students, I took the social reform gospel at least as seriously as the hell and damnation and, indeed, concluded that one could not be separated from the other. A literal reading of the teachings of Jesus, it seemed to me, had much more to do with our duties to the less-well-off around us than it did to the pursuit of our own salvation. In fact, it seemed pretty clear that Jesus had in mind to connect the two, that the path toward personal salvation lay more down the road of caring for others in need than in single-minded avoidance of sin.

People join the army and the church for many reasons. The same is true of politics. Some are ambitious for title, office, respect, and power. They find soliciting votes and money and negotiating compromise congenial, even enjoyable, and seek to make politics a career.

A minority, on the other hand, tolerate the tumult of politics as the price of service. These are idealists by and large who find they must choose between preserving that idealism or sacrifice it on the grindstone of pragmatism in pursuit of a career.

A surprisingly persistent question during a few years in public life was, Why did you decide to do it? This question's persistence is attributable as much as anything to a personality that did not measure up to traditional political standards. Another version of this question might have been Why is someone like you doing a job like this?

The easiest and often most understandable response came to be Because John Kennedy challenged my generation to give something back to our country. The more accurate, complex, and therefore more difficult to understand answer might have been Because I was compelled to.

It resulted this way.

Though I had no "calling" to be a minister, I preached my first sermon in the Ottawa, Kansas, Church of the Nazarene at the age of eleven. My text from Matthew 6:21 was "Where your treasure is, there will your heart be also." The minister,

Preston Theall, actually encouraged this unorthodox performance. The congregation of fifty or so appeared stunned.

Some years thereafter, happily, I fell under the guidance of Professor Johnson at Bethany Nazarene College. He was both a classical and an existential philosopher whose spirituality took John Wesley's social gospel seriously. I gradually came to understand that salvation went beyond the rescue of the individual soul for the hereafter to dedication to the improvement of the lives of others in the here and now. This revolution continued to the Yale Divinity School and then the ancient republican gospel according to John Kennedy: Civic duty is required of citizens of a republic, and that duty can be performed as public service. I never saw this mandate as idealism or even liberalism. I saw it as social justice.

The Kennedy challenge was not his own novel notion. One assumes his study of history caused him to know that our founders created a republic and that, since Athens, republics depended on involved citizens, citizens committed to resisting corruption and to pursuit of the common good. For me, the pursuit of social justice and performance of civic duty became intertwined and mutually reinforcing.

I was not compelled to become a politician, but I was compelled to be engaged in the life of the community and nation. Though of humble circumstances, I had received more advantages than many. My duty was to help the many. Political circumstances offered no other avenue than the post-Rooseveltian Democratic Party, then committed to a progressive-reform agenda and just beginning to loosen the hold of urban bosses and machines.

Before the Democratic Party could become the instrument of social change and justice, it had to reform itself. Nowhere was this more evident than in the chaotic 1968 Democratic convention in Chicago and its aftermath: Richard Nixon in the White House and the party split between young and old, white and black, men and women, industrialists and environmentalists, pro-Vietnam and anti-Vietnam.

When awakened to politics in my late teens, this conclusion led me inescapably into the Democratic Party. Now, as a fledgling senator in the late 1970s, I and the nation were confronted with a Republican gospel that held that righteousness had very much to do with rigid adherence to overturning *Roe v. Wade*, prayer in schools, unlimited gun ownership, the death penalty, and unilateral invasion of sovereign nations. This gospel was characterized by orthodoxy, rigidity, and intolerance—in short, resistance to all the liberal virtues— and seemed both to foster and feed upon public anger. My pursuit of philosophy and religious studies in divinity school gave me no education in dealing with this phenomenon. It merely intensified the confusion over the gap between what Jesus taught and what these people were teaching, ostensibly in Jesus' name, for political gain.

Somehow the political gospel of the Right also aligned itself with wealth, power, and privilege. Instead of the love of money being the root of all evil, greed became good and wealth, so long as large contributions were made to religiously certified Republican candidates, a clear signal of God's favor. Never mind that Jesus thought it easier for a camel to pass through the eye of a needle than a rich man to enter heaven.

Ironies multiplied, especially when in the war on terrorism an intolerant theocracy in America was aligned against the even more intolerant theocracy of Islam. The ultimate anthem of the American variety came in the triumphalist declaration by a neoconservative mullah in the White House when confronted with indisputable evidence that real facts did not sustain a new policy departure: "We create our own reality." The hair on the ghost of Thomas Jefferson stood on end.

For practical politics in the 1980s, this simply meant that a darling of this oddly constructed movement or collection of movements was in the White House and his party now controlled the Senate. The country had become more conservative, perhaps not to the extent those running things in the second-Bush years would believe, but nevertheless more Republican in almost every respect than Democratic. The qualifier is necessary because ordinary Americans remained more tolerant and even more progressive than those they were electing. These same everyday Americans, however, had lost confidence in the Democratic Party's ability to govern. Jimmy Carter was an exception because of Watergate, after which simple integrity was demanded, and Bill Clinton was an exception given the end of the Cold War and a third-party candidacy in his first election.

As a student of the thesis of cycles in American history, propounded most eloquently and persuasively by the late historian Arthur Schlesinger Jr., it seemed inevitable to me that the New Deal–Great Society era spanning 1932 to 1968 was bound to yield to some period of "consolidation" or conservatism.[24] I had come to assume in my early adulthood that American history was a continuum of almost uninterrupted economical, political, and cultural progress; new evidence mounted that things didn't exactly work this way. The Schlesinger thesis offered an alternative understanding of American history. That being the case, we were now in for an era of what Schlesinger called "consolidation" at best, and a rightward retrenchment at worst.

What no one could have expected, however, was the meanness, vindictiveness, and divisiveness of the early twenty-first century: right-wing ministers screening candidates for office; government services administered by favored religious organizations; dreams of empire in the Middle East; a willfully ignorant president; a bitterly partisan and eventually corrupt Congress; media empires dedicated to all these enterprises; and the leading established media cowed into submission and acquiescence.

A number of those elected to the Senate in the 1980 election gave evidence of all these trends, though they and their president never quite went to the extremes that followed. The American people had authorized a partisan shift, but hardly the social revolution the partisan revolutionaries had up their sleeves. There were a few moderate Senate Republicans, such as the estimable Howard Baker and Warren Rudman, to maintain balance and decorum. But even those thought of as conservative in that era, the Alan Simpsons and the Hank Browns, were to be replaced by many on the margin of, if not beyond, the ideological navigation charts of the day. In the 1980s, Senate Republicans by and large still believed in balanced budgets, caution in foreign military interventions, and resistance to government intrusion in its citizens' lives. These three traditional pillars of Republican orthodoxy were all cast overboard, first by the so-called Gingrich revolution in the House of Representatives in the mid-1990s and then by the Bush era that followed.

Some time back, in a book review, I observed that since the election of 1800 and even before, Americans have wanted to put national unity ahead of ideology and, like Jefferson, all be Republicans and Federalists, all Republicans and Democrats. Most Americans, in fact, think of themselves as citizens of the American nation before they identify themselves as members of a party.

Problems arise, however, because those who participate in party politics on a daily basis, grassroots activists as well as senior elected officials, do so out of conviction and belief. "The engine that drives the process," I wrote in the review, "is fueled by conviction, and that conviction produces individual and group identity and common beliefs."[25] People join parties and work for them to further causes and to perpetuate philosophies.

The history of American politics is bracketed by national identity on one side and party ideology on the other. The greatest periods of our history occur when one party's ideas and beliefs serve the national interest. This usually occurs in wartime or under great economic distress. Even then it needs always to be repeated that the Franklin Roosevelt New Deal was the product of pragmatism, not ideology. The conviction that separated him from the Republican Party of Hoover was that recovery was not possible without government action, a conviction recovered out of necessity by an incoming Obama administration in response to economic chaos.

To underscore the fact that our leaders are overwhelmingly ignorant of history and that ideologies rarely evolve, this same dispute would play itself out between the parties once again more than seventy-five years after Roosevelt's first election.

What makes some people liberal and some conservative, Democratic or Republican, is still a mystery unaccounted for simply by upbringing, economic class, or schooling. "I often think it's comical," sang Gilbert and Sullivan, "how nature always does contrive that every boy and every gal that's born into this world alive is either a little Liberal or else a little Conservative." We are what we are and, in the minds of some, what God made us.

Ideology by and large is harmless, at least until it seeks to stand athwart history, saying no, or derails progress or resists facts or frustrates the national interest. Then problems arise in battalions. On those occasions it becomes the duty of citizens to put the country ahead of a faction or a party, or its particular set of convictions.

Aside from the willfully ignorant, the only truly dangerous people I ever encountered in politics were those who believed they were right and everyone else was wrong.

You should not be in politics unless you treasure irony. To illustrate the point, I owed my 1980 Senate reelection to Barry Goldwater. The Colorado Republican Party had invited Senator Goldwater to speak at its annual Lincoln Day dinner early that year. The theme of the dinner was "Defeat Gary Hart." Barry came up from Phoenix that Saturday afternoon and was met at the Denver airport by the Colorado political press corps, eager for some attack quotes they could get in the Sunday papers. Barraged by questions about why it was important to defeat Hart, Barry parried and dodged, denying he was there to defeat me. Finally, overtaken by the impatience that had come to characterize him, he said, "Listen. I didn't come here to defeat Gary Hart. Gary Hart is the most honest and the most moral man I've ever met in American politics." Game, set, match. The Sunday *Denver Post* had a headline something like "Goldwater Praises Hart." By Monday we had 250,000 copies coming from the printer.[26]

Although I spent just over $1 million in my reelection, I had been outspent. By comparison, in my first election, six years before, throughout a lengthy primary contest involving six Democrats and, after nomination, a general election race against a wealthy two-term incumbent Republican senator, I had spent only $350,000. My average contribution had been $17. When I was replaced in the Senate by my colleague Tim Wirth in 1986, he spent almost $4.5 million. Now a Senate race in Colorado, a state of just under 5 million people, routinely costs $12 to $15 million.

Beginning in the first term in the 1970s and continuing into the 1980s, the issue of how we financed political campaigns became increasingly central for me. My own campaign-finance experience mirrored a national pattern that followed per capita demographics. Expenditures were increasing across the nation per vote until they reached astronomical proportions in the large states. Overwhelmingly the money went to buy media spots on television and radio. And in almost equal proportions, contributions from special interest groups overwhelmed individual contributions, especially small ones. A cycle evolved. Large amounts of money were raised from interest groups to pay for television advertising to elect candidates who would, at the very least, provide access to the contributing interests and their narrow agendas once elected, and politicians would increasingly become their representatives and

spokespersons. Though not strictly illegal, it was institution-
alized corruption and, as with other episodes in the nation's
history, led to a series of indictments and convictions of both
lobbyists and elected officials in the early twenty-first century.
It was all bound to happen, and was as predictable as the dawn.

America's government did not become a commercial
enterprise overnight, nor is political corruption a late-
twentieth-century invention. But sometime in the last quarter
of the twentieth century things changed. Elections became
more expensive. Politicians spent more time raising money.
The money increasingly came from special interests. Lobbyists multiplied and became the brokers between the special
interests and the politicians. They raised vast sums of money
for political elections in exchange for access for their clients
to the politicians who received their contributions. It became
all about *access*.

Very quickly thereafter, Washington became a commercial enterprise on a very large scale.

Except for Jack Abramoff and others like him, it was
not corruption on the traditional American political level.
Abramoff was clearly predictable. Something called the
K Street Project made it inevitable. A new breed of Republicans took power in the Gingrich years and beyond. The access
train—politicians, campaign contributions, lobbyists—left
the station. The K Street lobbyists in Washington increasingly became former Republican members of Congress. They
raised money for Republican candidates. The successful candidates opened their doors to the lobbyists' largely corporate
clients. Legislation favoring those corporate clients, including most importantly financial deregulation, was passed.

Everyone was happy. Elected officials had money for
reelection. Republican majorities would continue. The lobbyists made fortunes. The corporations and interest groups
got the legislation they wanted. So they gave more money.
And so on, and so on.

Lord Acton knew what he was talking about.

Though much of this commercialization of government has occurred during recent Republican years, my party, the Democrats, have largely joined the game. Candidate Barack Obama campaigned on a "clean up Washington" platform. And procedures have been adopted to break the insidious lobbyist-appointed official-lobbyist cycle. But even casual scrutiny of political fund-raising reveals the continuing contribution = access pattern.

There are additional innovations. First the wives, then the children of members of Congress became lobbyists. This would have been unheard of when I was elected to the Senate. It would have been worse than immoral. It would have been unseemly. But by the 1990s, there was so much money around. All you had to do was collect it from the client interest groups, give it to the election committees, and set up the meetings with the legislators and policy makers. It was even easier if you were all of the same party and belonged to the same country clubs. And you got rich.

Jack Abramoff, or one of many just like him, was bound for jail the day the K Street Project was announced. The system gave incest a bad name.

It would be comforting to believe this system ended the day Abramoff went to jail. But it would not be true. It would not be true because corruption in a republic is not defined by exchanging money for votes. Not at all. It is a much more serious proposition than that. Corruption in republics throughout history, and in the minds of our founders, consisted of placing one's narrow interest, or the interest of a small group, ahead of the common interest, or the interest of the commonwealth.

If we took the pledge of allegiance to our flag "and the republic for which it stands" seriously, more seriously than as a ritual gesture like wearing a flag pin, we would inevitably be required to face the fact that our republic is immensely corrupt, is indeed corrupt on an epic scale. Whether it is about contracts for weapons systems at the Pentagon, or consulting contracts at the Homeland Security Department, or permits to pollute, or tax breaks for the wealthy, it is all corruption. Our interest or our group's interest is more important than the national interest. And the incumbent's reelection is more important than anything.

Throughout these reminiscences I have reflected on the differences between many of those with whom I served in the Senate of the 1970s and many elected thereafter. Of the many senators of both parties with whom I first served and who gained the greatest respect, not one became a lobbyist. It was beneath their dignity.

Seeing this tide of corruption coming, campaign reform had become a cause and, along with others, I introduced legislation requiring a reasonable amount of free electronic media times for all legitimate candidates, limits on contributions, and limits on spending. Freedom of speech issues complicated this project. Campaign reforms enacted in the aftermath of Watergate slush funds, payoffs, and corruption faltered as the result of a Supreme Court ruling (*Buckley v. Valeo*) that limits could not be placed on the amount a candidate could contribute to his or her own campaign. Legislation I proposed in the early 1980s became the framework for the McCain-Feingold reforms in the 1990s, so watered down to enable passage that they achieved only a fragment of what is required.

So long as campaigns cost what they cost, and so long as vast amounts of money are raised from groups with narrow agendas—special interests versus the national interest—we will have legal or illegal corruption and public distrust of government. Many political scientists and practitioners believe that the national interest is nothing more than a total amalgam of all special interests. This view is sinister. It invites the kind of politics we have today and guarantees public distrust.

There is, instead, an identifiable and definable national interest above and larger than all the particular interests taken together. It includes all those things that the citizens of a republic hold in common: the public's resources and national wealth, our shared interests in security, our uniform interest in our children's future, the health of our natural environment, the composite of our legacy to future generations, good relations with foreign neighbors, constitutional ideals and principles, the rule of law, opportunity, equality, and justice for all, and a host of similar common interests. Protection and promotion of the national interest, dedication to its perpetuation, is not only the best politics, it is the only truly moral politics.

This national interest and all its elements are undermined and endangered by our current system of campaign financing. The dawning light at the end of a very dark tunnel is the Internet. Despite victoriously participating in the first American billion-dollar presidential campaign, Barack Obama revealed the massive potential of the Internet in political fund-raising and the therapy represented by literally millions of small contributions. Hopefully, technology may help achieve what legislated reform has not.

As I had written eight years earlier, Democratic defeats in 1980, as in 1972, resulted from too few ideas to address a raft of new realities. Though impossible to know at that time, the road back would require almost three more decades. The notable exception, of course, was the post–Cold War Clinton presidency. With the important exception of health care and possibly welfare reform, he did not seek and was not given a strong mandate to introduce new systems, but he rather focused on trying to change old ones. And most of all, he was faced with an overwhelmingly uncooperative Congress.

With regard to his overheated impeachment, the American people made clear that there were much more important things for the country to be dealing with. The media, and his political opponents, got a lesson in the great difference between what people find interesting and what they think is important. Most Americans gobbled up every detail of the nasty business they could find, but overwhelmingly disagreed with the proposition that, therefore, Clinton should be impeached.

The earlier dawn of "morning in America" was a reminder of the great difference between serving in a parliamentary body one's party controls and one the opposition party controls. In my second term, Senate Republicans set the legislative agenda, chaired the committees, and called the shots. Being out of practice, even up until the mid-1980s the legislative trains were still not running on time. Fumbling through the spring of 1985, then majority leader Robert Dole was engaged in his usual early evening effort to cajole senators into staying into the late hours when the ever-colorful Barry Goldwater, then on canes from painful hip replacement surgeries, objected. Dole countered by reminding him and others that "the Senate does its best work at night." Disregarding the galleries full of schoolchildren, journalists, and tourists, Goldwater said: "So do I, but not standing up."

The new majority had routinely come to insist on repeated votes on the emerging social agenda of prayer in schools, so-called right-to-life amendments overturning *Roe v. Wade*, antiflag-burning amendments, the occasional test vote on the ownership of assault weapons, and a variety of wedge issues meant to reassure conservative constituencies and make more vivid the partisan and ideological divides. Meanwhile Rome frittered, and the economy, failing to respond to the magic of massive tax cuts, produced only deficits and recession. And partisan divisions, predictably, grew.

A national candidate's experience in foreign affairs, based on extensive travel and familiarity with world leaders and his or her ability to defend the nation, have always been, to greater or lesser degrees, factors in national elections. And, particularly following World War II and the emergence of the United States as a great power, rightly so. It was, therefore, a shock to see Ronald Reagan's picture with European leaders at his first G-7 meeting, in 1981, and the accompanying text that stated that this was the first time he had met them. Something did not seem right here.

At the beginning of my second term I set out to organize what came to be called New Leaders conferences, get-togethers of younger parliamentarians and party leaders from allied democracies. A staff member, Doug Wilson, with the help of political sections in our embassies in Europe, identified a core group, we invited them to a conference in Sea Pines Plantation, Hilton Head Island, South Carolina, and the effort began. In retrospect, it turned out to be an illustrious group. Other cochairs included Gianni de Michaelis, an Italian senator in his thirties and a future foreign minister of Italy, and Chris Patten, a young British parliamentarian, future Conservative Party leader, and European Union foreign minister. A new parliamentarian named David Steel, a future leader of the British Liberal Party, also participated, among a number of other future leaders.

This very successful introductory gathering led to a follow-on meeting in Venice, which de Michaelis hosted. We put together a US delegation that included three young House members—Al Gore, Geraldine Ferraro, and Chris Dodd, who had just been elected to the Senate—all of whom were to have illustrious careers in American politics that more than justified their selection. Later, we convened a New Leaders conference for Latin America in Puerto Rico; an Asian conference was held in Seoul, Korea; and a Pacific Rim conference, focused on regional trade and security, was convened in Laguna Niguel, California. Participants included Abdurrahman Wahid, future president of Indonesia; Nobutaka Machimura, a future foreign minister of Japan; and Mike Moore, then member of the New Zealand parliament and later prime minister of New Zealand and head of the World Trade Organization.

In each case, almost all the attendees went on to become ministers, senior parliamentarians, and leaders of their respective countries. Many of the friendships I made in these conferences, including with Gianni de Michaelis and Chris Patten, continued throughout a lifetime. And I believe the same is true for many of the others. By that time the world was becoming too small and time too compressed for American presidents and other leaders to get acquainted only after they assumed positions of power. Out of the Venice meeting of our group, Aspen Institute Italia, a European affiliate of the Aspen Institute, was formed and continues to contribute to serious international dialogue.

During one of the Senate's legislative breaks in this same period, I went out to visit our fleet in the Indian Ocean. The ever-volatile Middle East was in one of its perpetual cycles of turbulence, and we had a carrier task group, and eventually two, on station in the region, available over the horizon if something broke. Following the 1980 election I had sought and was awarded a navy commission as a lieutenant (junior grade) in the US Navy Reserves and was in uniform, though not exactly on duty, throughout the visit to the carrier USS *America* and one of its escorting destroyers. My commission had been facilitated by Captain John McCain, then retiring as navy liaison to the Senate.

The trip confirmed the importance of a maritime strategy as an important element, if not the centerpiece, of a larger national security strategy. Within the security community, the traditional arguments are well known. With the large carrier centerpiece, a fleet, carrier task group, or even smaller complement of ships can come and go; require land-based facilities only for fleet headquarters, resupply, and port visits; and can remain far enough offshore in troubled venues so as not to become objects of protest and attack. When trouble arises requiring an American military response, carrier-based aircraft or short- or long-range cruise missiles can come into play, and the ships can land marines, special forces, or other expeditionary forces and can provide air cover for them.

The arguments pro and con often become so specialized and recondite that laypersons feel required to withdraw. But the basic reality is that long-term, land-based deployment of US military units, army or air force, require diplomatic negotiations with often undemocratic and unsavory governments. Base facilities are subject to closure with a change of governments or to physical assault if insurgencies occur. Large expenditures of "foreign aid" are required to convince foreign governments to cooperate, as well as for the United States to construct and maintain these elaborate facilities, including the housing, education, and health care of families. None of this is the case with maritime assets.

The 1982 biennial congressional elections provided no expansion of the Reagan revolution, with majorities not changing in either house. As a survivor of the previous landslide, however, and a new-generation senator from a western state, I received a considerable number of invitations to campaign with and for Democratic incumbents and challengers across the country. Accepting a number but by no means all, I crisscrossed the country and in event after event heard from party leaders and activists a constant theme: "We need new leadership and some new approaches." The strong consensus seemed to be that a continuation of past policies with established constituent groups and leaders was not going to work in 1984 and beyond.

Having now completed eight years in the Senate, I had evolved what amounted to a personal political philosophy. It consisted of basic notions: listen closely, look over the horizon, fashion new approaches to emerging new realities, persuade others that changing times require new ideas, encourage idealism, and refuse to compromise principles. When a national candidacy began to emerge, it was perhaps the ability to anticipate rising and shifting tides such as globalization, information, and the changing nature of conflict that led to greater success than most observers anticipated. It all amounted to achieving traditional progressive objectives by using new approaches.

As eyes were turning, at least within the commentariat and punditocracy, toward the next presidential election, the sense was that President Reagan could be defeated, but not by politics as usual. Preferential polls among Democrats showed former vice president Walter Mondale to be the front-runner, with approximately 50 percent support among those polled. This was considered by the experts to be prohibitive for any would-be challenger. A few of us saw the glass half empty. As a popular and particularly well-known figure in the party and President Carter's vice president, why did he have only 50 percent? Half the party wanted someone else.

During this period and after, a substantial number of offers of support, mostly from local, grassroots activists, came in for me to run in 1984. Ten years after the McGovern campaign experience, my political radar was sophisticated enough to be able to gauge sincere from casual offers of support and, given the credentials and experience of many of these people, they had to be taken seriously. After the 1982 election, discussions concerning the possibility of a national candidacy began with a few friends. Exploratory trips to Iowa and New Hampshire, two states I knew well, were in order, and invitations were forthcoming.

Meanwhile, a forerunner of sorts of the Iraq war two decades later was emerging in the early 1980s in Central America. The centerpiece was Nicaragua, where leftist insurgents called Sandinistas had overthrown a US-supported corrupt oligarchy and were socializing the nation. Neighboring nations, including El Salvador, were restive and combating their own long-term insurgent oppositions. By and large the United States, despite its revolutionary heritage, had opted for "stability" in the form of support for governments in power, whether democratic or not. The Reagan administration publicly denounced the Sandinistas and other rebels; sent increased financial and military assistance, often to repressive governments; and undertook a series of covert operations in the region.

Though rumors of covert operations existed, it became virtually impossible to get reliable information on what we were or were not doing. The Republican-controlled Senate was not eager to perform its constitutional oversight responsibilities, except to conduct hearings that highlighted the threat of Central American developments to US security. For a veteran of the Church Committee and its disclosure of covert operations run amok (and even worse, ones it chose not to disclose, ostensibly out of "national security" concerns but more often national embarrassment), it looked like history repeating itself. Sobriety and statesmanship were not enhanced by a Reagan speech promising that, left unchecked, the Sandinistas would take over Central America, then Mexico, and then march on the United States itself. Here the forecast of grossly overinflated and inaccurate threat assessments to justify a future war in the Middle East is inevitable.

Still Democratic, the House of Representatives and a minority of us in the Senate raised objection. We demanded at the very least greater proof than a frequently befuddled president had then offered. Receiving none, legislation in the form of the Boland Amendment prohibited expenditures for US military engagement in the region without explicit congressional authorization. Following Vietnam, the Pentagon Papers, and Watergate, automatic trust in the word of presidents had seriously eroded. Unwilling to recognize Congress's constitutional role in military actions, the Reagan administration went deep underground, and what got to be called Iran-Contra quickly evolved. In a word, this bizarre operation cooked up by behind-the-scenes figures like Oliver North, Elliot Abrams, and others sold weapons the United States had provided Israel to Iran and then used the proceeds to support CIA covert operations and the so-called Contras, government security and counterinsurgency forces in the region, in clear, purposeful, and blatant violation of US law.

It was nothing less than a covert program by the White House to subvert the laws of the United States. Once again, a precedent was laid down for the second Bush administration. In an effort to perpetuate their deception, Oliver North and Elliott Abrams committed perjury and became convicted felons, all to conduct a secret war based on badly flawed premises. The war was covert not to the Sandinistas, but to the American people and their elected representatives.

Frustrated by the inability or unwillingness of the Senate to find out what was truly going on, my colleague Bill Cohen of Maine (later secretary of defense) and I arranged to visit Central America in early September 1983. We flew from the funeral of Senator Henry "Scoop" Jackson, in Washington State, to Houston, and early the following morning flew in a small air force jet to Managua. Our escort officer was Colonel Jim Jones (later to become commandant of the Marine Corps, then NATO commander, and more recently national security advisor). Shortly after dawn, as we approached the Managua airport, the plane suddenly veered off and started back north. Colonel Jones ("Jim" to us) went forward and was told the airport was then under attack. Our backup airport was in Tegucigalpa, where the plane's landing gear collapsed on landing.

We were met by our ambassador, John Negroponte (later first director of national intelligence and then deputy secretary of state), who briefed us on events of the morning at his residence. Here is what had happened. Minutes before our scheduled landing in Nicaragua, a twin-engine Cessna aircraft carrying two five-hundred-pound bombs under its wings flew down the main runway at Managua with the purpose in mind of dropping one bomb on the three-plane Nicaraguan air force and the other on the three-plane national airline. Tipped off, the Sandinistas lined the runway with antiaircraft guns and promptly shot the plane down. It crashed into the terminal at the exact point where Bill Cohen and I were to be welcomed by the ruling commandante, Danny Ortega, and company some minutes later.

To compound the tragic farce, though the two men on board, one an American, were killed, the intact nose of the plane contained a largely undamaged briefcase that, on inspection, contained a wide variety of communications with the CIA. Furious, Bill Cohen got the director of the CIA, William Casey, on a secure phone from the embassy in Tegucigalpa and promptly read him the riot act. Cohen wanted to know if killing two United States senators was part of the original plan or just an afterthought, a bonus of sorts for getting rid of two troublemakers. Notorious for his inability or unwillingness to make sense, Casey mumbled excuses and surprised denials. Casey's response was reminiscent of the man accused of setting a hotel fire by smoking in bed and whose defense was that the bed was on fire when he got into it. A later translation of his virtually incomprehensible mumbles seemed to be "We didn't do it. But if we did do it, I didn't know about it. And even if I did know about it, I really didn't intend for you guys to get killed." As an announced Democratic candidate for the presidency in 1984, I had some doubts about the last part.

A replacement aircraft shortly picked us up, and we made the short hop down to Managua where we were met by Ortega, much of the Sandinista government, and every television camera in Central America. Ortega took the occasion to demonstrate the flight of the plane, survey the damage of the fire from the crash, exactly where we stood, and then laid out for our inspection the CIA documents. Our response was a more sophisticated version of "the bed was on fire when we got into it."

That night we were given dinner by a Sandinista minister named Nora Astorga, a tall, attractive woman in her mid-thirties. It was a pleasant evening at her home with a half dozen or so senior government officials. Only later were we told Senora Astorga's colorful story. She had studied medicine in the United States in the late sixties but returned to Nicaragua to become a lawyer and minister of justice in the Sandinista government following its overthrow of the Anastasio Somoza government. During the insurgent revolution she played a double life as a respected lawyer by day and revolutionary by night. In March 1978 she agreed to a long-sought tryst at her Managua apartment with General Reynaldo Pérez Vega, who bore the nickname of El Perro (the dog) and who was second in command of Somoza's hated National Guard. Arriving at her apartment that night, after his security detail had been sent away, he went to Sra. Astorga's bedroom where he found not the desirable Nora but three armed Sandinistas, who slit his throat.

The year after our dinner "La Norita", as she was called, became Nicaraguan ambassador to the United Nations, and she died in 1988 at the age of thirty-nine. On occasion, Defense Secretary Cohen, General Jones, and I reminisced about our dinner with La Norita and what difference it might or might not have made in our appetite had we known of the fate of El Perro.

We flew to San Salvador where US Ambassador Tom Pickering (eventually to hold virtually every senior post the US diplomatic service offered) who was fluent in five languages, including Spanish, briefed us on overt and covert operations in El Salvador which had become a principal base for Contra operations. We spent an evening with CIA agents, Contra operatives, and what were undoubtedly contract employees. The most we got out of them about the failed Managua bombing raid a couple of days before were vague denials, rolled eyes, shoulder shrugs, and preoccupation with shoe laces.

The next day we took an Army helicopter from a midtown school yard to a village up country that had been "pacified," that is purged of rebel elements. Bill Cohen monitored the takeoff with earphones provided by the crew and I chose to study the city from the open-sided chopper. As we rose to about 1,500 feet Bill tapped me on the shoulder and, pale, gestured at the earphones. I smiled and shrugged.

When we landed, he said: "Do you know what happened?" I had no idea. "When we got to altitude the chopper totally lost hydraulic pressure in the main rotor and the pilot said to the co-pilot, 'Holy ****, I've gotta put this ************ down." He started banging on the hydraulic gauge as hard as he could with his fist and, as we hung in the air, the pressure needle finally rose. As we saddled up later, after touring the village with the Salvador military, we asked the pilot about it and he nonchalantly said, "Well, it's an old helicopter. What can you expect?"

While the United States remained distracted by a Reagan preoccupation with a threatened Sandinista invasion of Texas, the Cold War dragged on. The Soviets continued to modernize their strategic—that is, nuclear—forces, especially by increasing the size of their intercontinental ballistic missiles. The Reagan administration and its supporters in Congress insisted on response with a new generation of US missiles. US technological superiority (the groundwork for which was laid by German rocketeers, notably Wernher von Braun, brought to the United States after World War II, leading to the taunt "Our Germans are better than their Germans") enabled us to build more accurate missiles that, therefore, did not need to be as large as those of the Soviets. Being less accurate, Soviet missiles had to be larger to carry larger warheads in order to destroy targets, which we could do with more accuracy.

But increased accuracy was destabilizing, in the arcane logic of the Cold War, because accurate missiles, or even for that matter larger missiles, could preemptively wipe out the other side's missiles, known in the language as "the deterrent force," and thus accuracy represented a temptation to strike first and eliminate any response. This was less a threat to us because our strategic planners had created a "triad," dispersing our nuclear forces among land-based, silo-launched missiles; long-range, nuclear-armed B-52 bombers; and the Trident submarine fleet, carrying sea-launched nuclear missiles. The theory was that, even if our land-based missiles were attacked and mostly destroyed, we could respond with our air and sea capabilities, thus causing the Soviets to think twice or thrice about starting anything. Lacking the latter two legs of the triad, however, the Soviets had put their nuclear eggs in the land-based basket.

Even so, as the Soviets built larger missiles, hard-line American thinkers saw this as a threat and attempted to devise means to make the first leg of our triad, the silo missiles, less vulnerable. And this led to schemes of hide-and-seek, moving missiles from silo to silo, a cumbersome process to say the least, or taking the missiles out of the silos and putting them on giant trucks or trains. To complicate matters even further, nuclear geniuses (our Germans) had perfected ways of putting multiple warheads on individual missiles and making them independently targetable. Thus the single missile X could hit targets A, B, and C, and eventually D, E, F, and beyond.

All this existential chess led to the introduction of a proposal to build the MX missile, a multiple-warhead missile carried on railroad cars all across the western United States. The cost was enormous in a time of huge deficits (by the lesser standards of that day), it would further accelerate the extravagant arms race, and it would divert resources from urgent domestic needs. Much like the missile defense system, dubbed Star Wars, that Reagan had become entranced with and that would plague us down to the close of the second-Bush years, no one knew whether the mobile missile scheme would even work. And, back to Strangelovian Cold War logic, the MX increased our ability (and temptation) to strike first, and thus destabilized the balance of terror based on mutual assured destruction (MAD).

By now, the fall of 1983, I was an announced and active candidate for the Democratic nomination for president and busy on the campaign trail in Iowa, New Hampshire, and elsewhere across the country. Suspension of campaigning to try to defeat the MX in the Senate while half a dozen rivals continued on made little political sense, but it seemed at the time, and even today, to be the right thing to do. My candidacy had been announced the previous February to a modest crowd on a cool but sunny day on the steps of the Colorado Capitol, and thereafter I had managed to double my standing in the Democratic preferential polls, from 1 to 2 percent. Months later we had identified and organized small bands of volunteer supporters in almost every state, and hired an even smaller political staff in Washington. Our financial resources were meager and never rose above modest.

My economic proposals focused on transformation, preserving what we could of our industrial base while resisting protectionist measures, but investing in education and training of the workforce, new and high technologies, and increasing trade in technology, information, and services. My foreign policy focused on diplomacy not confrontation, caution in military interventions, overt rather than covert relationships abroad, and integrity rather than Machiavellian manipulation. My defense theories were heavily based on military reform principles. My shorthand label would be that of reformer promoting new ideas. But I would continue to face the question of electability by both political pundits and activists. Customary and predictable questions focused on "how": How are you going to raise the money? How are you going to emerge? How can you defeat Mondale? In response, my mantra got to be "An unlikely possibility is preferable to a likely improbability."

We were sustained then and thereafter by the belief that Ronald Reagan could be defeated (though not without difficulty) and, more importantly, should be. It would not happen, however, with traditional leaders proposing conventional programs. For a number of months I had waited to determine the field of contestants on the Democratic side. If my belief was correct that this would be a generational election as much as an ideological one, both within the Democratic Party and against the Republican president, then the first hurdle would surely be a contest for leadership of the next generation of Democrats. As time passed, however, no other elected officials of my generation stepped forward. In addition to former vice president Mondale, the field came to include Senator Alan Cranston of California, Senator Ernest "Fritz" Hollings of South Carolina, former Florida governor Reubin Askew, Reverend Jesse Jackson, eventually George McGovern himself, and most notably John Glenn. As a two-term senator from a large industrial state, Ohio, it was generally assumed that Glenn would be the competition for Mondale if for no other reason than that he was universally known as a brave astronaut whose exploits were then being dramatized in the movie version of Tom Wolfe's book on the original seven Mercury astronauts, *The Right Stuff*.

As an instrument in the frustration of the traditional Democratic Party and its power structure in 1972, I had been in an awkward position with former competitors for the party's nomination who were or had been Senate colleagues—Hubert Humphrey, Scoop Jackson, Ed Muskie, and others—but also with party regulars at the state level. The sharply edged contest in Illinois between the "regular" Daley delegation and the reform Jackson-Singer delegation was a distinctive case in point. Intermediaries organized a break-fast in Chicago with some of the state party's successor generation of leaders in the fall of 1983. Mike Madigan, future Speaker of the state legislature, Neil Hartigan, soon to be state attorney general, Ed "Fast Eddie" Vrdolyak, president of the Chicago City Council, and a dozen others gathered in a conference room at the University Club, and when I came in they were seated and silent. I went around the table introducing myself to notable coldness, even hostility. Finally, seated, I looked expectantly across the table at Vrdolyak who stared at me, stony-faced, then said, "Let's see. You're the guy who kept us out of the 1972 convention. Right?" Spluttering, I started to deny culpability and then, having pulled off the stunt, they all broke into laughter.

Resistance from political "regulars" was not the only hurdle. My campaign would never pass 2 or 3 percent in the polls prior to New Hampshire. Pundits and pollsters awarded the nomination to Mondale before a vote was cast. Our state organizers and staff in early primary states went unpaid for weeks. There was no money. Finally, in January 1984, completely strapped, I did what I had pledged never to do when I entered public life: I put a $50,000 mortgage on our Washington home. That tiny amount, by today's standards, enabled us to run a very limited amount of television and radio spots in New Hampshire. This was small reinforcement for the days, weeks, and months of house parties and small meetings in almost every town in the state.

Despite a raft of misdiagnoses, I finished a distant second to Mondale in the Iowa caucuses and then soundly defeated him in the New Hampshire primary days later. Thereafter, the back-and-forth primaries and caucuses continued throughout the fifty states, with each of us winning about half the states. One of a number of media myths persists to this day that my campaign somehow "peaked" in New Hampshire and faded quickly thereafter. This is not true. We won all the New England states, seven of the nine so-called Super Tuesday states, including the largest southern state of Florida, won Ohio, came close in Illinois, and finished by winning eleven of the last twelve primaries, including a sweep of California and virtually all of the West. Such things matter little, except facts would seem to be important, even in the journalistic world.

The 1984 Democratic convention in San Francisco was the first convention featuring what were called superdelegates, those party leaders and elected officials given automatic delegate status. Unlike under similar circumstances in the next contested nomination, in 2008, virtually all these elected and party officials endorsed Mondale, most even before the primaries began, and he had their unanimous support at the convention, thus ensuring his nomination despite my late western surge. When Lee and I called them all between the last of the primaries and the convention, some expressed regrets at their early endorsements and more than one disclosed that they or family members were threatened with the loss of public service jobs if they voted for me.

The weekend before the San Francisco Democratic convention convened in July 1984, opinion polls showed that I came within five or fewer percentage points of Reagan, while Mondale ran twelve to fifteen percentage points behind. My name was placed in nomination, and I received 1,201 votes, but Mondale had a majority. Immediately thereafter I sought recognition from the convention chair and, from the podium, moved the nomination of Walter Mondale by acclamation. That fall I campaigned for Mondale in more than fifty campaign events, both with him and on my own, though it mattered little in the final outcome. Asked what I thought about so-called superdelegates later, I said, "Whatever made them super did not also make them smart."

As if to add insult to injury, the Friday after the convention closed, a somewhat unnerving incident occurred.

Steve Ramsey, head of the Secret Service detail, knocked on the door of our seventh-floor suite at the St. Francis Hotel just after noon. Walter Mondale had been nominated by the Democratic Party the previous evening, the campaign was now officially over, and Lee and I were on our way across the Golden Gate Bridge to Sausalito for a final lunch with campaign friends and supporters.

We descended a few floors on the elevator on the Post Street side of the hotel, the entrance where Sara Jane Moore had taken a shot at Gerald Ford nine years before, when Steve suddenly stopped the elevator, reversed direction, and hustled us unceremoniously back into our suite. After half an hour, he knocked again, we went down to the street, waved to a crowd of two or three hundred across the street, and set out in our five-car motorcade for the bridge and Sausalito.

Minutes passed, and Ramsay said nothing. Knowing something unexpected had transpired, I said, "Steve, what happened?" He looked back from the front seat and replied, "Our site agents [Secret Service agents in street clothes] were working the crowd and saw a kid they didn't like. He had a backpack, kept changing positions for a better view, and fit the profile," i.e., the characteristics of what the Secret Service called a "shooter" or sometimes "the Jackal." "They confronted him, showed their identification, and he bolted. They caught him, threw him down, and found a loaded .38 in his backpack." He continued, "We've got him down at the San Francisco police headquarters and are asking him some questions."

We continued on to the bridge. After several minutes I tapped Steve on the shoulder and said, "Ask your guys to ask the kid if he knows I did not get the nomination." Steve laughed, then relayed the message to his people at the SFPD. Five more minutes passed, then Steve listened to his earpiece. He turned and said, "We asked him if he knew you did not get the nomination. The kid said: 'He didn't?'"[27]

Life thereafter resumed some degree of normality, but with a difference. Ten years of Senate experience had begun to reveal that institution's more intricate layers. It was surprising to discover different types of senators, in at least three regards, from what would expect. One was the difference between the campaigners and the legislators. Basically the campaigners loved the hurly-burly of campaigning, the speeches, handshaking, banners and bands, backslapping and glad-handing, and even, shockingly, asking for money. By comparison, the legislators suffered through campaigns in order to engage on a national level in formation of policy, in committee hearings and the markup of legislation, in the competition of ideas, in debate on the Senate floor. Campaigners were bored with governance, and legislators disdained, and in some cases were intimidated by, the prospects of the next election. The number of shy United States senators was surprising. How could one be shy yet rise to that level of politics? In some venues, apparently, constituents will excuse limited campaigning skills to obtain good legislation.

There was also a divide between leaders and followers. Almost by definition a United States senator is a leader. How else could he or she have gotten there? Once on that stage, however, some acquiesce in leadership by others, *leadership* in this case defined by introduction of proposed bills and amendments, suggestions in party caucuses for new directions, and redefinition of old issues in new ways. It really got down to who would define the issues and how. The activists, a minority, defined or redefined issues, and the followers voted for or against.

This difference highlighted a third divide: between careerists and self-limiting public servants. Careerists included those who liked the Senate so much they wanted to stay there for as long as they could. Others saw their time as limited and sought to accomplish what they could in one, two, or three terms. Careerists left only when defeated. The rest retired voluntarily. A small number unaccountably hated the place, complaining and grumbling daily. Why had they struggled so hard to get there? It wasn't as if there were not libraries full of books on government that told them what to expect. A small number of senators, mostly those already singled out, could stay longer in the Senate without succumbing to the charms of the special interest lobbyists. But they were rare. With some exceptions, the careerists solidify their political base at home, make their arrangements with the interest groups, court contributors, and look to the next election.

Early in my first term I was surprised by the number of Colorado citizen delegations that came to Washington. Particularly in the spring and fall, a good part of each day, often outside committee rooms, was dedicated to meeting with these home state groups. Often they were there attending national conventions of their organizations. Sometimes, though, they were summoned to Washington by their national lobbyists to urge congressional support for or opposition to some pending legislative measure. In many cases these were rural or small-town people or health-care providers or teachers who were paying their own way at a sacrifice. I averaged a day a week in Colorado over many years, at least until the all-consuming presidential race, and always urged these constituents to save their money and meet with me in the state.

Some seemed surprised to learn that I was home that often and available in various corners of Colorado. This too represented a revolution. Meeting the venerable John Stennis of Mississippi, a perennial chairman of the Armed Services Committee, when I first arrived, I was dumbfounded when he said that he went back to Mississippi four times a year when he was first elected but now found it necessary to double that.

The exercise of representation has evolved over the decades, but the fundamental nature of representation has not changed. Small republics throughout history, from Athens through republican Rome to Venice, the Swiss cantons, and beyond, could be governed on a day-to-day basis by councils of one kind or another, themselves regularly directed by citizen assemblies. Large republics, America among the first, required two innovations: federation and representation.

On one level the idea of representation is straightforward and self-evident. Regular elections involving competing parties, interests, and candidates produce elected representatives to city councils, county commissions, state legislatures, and a House of Representatives and a Senate. But there is another level to representation that is more complex and perhaps even mysterious.

Thomas Jefferson wrote that a public official becomes, upon entering office, public property. Assuredly, he did not mean the kind of present-day celebrity property to be batted about by the popular press in the same manner as musicians, actors, and people famous for being famous. In a way, he meant, those we elect belong to us, are accountable to us, must *represent* us, but must also *educate* us involving the public life and issues of the day.

And it is at the intersection of representation and education that the mystery lies. Literal representation can be accomplished by regular public-opinion polls on the issues of the day and binding the elected representative to reflect majority opinion and vote accordingly. But if that is what representation truly means, it requires only an automaton, literally, to push a button in a state capitol or in Congress.

But, as the conservative parliamentarian Edmund Burke famously stated, he owed his constituents, those who elected him, his *judgment,* holding open the real possibility that his own judgment, honed by what he learned in Parliament, might differ from public opinion. When that possibility actually occurs, the elected representative has a duty to explain why his or her judgment differs from constituents', to share information and wisdom gained in hearings and debates, and to convince the electorate that its majority opinion may be in error or simply incomplete.

It is at this juncture where leadership has failed. Too many elected politicians, unable or unwilling to exercise judgment or educate constituents, vote according to popular opinion, even when wrong. They do so, in too many cases, out of the desire for a political career. And they do so at the expense of the long-term national interest. In a word, they place their own career interests ahead of the nation's interest.

The mystery of representation rests in its moral component. The vast number of votes in Congress are not what might be called "profile in courage" votes. The number of times self-interest conflicts with national interest are relatively few. But they do arise often enough to define character and to separate genuine leaders from careerist politicians.

The American republic, a federated republic dependent upon representation, requires its representatives to demonstrate courage, vision, and leadership. Leadership requires an ability to see over the horizon, the creativity to provide new solutions to new challenges, and the courage to educate the people that old policies, ones that comfort them, must give way, and to sacrifice office if they refuse.

Beware the politician for whom office becomes too important.

During the 1970s and '80s there was also a small wave of retirements—some very good legislators, but almost all senior members. Faced with the new realities, television and money, they saw no future. It was the passing of an age, an age in which public oratory featured grand gestures, shouted stump speeches, county fair rallies as entertainment, and "pointing with alarm and viewing with pride." This style did not work on television, which converted arm waving into madness and storytelling into buffoonery. During this period politicians became younger, had more hair, and spoke more normally.

My own innate reserve was a cause for discounting among the pundits. Most candidates produce "keys on the typewriter," that is, clichés that become identifying taglines and, like crows flying from the power line, are adopted as shorthand by most reporters. Mine was "cool and aloof." Gary Hart, "cool and aloof," today announced, and so forth. The most successful political figure at bridging the gap between the old and the new later became Bill Clinton, whose fluency made him effective on television but who also had the charm to "work the room." This cliché meant traditional backslapping, small-talking, and demonstrations of care and affection toward strangers.

Following my unexpected victory in New Hampshire in 1984, "cool and aloof" gave way overnight to "media surfing" accusations by the media clamoring for interviews. How a reserved candidate who preferred to campaign with his back to the wall, in the (surprisingly successful) hope of drawing people to him, came to become overnight the Jim Morrison of American politics right before our very eyes was never carefully explained. The people of New Hampshire knew me very well as the former, the rest of the country had to adapt itself to me, or me to it, as the latter.[28]

Then, after the 1984 election, my family and I visited the Soviet Union in the winter of 1985 as the guests of then foreign minister Andrei Gromyko and the US-Canada Institute. On the way we stopped in Paris, where I was invited to meet with President François Mitterrand. To compensate my children, Andrea and John, for the burdens politics had imposed upon them, I sought opportunities to introduce them to significant leaders. At ten and eight when we moved to Washington, the only important person they wanted to meet was my new colleague John Glenn who, by then, was well established in their American history books. In 1985, by prearrangement, I took John, then a lanky nineteen-year-old, with me to meet the French president. In the limousine to the Élysée Palace

I straightened his wayward tie and tried to tuck in his shirt. Once in the grand office designed by no less than Charles de Gaulle himself, we sat before Mitterrand's elaborate desk and began a cordial visit on the great issues of the day.[29]

Following the campaign there was also a subtle change in my role in the Senate. The institution is much too historic and august to change dramatically, especially with regard to any individual member. But once one has established some degree of credibility on the national stage, quiet differences in attitude and respect arise. Thereafter, on the occasions when I would speak in the Democratic caucus lunch on policies or party positions, I knew I was being listened to in a keener way. From the day I entered the Senate in January 1975, for example, I repeatedly argued against increasing dependence on Persian Gulf oil, including in a number of speeches and published articles in the late seventies and beyond, saying that this dependence would inevitably lead us into Persian Gulf wars. Before announcing for president, I had introduced legislation to tax imported oil at $10 a barrel to reduce this dependence. Advisors said I had to abandon that idea in New England states, where imported oil was used for heating homes. Instead, I campaigned consistently and vocally for the tax.

When energy legislation emerged on the Senate's agenda in the fall of 1984, I urged my Democratic colleagues to adopt the principle of an oil-import tax. A number of leading senators rose in protest, calling it everything up to and including political suicide. Fritz Hollings of South Carolina, a former competitor on the campaign trail, took the floor of the caucus. Pointing at me he said, "Don't tell me it can't be done. This man never abandoned this idea and he won every New England state."

Had we adopted an import tax of this sort a quarter of a century ago, we might be free of Persian Gulf dependence and a trillion dollars or so would have been added to the national treasury. From 1974 on, the nation's failure to combine energy conservation with increased production of sustainable supplies would be both mysterious and confounding.

Together with the energy picture, Cold War ups and downs made concerns for arms control serious. The debate over the new MX missile in 1983 came against the backdrop of an arms buildup on both sides and very little progress in arms control negotiations in Geneva. During the Carter years, Senator Robert Byrd succeeded Mike Mansfield as majority leader and had the productive notion of appointing several senators to be "observers" at the Strategic Arms Limitation Talks (SALT II) in Geneva. In the hope that a treaty might be negotiated and submitted for ratification, the observers would be prepared to lead the debate in support of a treaty some of whose provisions might be arcane and be able to explain its advantages to fellow senators. As one of the appointed senators, I made several trips to Geneva to observe the negotiations and participate in informal discussions with the Soviets. Given the imbalance and lack of symmetry between the nuclear arsenals of the two sides, it was always a process of comparing apples to oranges and trying to decide how many apples equaled how many oranges.

Limiting disparate arsenals and reducing overall totals of specific weapons systems occupied most of these negotiations, but other issues, for example, such things as confidence-building measures, were important. These had to do with what one side could do to assure the other side that no steps were being taken to prepare a surprise attack, or to unnecessarily conceal weapons, or to develop purposely destabilizing practices or weapons. The expert diplomatic negotiators steeped in arms control language and concepts were ordained into the priesthood of all this, but even those observers such as myself who tried to stay current on these arcane developments had a difficult time tracking the complex twists and turns.

In any case, the Soviet Union invaded Afghanistan, Americans were taken hostage in Iran, and President Carter would not possess the personal popularity and political clout to submit a SALT II treaty to the Senate and get it ratified.

During the early and mid-Reagan years, arms control slowed down a great deal. Surrounded by much harder-line advisors who convinced the president that we could only negotiate from strength, and strength meant a major arms buildup, serious limitation and reduction talks suffered. Nevertheless, discussions continued in Geneva, though without much intensity, and I observed them on a couple of occasions. Reagan had sent the distinguished diplomat Paul Nitze to Geneva to try to negotiate a limitation on intermediate range missiles (with ranges between five hundred and fifty-five hundred kilometers). Little progress was under way when I visited in 1982, in part because Reagan policy makers in Washington were only in favor of treaties requiring the Soviets, but not the United States, to disarm. Ambassador Nitze, however, took his job seriously and invited me to join him for an informal lunch with his Soviet counterpart, a youngish Yuri "Yuli" Kvitsinsky, at La Perle du Lac restaurant on the shore of Lake Geneva.

Operating with one political hand tied behind his back, Nitze continued to explore ways that might work. Loyal to the president, but less so to his inferior arms control bosses in Washington, Nitze proceeded to involve me in one of his "walks in the woods," a series of informal discussions he and Kvitsinsky carried on for some time in which offers and counteroffers were unofficially explored. Nitze's theory seemed to be that he might deliver an offer to the Reagan administration it could not refuse. After a few niceties, Nitze turned to me and said, "Ask my Russian friend how he might respond if he were to be offered the following proposal..." Confused, I turned to the Soviet and conveyed Nitze's idea. Kvitsinsky said, "That's an interesting notion. Please tell my friend Paul that if such a proposal were to be made, it would attract great interest in Moscow." By now even I figured out the game and proceeded to play the role of unofficial courier. Rather intricate formulas were tested and revised. Specific numbers were exchanged. At no time did one diplomat address the other directly. At no time was a record made of an offer or response or bargaining position that later could be dubbed official. They were walking through the verbal woods, and I was the hollow log in which each side was leaving messages for the other.

It finally worked; after Paul Nitze left Geneva, an Intermediate-Range Nuclear Forces Treaty (INF) was signed by Reagan and Gorbachev in Washington, in December 1987, during the great thaw and Reagan's late-term conversion to arms control. Nitze was effective. Of the 2,700 missiles destroyed, the Soviet Union contributed almost 1,900 of them.

A former colleague, John Tower, was sent to Geneva to negotiate a Strategic Arms Reduction Treaty (START I), and I was part of a delegation, with Senators Kennedy, Gore, and Nunn, that joined those talks briefly in the mid-1980s. Like Nitze, up until this stage of his life Tower had never been a fan of arms control treaties. One night while I was dining alone at the Hôtel de Ville restaurant in the old city, Senator Tower and two of his daughters passed by and invited me join them for dinner upstairs. Knowing from experience that he saw his family seldom, I declined, but did join them briefly for coffee after. In April 1991, Senator Tower, together with one of those daughters, Marian, died in a plane crash in Georgia. Three months later the START treaty was ratified. One month later the Soviet Union began to dissolve, and five months later it disappeared.

A political deadline was looming in 1986, and a decision was required. My second term was ending, and the possibility of a second national race, starting from a much stronger base, was a very great possibility. Having missed

a number of Senate votes in the 1983–84 period and substantially reduced constituent trips to Colorado during the
first national campaign, it did not seem right to seek a third
Senate term with the thought, if successful, of immediately
starting a grueling second presidential campaign. The people
of Colorado deserved better. In early 1986 I announced that
I would not seek another Senate term, and a House Democratic colleague and friend, Tim Wirth, announced for and,
happily, won the Senate seat that year. Following one Senate
term he served as an undersecretary of state in the Clinton
administration and, most notably, the first president of the
United Nations Foundation.

The year 1986 was eventful. In July of that year, Lee and
I, with staff members Elsie Vance and Doug Wilson and a
few friends, spent ten days in the Middle East, starting in
Amman, Jordan, then to Cairo, then to Tel Aviv and Jerusalem, and finally, unexpectedly, back to Amman. In Amman
we were guests of King Hussein and Queen Noor. After meetings with the king, his prime minister, Zaid al-Rifai, and his
defense chief, Field Marshal Sharif Zaid bin Shaker, we were
invited to spend part of a weekend at the summer palace,
simply a very nice house with compound, at Aqaba, on the
Red Sea. My personal impression after this visit and based on
previous meetings was that King Hussein was genuinely one
of the most humane and decent world leaders I was to meet.
Complex political circumstances involving Palestinian refugees from the 1967 war and thereafter, formation of terrorist
cells, and indigenous threats to his personal safety caused
the Hussein regime to adopt what some considered overly
repressive security measures within Jordan. Regardless, he
was the epitome of classic Middle Eastern hospitality.

In Aqaba we were guests of honor at a small dinner in the
home of the royal couple with the Rifais, the US ambassador
Paul Boeker and his wife, and the king and queen. After dinner, King Hussein asked me to join him in his upstairs study.

There he quietly described detailed and complex secret negotiations under way between himself and then Israeli prime
minister Shimon Peres, designed to establish a peace agreement between the two countries and to lay the foundation
for a broader regional peace arrangement. This was stunning
news. In theory at least, the two nations were still at war.
He asked me to confirm this when I met with Shimon Peres
and to organize an effort in the Senate and with the Reagan
administration to underwrite this historic effort with political and financial support. He received my commitment to
do all I could, and I began to plan how to organize such a
bipartisan effort.

The following afternoon the king and queen and two of
their young children took us out on the Red Sea in his fast
boat flying the royal pennant. A mile or two up the seacoast,
from the Israeli port of Elat, two equally fast coastal patrol
craft, flying the Israeli flag, set out. They maintained speed
but kept their distance. Seeing my surprise, and some concern, King Hussein smiled and said, "It always happens. They
consider that they are protecting me." Very little is simple
in the Middle East.

The next day we were received by Hosni Mubarak, president of Egypt, and his senior cabinet. It was becoming clear
that at least one or two leaders thought I might become president and wanted to develop relationships. Though cautious
in his comments, and inserting the usual criticisms of Israeli
policies, Mubarak offered a moderate assessment of the state
of affairs in the region and made it clear that his government
had no interest in departing from the peaceful relations with
Israel for which his predecessor, Anwar al-Sadat, had sacrificed his life. He also made it clear that he expected US financial assistance, then as now the second highest in our foreign
aid menu after Israel, to continue in exchange for his efforts.

We then went to Tel Aviv for meetings with Prime
Minister Peres, his foreign minister, Yitzhak Shamir, and

a small group of younger leaders, including Ehud Olmert, who would later rise to power in both the Likud and Avoda (Labor) parties. At this time Israel had a complicated coalition government in which both major parties participated in a power-sharing arrangement that required Peres to surrender the prime minister position to Shamir that coming October. Peres hosted a lunch in our honor with thirty or forty national leaders. Beforehand we met privately. In a small room at the restaurant I revealed my discussion with King Hussein and asked for his response. He confirmed the secret negotiations, confessed they had been going on for some time, including in Paris and elsewhere, and also confirmed that for an agreement to succeed it would require the wholehearted endorsement of the US government, both White House and Senate. He urged me to do all I could to lay the groundwork.

Afterward, I asked our ambassador Tom Pickering, the same ambassador who had laid out the covert Contra operations to Bill Cohen and me in San Salvador a couple of years before, to meet me at the King David Hotel, where we were staying in Jerusalem. Being a sophisticated diplomat, Pickering knew some but perhaps not all of what I had picked up from Hussein and Peres. I asked his help in two regards: first that he arrange for me to return, unplanned, to Amman so that I could clarify details of what Peres had told me; and second, to request a meeting with Secretary of State George Shultz on my return to Washington three days later. I suspected Israeli intelligence was picking up all of this and selected my words accordingly.

I had requested some time with the Israeli military services, hoping to pick up ideas for military reform, and got the full treatment. The day started with a tank battalion on the Golan Heights near Banyas, where I participated in maneuvers and could view Damascus in the distance, then a helicopter trip to a fighter airbase in north-central Israel near Zefat,

and ending with an evening patrol with the Israeli navy off
the coast near Haifa. Before leaving the tankers, they insisted
I join them in a hearty buffet lunch laid out on a long table.

An hour later I was suiting up in a G suit, ready to go on
a combat patrol in an F-4 fighter with the base commander.
His eyes merrily dancing, he laughingly insisted that I put a
couple of plastic bags in the cargo pockets and off we went.
The plane had to be rolled out of its hillside hiding place, standard practice, and we took off over the Mediterranean. After a
few maneuvers he headed up the Israeli coast toward the Leba-
nese border, turned a hard right at considerable speed, and
flew along the border until momentarily we got back to the
Golan Heights. The pilot then performed a high-level bombing
run, involving driving straight up about ten or fifteen thousand feet, dropping the nose over, and then powering straight
down at high speed. Our target was an abandoned farmhouse
with the roof painted white. Over the pilot's shoulder I saw the
planet Earth racing toward us at hundreds of miles an hour.
At what seemed the very last second, he threw on the brakes,
theoretically released his bomb, and pointed the nose skyward
once again. He counted off the g-forces during this maneuver:
"Four g, five g, six g, seven g...You okay, Gaary?"

We leveled off and went out about ten or fifteen miles.
We did a 180-degree turn and this time, *Star Wars* fashion,
we came in on the deck, literally flying through and around
rock formations and outcroppings, over treetops, around
buildings, at an altitude that seemed about ten feet off the
ground and a speed of more than five hundred knots per
hour. We approached the same target building, the pilot
threw on the brakes, looped up, and we once again released
our theoretical armaments. This building sure as hell was
destroyed now, or at least as destroyed as I cared to make it.

Up we went and took another hard right and proceeded
south down the Israeli-Syrian border. The pilot gestured
left and said over the intercom, "Down there, Gaary, is the

biggest ground-to-air antiaircraft battery in the world," then the afterburners kicked in and we took off like a rocket. After his repeated question "You all right, Gaary?," checking to see if I had by now resorted to the plastic bags, he turned right again and proceeded across northern Israel out over the Med and turned the controls over to me. From the backseat (this being a US Air Force version of the F-4, structured for a copilot) I performed a couple of barrel rolls, a series of full loops, some dives, and some climbs. Rivaled only by my carrier flights, it was huge fun. I didn't want to land.

Back to the base, where I turned over to the pilot my unused plastic bags with a great flourish. It had required monstrous self-will not to use them. Sometime later I inquired as to what happened to the pilot and was told that he might have become chief of staff of the Israeli Air Force.

There is an amazing footnote to this adventure. In the spring of 2002, I was teaching a seminar at the Yale Law School on Monday mornings and auditing a graduate seminar on grand strategy taught by Professors Paul Kennedy and John Lewis Gaddis on Monday afternoons. One afternoon the professors had invited several wealthy guests from New York to visit the seminar in the hopes that one or more might contribute to the development of a center on strategic studies. Against the wall two seats down from me sat a very fit man, built like a gymnast, who from time to time looked my way. I thought him to be vaguely familiar. Presently he leaned forward and whispered, "Did you run for president?" He had a slight accent. I nodded yes. He whispered, "Did you visit Israel?" I nodded yes again. He pointed to himself and whispered, "I was your pilot." He had not become air force chief of staff. Instead, he immigrated to the United States and, a genius mathematician, made a fortune in sophisticated software development.

Ambassador Pickering, having negotiated a rare passage across the Allenby Bridge dividing Israel from Jordan, and

I went by car the next day back to Amman. The bridge was guarded by imposing military figures on both the Israeli and the Jordanian sides. The embassy car halted at the end of the bridge on the Jordanian side, and a very distinguished officer in uniform approached the car. The driver identified the passengers, whereupon the Jordanian officer put his head in the window and shouted, "Gaary Hart? Gaary Hart? I watched your presidential campaign when I was studying in Nebraska!" He saluted elaborately, we shook hands vigorously, and I signed a picture "For Mohammed, with very best wishes, etc." The odds are quite small, but perhaps the picture is still in the guard post at the Allenby Bridge.

Once in Amman, I went directly to King Hussein's office and repeated the content of my conversation with Shimon Peres as accurately as I could. As an amateur in the diplomatic world, it seemed imperative to get the details correct, and I would make no mistakes in relaying an account of these meetings to Secretary Shultz. The king confirmed Peres's understanding completely.

Before leaving that afternoon for Paris, Prime Minister Rifai invited us to lunch at his house. Zaid Rifai, who became a highly valued friend from that time forward, entertained us with the story of an event that had recently happened. Experiencing fatigue and stress from his intense days in office, his doctor ordered him to take up a hobby. He chose flying, and proceeded to take lessons. On the verge of qualifying for a license and needing only flying hours, he was summoned to a meeting with the king at the palace in Aqaba and decided to take his instructor and fly down. It took less than an hour, and after landing, he was driven to the seaside home, carried out his business, and returned to the airport to fly home to Amman. His regular instructor had told him to expect another pilot to accompany him on the return.

At the plane a young man waited. Rifai gestured for him to get in and took the left-side pilot's seat himself. They taxied out and were given clearance to take off by Aqaba tower. The takeoff was smooth, and they headed north. Rifai said, "What is our heading?" The young man looked baffled. Rifai repeated the question, and the young man, now called in the story "the kid," said, "I don't know" and shrugged his shoulders. Rifai said, "What do you mean, you don't know?" The kid said, "I don't know. I've never flown before. I was told at the airfield that if I hung around, someone might give me a ride to Amman."

Puffing on his customary cigar in the telling, Rifai said his knees began to shake. If he had to crash-land, he knew the Amman airport had more emergency equipment and better hospitals than Aqaba. So he told the kid to look out the window and give him directions to the right or left to follow the highway down below that went north/northeast toward Amman. Not knowing exactly how the radio worked, Rifai managed to get off an emergency call that alerted the Amman airport, and virtually all of Jordan, that the nation's prime minister would soon be making an emergency landing. Fighter aircraft were scrambled as escorts, and fire trucks and ambulances lined the runway ahead. Knees trembling, arms braced, and the kid reading off altimeters and airspeeds, Rifai put the plane down in a series of high bounces that finally led to a careening halt.

"That was it," Zaid said. "I never got my license, and I never got back in a small plane."

After an overnight stop in Paris, I went directly to Washington, and from Dulles Airport, thanks to Tom Pickering, directly into Secretary Shultz's office in the State Department. Though I had attended briefings and testimony he had given in the Senate, I had never had a direct conversation with him. He knew the topic had to do with developments during my trip to the Middle East, and he had half a dozen senior staff and officials in attendance. I relayed in explicit detail the upstairs meeting with the king in Aqaba, the private meeting with Peres, and the second meeting with the king in Amman. Having given thought to the matter during the return flight, I committed to finding Republican senators to join fellow Democrats in introducing and passing a package of assistance measures, both humanitarian and military, to both countries, and stated I would fully cooperate with the administration in encouraging public support, directly and through the media, endorsing this breakthrough peace plan. Shultz said nothing. Sensing that there might be domestic political concerns, I solemnly swore not to have my name on the legislative measures, nor to seek any recognition for them. Then I was done.

The secretary was silent, Buddha-like, and then blunt. "We do not see any political advantage for us [the Reagan administration] to be engaged in the Middle East at this time," he said. I assumed he had not understood or that I had not been clear. I summarized the intense if not urgent desires of the Jordanians and Israelis once again and emphasized, as both Hussein and Peres had requested me to, that the coalition government in Israel was to reverse leadership that October, some one hundred days away, and a Shamir/Likud-led government would be much less inclined to pursue the initiative. Shultz responded, "I don't believe we want to go forward with this right now." That was that.

Though sorely tempted, I chose not to hold a press conference or even leak the story to some national news service. I did not want responsibility for endangering the peace process and possibly increasing the political and personal jeopardy of the two leaders involved, and a lesser consideration was the potential for the administration to accuse me of practicing diplomacy without a license or seeking to feather my own political nest. This story was never told. It would be a full eight years later, in 1994, before the Israeli-Jordanian peace agreement would be announced by President Clinton in the White House.

An even more significant trip took place in December 1986. Following the latest of the New Leaders conferences in Seoul, with my daughter, Andrea, I flew to Moscow, by way of Tokyo, to meet with President Gorbachev. In Tokyo, we stopped at the US Embassy to reunite with my old friend and mentor Ambassador Mike Mansfield. He not only summarized development in Japan and took us on a briefing tour of the entire Asian region, he also had sage advice on avenues to explore with the new, and dramatically different, Soviet leader.

We arrived in Moscow on Sunday night and were joined by fellow Americans Stephen Cohen and Katrina vanden Heuvel as well as a Denver friend, Robert Loup. Steve Cohen, I believed then and still, has the keenest and certainly one of the most perceptive minds around on developments in the Soviet Union. Monday morning I was taken to the Kremlin to meet President Gorbachev and, with the approval of the Soviet Ministry of Foreign Affairs, took Andrea with me so that she could meet the Soviet president. Our friends toured the Kremlin complex.

Accompanied by Anatoly Dobrynin, longtime Soviet ambassador to the United States and his principal advisor on American matters, Gorbachev was friendly and markedly different from previous Soviet leaders I had met. He waved us to his conference table and, confused, I asked Dobrynin what should be done with Andrea. She was then twenty-two years old and a graduating senior at the University of Denver in US-Soviet studies (the department of the same university, it turns out, from which future secretary of state Condoleezza Rice had recently graduated). Receiving the translation, Gorbachev immediately said, "*Da, da, da.* She is welcome to join us."

What I assumed from past experience would be a half-hour perfunctory handshake meeting lasted until after one in the afternoon. In October, less than two months before, Gorbachev had his first full summit meeting with President

Reagan, at Reykjavik, Iceland. By all accounts, it had not gone well. I believe I was the first American political figure to meet Gorbachev since this event, and he wanted an audience. He proceeded to describe what had transpired hour by hour. It was in considerably greater detail than had been contained in US press coverage, which had been dependent, in any case, on administration briefings, and provided a Soviet-eye interpretation of the event.

In a nutshell, Gorbachev was confused and was tempted to believe that he had been misled or set up. His condition for agreeing to the summit was that both leaders come with a detailed agenda. When the first session began, he put an outline on the table and asked for President Reagan's proposed agenda. Reagan had none, and simply agreed to operate from Gorbachev's agenda. Then, Reagan surprised Gorbachev by suggesting they dismiss the considerable number of advisors joining them both and proceed to talk man-to-man. Having come to understand that Reagan was not a man of detail, to put it mildly, Gorbachev was surprised. But, fully prepared himself, he acquiesced.

Thereafter, for two and a half days, the pattern went as follows: They would discuss a proposal for about two hours, then break to meet with their advisors. They would then resume using the same timetable. After the first break and those that followed, according to Gorbachev, Reagan, having agreed to accept fairly bold and in some cases sweeping reductions in nuclear arsenals, would return to say that, though they had had very good discussions, nothing had been agreed to. This pattern characterized every meeting. Gorbachev concluded that, left to his own devices, Reagan was personally inclined to dramatic action but that, once in the hands of advisors, whether merely seasoned or hard-line, he was convinced to back off.

Frustration mounted on both sides until, faced with no breakthroughs and little progress, the leaders were required to face the press. Reagan used the usual "frank and fruitful," "direct and productive" diplomatic clichés. Gorbachev, making no effort to conceal his disappointment and frustration, concluded that he was dealing with a government uninterested in ending the arms race at that time and essentially said that the Cold War would continue. When I met with the Soviet foreign minister, Eduard Shevardnadze, the following afternoon, he said that he had known Gorbachev since their early days as regional party leaders and later junior Politburo members and, in the car going to the press conference, he had never seen Gorbachev so upset and feared that a real war was going to break out.

Following the detailed deconstruction of the Reykjavik summit and the issues of nuclear arms reduction, my discussions with Gorbachev expanded to human rights and other issues. It was obligatory for American politicians visiting the Soviet Union to raise the plight of refuseniks, protesters against the regime, those seeking to emigrate to Israel, and exiled dissidents, and to make specific requests on behalf of named individuals. I continued this tradition, naming particularly Andrei Sakharov, the famous nuclear physicist, human rights activist, and 1975 Nobel Peace Prize laureate, exiled to Gorky; a cancer patient named Rima Brava; and several others seeking to emigrate. Gorbachev dismissively waved his hand and chastised me and others like me for interfering in the Soviet Union's internal affairs. "Don't you have enough problems in your own country to worry about?" he said. "Let us solve our problems in our own way." This was a fairly standard response and a semipolite way of saying, It's none of your business.

Gorbachev then turned to Andrea and spoke to her in Russian. Though she had studied the language she did not feel confident enough to test her language skills on the president of the Soviet Union. In translation, he said, "I know you are studying my country and our politics and culture."

Leaning back in his chair, with a grin and expansive wave he continued, "Why don't you come over next summer, spend the whole summer traveling Russia and the Soviet Union as my personal guest." I nudged her under the table and gave a definite positive nod. Andrea said, "That is very kind, Mr. President, but next year my father may be involved in a national campaign and I'll need to help him." Gorbachev said, "I know, and having a daughter like you, I understand. But the offer will remain open."

The following afternoon I met for three hours with Shevardnadze, who provided more details on events at Reykjavik and gave a sweeping analysis of the US-Soviet goals and Soviet intentions in the world. I was struck, yet again, with how different these new leaders acted and sounded—more relaxed, more open, more expansive—than their traditional predecessors. Neither of the two had traveled enough to be men of the world. They relied heavily on advisors like Dobrynin. But, a few years later, after the Soviet Union dissolved and he was out of office, Shevardnadze confided to me that he and Gorbachev and those they brought with them to the top were stunned to open the national treasury's books for the first time and learn how desperately underfinanced the Soviet domestic economy already was and how much disproportionately was being spent on the military and the Cold War. Though they were rich in energy and minerals, they had not developed their resources to any degree that would permit foreign sales and thus generate hard currency revenues.

The conventional view is that the US arms buildup begun under Carter and continued under Reagan, and the prospect of competition in a costly, high-technology race centered on Star Wars brought the Soviet leaders to their knees and caused them to surrender. Based on my experience, the picture is much more complex. The arms race, begun and continuing well before Reagan, was driving Russia and its dependent Eastern European allies into third-world status, and a new generation of leaders was willing, and some might say honest and courageous enough, to acknowledge this picture and set a different course. In any case, an accurate historical analysis will be much more nuanced than the favored American political view.[30] That view is dangerous if used as a precedent, one that leads us to believe all we have to do is buy more weapons and spend more money and we will cow any rival or peer competitor—say, China—into submission. Down that road lies bankruptcy, but next time for the United States.

Given my lifelong fascination with Russian history and literature generally, nineteenth-century Russia more particularly, and Leo Tolstoy especially, the Soviet hosts organized a trip to Tula, over two hours south of Moscow by car, to visit the ancestral Tolstoy estate Yasnaya Polyana, where the great writer was buried. Our small group toured the estate and the large two-story Tolstoy house, including the writing study where much of *War and Peace* had been written. We were also reminded of a story from Tolstoy's youth, when his older brother told him the legend of the "green stick," a stick buried on the property that once found would have magical qualities guaranteeing every wish. Tolstoy mentioned his desire to find the green stick on a number of occasions throughout his life. I visited the great writer's grave and signed the visitors' guest book.

There were meetings with a distinguished diplomat, Arthur Hartman, then US ambassador, and other embassy officials, and a speech at the Institute for US and Canadian Studies, the perennial interlocutor for US-Soviet exchanges. Steve and Katrina also organized a dinner for the four of us at the dacha of Yevgeny Yevtushenko, the iconic national poet, outside Moscow. Many toasts preceded dinner, that is until the vodka ran out. Anticipating his remarriage a few days hence, Yevtushenko had stocked two cases of wedding wine. During and after dinner we dipped into the wine to celebrate his wedding in advance. The week ended, and we went to Sheremetyevo Airport to return to the United States.

Awaiting us at the airport were Rima Brava and others whose emigration I had requested, and a short time later Inna Meiman, who was on the list I provided Gorbachev, was to follow. It had occasionally happened that, to show favor to a visiting political figure, individuals on whose behalf they had intervened would be granted release from confinement or the right to emigrate. It was moving to see the tears of gratitude in Ms. Brava's eyes as we met for the first time at the steps of the plane and she thanked me.

That morning, even more momentously, Gorbachev called Andrei Sakharov in Gorky and welcomed his return to Moscow. This was worldwide news and a huge signal that things were finally changing in the Soviet Union. I sought no credit, nor was any given. But the coincidence of timing was not lost on me at least. As I boarded the plane, it occurred to me that I might have discovered Tolstoy's green stick.

In early April 1987, I announced my candidacy for the presidency against the backdrop of the stunning Red Rocks Park outside Denver and again at a downtown rally at midday. There had been some preliminary preparations, including a visit to Ottawa, Kansas, where I was born and grew up, and where my parents were buried. Before a speech at Ottawa University honoring my hometown and expressing my gratitude for the impact growing up there had had on my life, I had a reunion with my relatives. I had over twenty aunts and uncles and, therefore, dozens and dozens of cousins. My mother came from a family of thirteen. Her father, Willard, a railroad man and nurseryman most of his life, believed the biblical admonition to "marry, multiply, and replenish the earth." My father was from a family of eight. Neither of my parents had the opportunity to graduate from high school, being required to join the workforce in their early teens. I expected perhaps a dozen people at the reunion. Instead, in the room set aside for the occasion there were at least two hundred people, many of whom I had never met and who turned out to be spouses and children of the many cousins.

Ottawa's population was ten thousand when I was born, and it was ten thousand when I returned. The county seat of agricultural Franklin County, it seemed hardly ever to change. There was a fairly new high school building for the appropriately named Cyclones, and Main Street shops changed hands from time to time. But it was and is as solid a midwestern community as could be found anywhere. With my father and my cousin Jon, I had hunted its fields and fished its streams outside of town. And I had earned my way through college, then graduate school, then law school on construction crews and on the tracks of the Santa Fe Railroad, whose double-rail main line heading west bisected the north–south Missouri Pacific line in downtown Ottawa. Ottawa was a railroad town, and that is what had drawn my mother's family from Deepwater, Missouri, in the Ozarks in the 1920s. My father's family had emigrated to the United States fifty years before the American Revolution. The Hart-Pences settled in Hunterdon County in western New Jersey by the early 1730s, and each of my ancestor grandfathers migrated one state westward with the progress of the national boundary, across Pennsylvania to Ohio, then next to Indiana, then to Illinois, then across Missouri to Kansas, where my very old grandfather claimed to this very small boy that he had been a frontier marshal in Burlington, Kansas, and had joined posses that chased the bank-robbing James brothers, Jesse and Frank, back to Missouri. According to legend, the family first hyphenated its last name, then combined the names to avoid the impression, during the Revolutionary War, that they were Hessians. In my early twenties, my parents and Lee and I shortened the name to Hart, pure and simple.

I left Ottawa at the age of seventeen to attend Bethany Nazarene College, now Southern Nazarene University, in

Bethany, Oklahoma, a town whose literary claim to fame was as the site where the Joad family in John Steinbeck's *Grapes of Wrath* spent its first night on the road to California during the Great Depression. Except to visit my parents and see high school friends, I never returned to Ottawa for long. But it is true that the place from which you start out stays with you the rest of your life.

My parents, Nina Lavone Pritchard Hartpence and Carl Riley Hartpence, dedicated their entire lives to my sister, Nancy, and me. They lived simply and humbly and sacrificed comforts to see us educated. They gave us as much as the wealthiest family in America gives its children. Though they lived to see me through Bethany Nazarene College, my mother barely well enough to drive to the commencement, and a few years beyond, they did not live to see much of the thunder and the sunshine that followed. A day does not go by that I do not think of them and thank them for the extraordinary sunshine that has been mine.

Needless to say, I was not to become president. The circumstances are too well known, and to some degree still too painful to require repetition. And for most they would be beside the point. There were, however, lessons provided, and some of them deserve summary.

In the prelude to the 1988 election, polls showed me to be well ahead of other suggested Democratic contenders and almost as far ahead of the leading Republican contender and eventual president, George H. W. Bush. Shortly after announcing my candidacy, I chose to withdraw from the contest in a flurry of stories, some of which were true, some of which were partly true, and many of which were simply wrong. The controversy, carried for five days as a siege to the very gates of my mountain home, made it impossible to campaign. This decision to withdraw was not made lightly, nor without deliberation. In the aftermath, it would be widely reported that I was "driven" from the race. The events as viewed through my eyes caused me to *choose* not to continue. The difference is not a matter of semantics. No office this nation has to offer is worth the sacrifice of the privacy of my home and the protection of my family.

Other important considerations simply got swept away in what the press itself soon came to call a media feeding frenzy. But the principals in the event were immediately swept up in myths that only a Homer could truly appreciate.

The most pernicious and self-perpetuating myth was that I was placed under surreptitious surveillance by a team of newspaper reporters because I dared or challenged the press to follow me. This is simply not true. The facts are categorically otherwise. I invited one journalist from a leading paper then preparing a magazine profile to join me, openly and visibly, in my daily routine.

Starting years before, in the McGovern campaign, I had worked with the press, knew its principal figures nationally and locally, and had great respect for its professional members. In virtually all cases I had been known to them in my public, and in some cases private life for more than fifteen years. A number of leading American journalists had been guests in my home, and Lee and I had developed family friendships, and even exchanged holiday gifts, with several of the best known of them. The proposition that I would dare or challenge reporters to follow me, and particularly dare them to invade the privacy of my home, is preposterous on its face. As the controversial weekend established, I was capable of errors in judgment, but inviting, let alone daring, the entire press corps to become a private and secret bureau of investigation was not one of them.

The newspaper that did place me under surveillance and did invade the privacy of my home began to do so well before the profile containing my invitation to its author appeared. Its actions in the matter, placing a candidate for president under secret surveillance by a team of investigators, so troubled one major national newspaper, and to my knowledge only one, that it sent its own reporters to interview these journalists and their editors to explore their motivation, something perhaps never before done in American journalistic history. They were turned away at the paper's door. The investigators would not be investigated. Journalism dedicated to reporting the truth has its limits.[31]

Language, the tool of the journalistic trade, also suffered. To this day, the words *scrutiny* and *scandal* are open wounds. *Scrutiny* is a mild word for a vicious process, at least for the subject of the scrutiny. It has been used to justify virtually any behavior including, as mentioned, peeking in the windows of the homes of public officials, obtaining their phone records, filtering through their trash, and asking totally inappropriate questions of their friends. *Scandal* has been used so often in a narrow sexual context that it is rarely used even to discuss serious social ills, such as, for example, the scandal of elderly people without medicine or children without food. Words debased, particularly by those whose trade is in words, become meaningless.

It was argued at the time that excessive zeal was justified on the grounds that character in a nation's leaders matters. Without doubt. But character is demonstrated over a lifetime, and in many ways. And it is not by accident that the founder of the Christian faith advised his disciples "Judge not, that ye be not judged." For judgment of character would seem to require the establishment of character. For that, those who seek to set themselves up as self-appointed judges of character in others must look first to the superiority of their own character. Perhaps we should be led by those who are morally superior, but that would have eliminated Presidents Roosevelt, Eisenhower, Kennedy, and Johnson, just to name a few.

None of this is an argument for moral relativism, self-ishness, or betrayal. It is a plea for a small margin of tolerance for the personal relationships of others whose intimate details we will never and should never know. If we actually choose not to judge others whose private lives we can never know, not only would we not be equally judged, we might actually improve the caliber and quality of those who seek to lead us, as we were in our prejudgmental history.

At roughly the stage in life of Tennyson's *Ulysses*, a political warrior, increasingly described as "senior," would often be asked for some distillation of wisdom gathered over the years. On these occasions, I find myself remembering, indeed never forgetting, a remark made early in my Senate years by Mike Mansfield. He was not given to lecturing or even offering unsolicited advice. But in an early struggle over a complex interpretation of Senate rules, an interpretation that pitted competing desired outcomes, achieving worthy objectives against upholding historic institutional precedents, I sought his judgment. He said, "Draw a line. Never cross it."

I knew then what he meant, and I know it still today. It was the best advice I have ever been given. Decide early on what principle is more important than political ambition, what principles cannot and should not be violated regardless of the personal consequences. And never, ever abandon those principles. In office and since, I have always tried not to cross that line. That line is meant to keep perspective on politics and political ambition, but it is also the standard for defining integrity.

Long life has provided the chance to consider the relative merits of age and youth. Youth is experimental, imaginative, and creative. Age is seasoned, experienced, and cautious. Young people are liberal. Older people are conservative. Or so we are told. There are always exceptions. Some of the most cautious people I have met were young. And some of the most creative were old. Sweeping categories are dangerous and often wrong.

Yet in politics and government, at least young leaders are more inclined to try new ideas and approaches. Older leaders have often seen ideas younger ones consider new to have been tried before and to have failed. It is not as if they are against the "new." It is that they are against repetition of failure. But observation of repeated human failure is often the cause of lassitude and sometimes cynicism among the older.

Thus, young leaders are needed for innovation, often mistakenly called liberalism. Older leaders, hopefully statesmen, are needed for a sense of history, always mistakenly confused with conservatism.

Heraclitus said we could not step in the same river twice. The one constant in life is change. The 1960s were not the seventies, the seventies were not the eighties, the eighties not the nineties, and most of all, the twenty-first century is not the twentieth. In its effort to preserve tradition, the conservative mind, too often associated with the elderly, seeks to deny, Canute-like, the tides of change. That mind, as Arthur Schlesinger Jr., said, is characterized by gravity, custom, and fear.

Ideally, we would produce leaders who, regardless of age, combined the experimentalism of youth to respond to changing times with the sagacity of age to resist repetition of error. These we call statesmen. It is fashionable now to say there are no statesmen, and to an unfortunate extent this is true. I am fortunate to have met a few—Averell Harriman, George Kennan, and Dean Acheson. They not only made history, they understood history.

And if there is one cause for the demise of statecraft, it is the failure to know history. The Age of Reagan was characterized not only by a suspicion of science, it was also suspicious of history. Of course, a handful of conservative commentators could recall the glory days of bygone eras, usually nostalgically remembering the good but not the bad. Of the application of the lessons of the past to the realities of the present, however, there was little.

The mistakes of Vietnam, let alone centuries of colonial occupations, held no lessons for Iraq. Unregulated Hooverian markets held no lessons for market deregulators of the 1990s and 2000s. History's trail of failed empires lent no wisdom to the arrogant imperialists brought to power in the George W. Bush era.

Likewise, as with the earlier McGovern experience, with the passage of time I came to understand that the business of politics went beyond gaining power. At its best it can be the vehicle for channeling human energy and idealism. Out of the second national campaign, which scarcely had a chance to be born, emerged many extraordinary people—"souls that have toil'd, and wrought, and thought with me." Debbie and Billy Shore founded Share Our Strength, one of the nation's leading hunger relief organizations and a template for a host of other humanitarian efforts. Alan Khazei founded City Year, which gave opportunities to young people to perform community service across the country and then became the prototype for America's largest and most successful public service program, AmeriCorps. Dennis Walto has given his life to Save the Children and other humanitarian causes abroad. Peter Gold founded First Book to provide disadvantaged children the opportunity to own their own books and learn to love to read. David Lane is now director of One foundation and Doug Wilson helps direct the Howard Gilman Foundation. Kathy Calvin is vice president of the United Nations Foundation. Laurie Mathews has given much of her life to humanitarian relief in Nepal. Martin O'Malley became governor of Maryland.[32] Jeannie Shaheen became governor of New Hampshire and then, in 2008, the first female US senator from that state. Kathleen Sebelius became governor of Kansas and later secretary of the Department of Health and Human Services. The list could cover pages, but these are examples of many idealists empowered by campaigns and by politics, by the thought that one person can make a difference, and by the ancient notion of civic virtue and service as superior to wealth, acquisition, and luxury.

A sense of idealism in public life has been missing—that is, until the remarkable campaign of Barack Obama—for many years. In the interim it became difficult for a generation or two of young Americans to appreciate idealism's power. Personal pursuits, acquisition of wealth, and consumerism replaced for a time the sense that we are all in this together and that one life in service can make an impact. Idealism, the sense that wrongs must be righted, that injustice must be fought, and that a better society is achievable, is among the most powerful of human forces if called upon and empowered by leaders. At least in our early years, almost all of us listen for that summons.

I believe I would have been a good president, possibly even a very good one. I am encouraged in that thought by the letters I received from presidents, prime ministers, and others I had come to know, and a considerable number of everyday people whom I did not know, regretting what happened and regretting that we would not have the chance to work together to try to improve the world.

As an example of the kind of administration I had in mind, if elected in 1988, I had resolved to seek to quietly and unofficially negotiate a comprehensive set of agreements with Mikhail Gorbachev between the time of the election and the inauguration, to invite the Soviet leader to Washington to witness the inauguration, and then formally execute the agreements while he was there. The purpose and effect would have been to end the Cold War years before it ended itself.

Later, in the mid-1990s, I was active in Global Green, the US chapter of Gorbachev's international environmental foundation Green Cross International. We were in Geneva for an annual meeting of the foundation's international leaders. I had not seen Gorbachev for some time. When he came in the room he made his way toward me and, in a gesture not common for him or traditional Soviet leaders, at least regarding American politicians, threw his arms around me. Over dinner I told him of the idea of how a Hart administration might have started, including with his presence at the inauguration, and asked what his response might have been. "Of course," he said, "I would have done it immediately."

Thanking supporters.

Man bites dog.

With Lee, campaigning in 1984.

Saying thanks to Barry Goldwater at the Air Force Academy.

Andrea, Doug Wilson, and me with President Mikhail Gorbachev, 1986.

Democratic primary finalists.

Signing the guest book at the Tolstoy estate, Yasnaya Polyana.

With Lee at the 1984 Democratic National Convention in San Francisco.

With French President François Mitterrand.

Congressional delegation with Prime Minister Margaret Thatcher.

With Israeli Prime Minister Shimon Peres.

With Egyptian President Anwar Sadat.

With President Hosni Mubarak in Cairo, 1986.

Wreath-laying at the Tomb of the Unknown at the Kremlin, 1986.

Fidel Castro with a Colorado buffalo.

Presenting the Hart-Rudman Report to Defense Secretary Bill Cohen.

In Colorado.

PART IV

AN ODYSSEY CONTINUES (1988–2008)

As he rises from his stony perch above the harbor, Ulysses tells his mariners that he is prepared to sail beyond the sunset "and the baths of all the western stars," until he dies. This last odyssey offers no return. He fears nothing. We must be prepared, he notes, to perish in the wine-dark sea ("it may be that the gulfs will wash us down") and even to greet the great Achilles one more time somewhere in the Happy Isles of eternity.

Even in old age, even with his powers of body diminished, "tho' much is taken," and though he and his mariners no longer possess the power to move heaven and earth as before, "much abides" and "that which we are, we are." If we mean to journey forth "to follow knowledge like a sinking star," more important than our youthful bodies and muscular strength is our dedication, our wisdom, our determination. We may have been stronger in body then, but now we are stronger in spirit and in will.

What we now have to share with each other is the equal temper of our heroic hearts. These hearts may have been weakened by time and fate. But that weakness is more than made up for by the strength of our will. And the strength of our will, the fierceness of our spirit, enables us to sail beyond the sunset till we die and, on that classic charge, "to strive, to seek, to find, and not to yield."

Our ancient mariner, the great Ulysses, will not die idle on his barren rocks. He cannot. Otherwise, he would not be great and he would not be Ulysses, and we would not still care about him throughout the course of Western history. His is the standard to which we repair in our search for purpose and for strength. If he can do it, if he can summon his mariners and launch out one last time, if he can sail beyond the sunset, if he can smite the sounding furrows, then so can we.

Age is neither a reason for delay nor an excuse from effort. To believe once that a newer world exists, that a better destiny beckons, is to believe it always. In modern times to seek a newer America is not a career. For some it is a kind of destiny, not one of choice but one of necessity. The idleness and the barren rocks are but symbols of decrepitude and not warrants from duty.

It is too much to think or even suggest that we are all Ulysses. But it is not too much to believe that there is a touch of the spirit of Ulysses in all of us, that we are all on one kind of odyssey or another. For if life is not an odyssey, then what is it? If there is no reason to search for knowledge "beyond the utmost bound of human thought," if my only purpose is "to store and hoard myself," then life is too little and time is a commodity of brittle value to be squandered at ease or in a never-ending search for material wealth.

Our Ulysses is a king. But we do not have to be kings to share Ulysses' spirit. All possess a kingdom of some scale and some dimension. Not all are ready to risk a last voyage from that kingdom in search of either knowledge or a newer world. But some, those with the hungry heart, must. Otherwise, we become dull and rust unburnished.

One person's life, this author's, has been an odyssey of sorts, an odyssey largely played out in politics but not confined to that arena, an odyssey of modest dimensions but occurring during momentous times. Life has been piled on life, and that has still not been enough. Hours are being saved from that eternal silence, but for what? For another voyage? If so, where to? To sail beyond the sunset, and to seek a newer world out there.

Like our aging mariner, the first step on the last voyage is simply to put to sea and to sail toward that horizon where the margin fades forever and forever when we move, to pass through that arch through which gleams the untraveled world.

Perhaps out there the newer world is to be discovered. We will never know until we set to sea one more, perhaps one last, time.

Stories of our experiences, in almost all cases unique to oneself, offer lessons and possibly even marker buoys on the dark sea ahead. For those who have sought a newer world in the public arena, those stories are to be found in that arena. But for one who has lived part of life on the public sea and part on the sea of the private world, both worlds, both seas, offer different instructions.

Some events offer little direction. They are simply what they are. A Cyclops here, a Circe there, a descent into Hades, then Lotus Eaters and a Calypso. Lessons have to be sought where lessons exist. But the search for any meanings life may offer is a search for patterns. And in the author's one life, patterns there have been. They are derived from odyssean adventures in the murky world of intelligence and secrets, in the uneven venue of the former Soviet Union and its return to historic Russia, in the unique chamber of the United States Senate, in the treacherous passage through the Scylla and Charybdis of politics, in the passage from the age of Roosevelt to the age of Reagan and then to a political era now being defined by a leader named Obama, and in the voyage of one very modest craft from small-town America to the capitals of the world.

We shall see whether the lessons of a multilayered life offer interest if not also instruction to others, and only time will tell. But time has never been on the side of our aged king and his mariners, or of any of us as we shuffle across and then off this mortal coil.

So now each of us must tell our own stories and sing the song of our own lives, as a means of creating our own arch through which untraveled worlds gleam, worlds we may discover if we have the courage to seek them, to travel on, to strive, to seek, to find, and not to yield.

———————————————————————————

The Soviet ambassador in Washington, the career diplomat Yuri Dubinin, called in early 1988 and suggested that he had a project to discuss. Earlier I had met with him to determine whether there were ways to build economic bridges between the United States and the Soviet Union. He seemed skeptical but promised to check "with Moscow." As it turned out, "Moscow" was President Mikhail Gorbachev himself. A few days later I traveled to Washington and met with the ambassador.

Not having had the opportunity to negotiate an end to the Cold War, relations with the Soviet Union were still critical to US interests, and efforts to bring Russia closer to the West seemed increasingly important. Plus, it seemed to me Gorbachev was looking for ways, both within and outside normal diplomatic relations, to cooperate with the US and Western democracies and to prove to the hard-liners around him that glasnost would pay off for the Russians.

"We have a very big project," Dubinin said when we met, "and our government would like to know if you are interested and can help find an American communications partner." He provided only the most general outline, but it eventuated that the project was huge. The Soviets proposed to construct a dual fiber-optic cable all the way across the Soviet Union, ultimately linking London with Tokyo, transiting through Copenhagen, Leningrad, Moscow, across the country to Nakhodka on the southeastern Russian coast, and then under the Sea of Japan to Tokyo. The cable would complete a twenty-five-thousand-mile global fiber-optic network. Among other things it would require digging a trench about nine thousand miles long in which to bury the cable.

After I retired from the Senate, Lee and I returned to

Colorado and made our home in a rickety cabin begun in 1880 by an early prospector on some unspoiled acreage twenty-five miles west-southwest of Denver, and I joined a Denver law firm. We had bought our property in two parcels in 1985, while I was still in the Senate, with an option to purchase the second, larger parcel two years later, in May 1987. Some financier friends had offered to provide a mortgage at market rates in a friendly gesture toward someone they thought might be president. The option came due the chaotic week I abandoned the presidential race, and the financiers were not to be found. We stood to lose the place in the space of days. With some notable exceptions, including Rev. Jesse Jackson and a personal friend since the McGovern days, Warren Beatty, our phone was not ringing. During one conversation with Warren that week I mentioned that, among other things, we were about to lose our home property. He wondered why, and I tried to explain that our financing had disappeared and that I had no money. "I do," he responded, and promptly arranged to loan the necessary funds to save our home property. Given some hard work, within a short time he was fully repaid, with interest.

Some months later, while struggling to construct a professional base, I was introduced to an executive at US West, one of seven Bell operating companies created by the breakup of the national AT&T network a few years before, and now headquartered in Denver. US West was shortly to create a subsidiary, US West International, to explore telecommunications opportunities worldwide, and Richard Callahan would be made its president. The US West leadership had many areas of the world in mind other than the Soviet Union.

Though the collapse of the Soviet Union was to come within three years, in theory at least, our two countries were still locked in the Cold War. Very few Fortune 500 companies were engaged in any major projects in the Soviet Union at this time, and none was engaged in an infrastructure project of the magnitude of the proposed Trans-Soviet cable. Leaving aside the size and scope of the fiber-optic project, the idea of an American telephone company building the backbone of a new Soviet communications system was staggering in and of itself. The diplomatic and intelligence implications of this project were both intricate and stunning.

Looked at objectively, the project offered insights into Gorbachev's revolutionary thinking: he understood the need for dramatic technological breakthroughs in the Soviet Union; he was open to US participation; he was abandoning traditional Soviet paranoia and isolation; and he was opening his closed society to the world. Neither the Soviet government nor US West sought media attention to the project, but its political implications were breathtaking.

US West executive Richard Callahan was to be the key figure in this project, and he was an interesting one. The product of a small South Dakota town and a star player on a nationally ranked Nebraska football team, he had started a telecommunications career at the local and state level and steadily moved upward. Though not widely traveled internationally, he seemed undaunted by a gigantic project in the Soviet Union. In fact, he immediately saw it as both a business opportunity and a technological challenge. He authorized me to travel to Moscow to get as many details as possible. I met with Gennady Kudriavtsev, deputy minister of communications, who laid out the proposal, literally, on a gigantic map. The Soviets knew exactly what they wanted to do, and they wanted an American partner to help by providing the technology while they provided the manpower.

Back in Denver I briefed Callahan, and he arranged for me to present the proposal to the US West board. The US West board, like most corporate boards, was composed of conservative businesspeople. Nevertheless, a decision was reached to permit Callahan to pursue the project, and he and I traveled to Moscow to open discussions.

Efforts by my Denver law firm to establish international reach proved unsuccessful, and I relocated to an extraordinary international law firm, Coudert Brothers. Established by three French-American brothers in 1852 and headquartered in New York, Coudert had more than thirty offices worldwide, and its partners spoke twenty-five languages among them. Coudert permitted me to remain in Colorado and, unlike most law firms of that day and since, did not lobby the US government and, happily, did not insist that I do so. When I left the Senate I had determined that I would not lobby my former colleagues, and I have never done so. Fortuitously, Coudert Brothers had opened the first American law office in the Soviet Union in 1988, and its international network would suit US West's needs as the company ultimately developed wireless (cell phone) and cable telephony (television and telephone) systems in more than two dozens countries around the world.

The Coudert association, as well as the work with US West and its successor companies, would last throughout the 1990s and until late 2005, when the firm would sadly dissolve after 152 years of existence. It was a historic law firm, composed of superb lawyers who were also dedicated internationalists. The firm pioneered in Russia, China, Hong Kong, Vietnam, and other newly opened markets, and helped establish American business presences in a wide variety of new venues where US companies had not gone before. In the meantime, my years with Coudert were characterized by extensive international travel, many dozens of trips to the Soviet Union and soon Russia, Eastern Europe from Poland to Bulgaria, China, Vietnam, the Philippines, Jordan and Lebanon, Argentina and Ecuador, and dozens of other nations.

Association with an international law firm and representing corporate clients doing business around the world made considerable travel necessary during these years. Though I was trained in the law, years in public service had made other, sometimes younger, lawyers much more adept at drafting contracts and examining securities filings. My principal stock-in-trade at this point was a network of contacts and friendships in foreign capitals, which proved helpful to the award and completion of major infrastructure projects in many foreign venues. Given some of the extraordinary experiences that occurred during these years, a measure of travel was both interesting and rewarding. It was the best way I knew to make a living without falling into the Washington lobbying trap, a trap baited by solicitation of campaign contributions as a means of guaranteeing access, for clients and high fees, to policy makers and legislators.

But the centerpiece of all this international activity was Russia and the Trans-Soviet/Trans-Siberian fiber-optic cable project. Callahan put together a small negotiating team composed of technical experts, communications financing personnel, and experienced project operators. Over the course of several trips to Moscow spanning 1988 and 1989, US West and the Soviet Ministry of Telecommunications negotiated a partnership to build and operate the system. It was to be a dual cable because the Soviet government would use one cable as the backbone of a new national telecommunications system, and an international consortium of subscribing nations would have access to the other cable to carry international communications traffic between Europe and Asia and then throughout the world. Structuring the original partnership was legally and politically intricate, to say the least. Organizing a European-Asian consortium of a dozen and a half national financiers and users was more complex on multiple levels.

In the age before privatizations, the history of telephone systems was characterized by government ownership, or at the very least government regulation. The operators in most countries were ministries of post (mail), telegraph, and telephone—or in the shorthand of the business, PTTs. Word of the US West–Soviet partnership and the Trans-Soviet project moved swiftly throughout the closed but complex world of PTTs and telecommunications. Within a number of months, most western European and Asian PTTs had indicated interest in joining a consortium of nations that would finance and then have access to the new fiber-optic system. It required very little mathematical extrapolation for operators and users to understand the huge commercial opportunities access to the new network offered these national operators and their customers.

Even as negotiations continued between US West and the Soviet ministry, several meetings involving the international consortium were organized. One of these took place in Vilnius, Lithuania, in 1990. By now, Kudriavtsev had become the Soviet minister of telecommunications, and he had several railcars added to the scheduled overnight train from Moscow to Vilnius. About sixty representatives of the two principal partners and the PTTs of Europe and Asia collected in Moscow, and the train departed around 8:00 PM one Sunday evening. Our host, Kudriavtsev, was by any measure colorful. He had started as a postman in rural Siberia and had risen by force of ambition and personality, and perhaps friendships cultivated with powerful people, to the top job in the second-largest Soviet ministry, employing over 850,000 people. As host of the trip he brought on board Mason-jar-sized containers of caviar, boxes of homemade bread and exotic Russian pastries, *zakuskis* (hors d'oeuvres) of every kind, beer and Georgian wine, and a small lake of vodka. Once the train was under way and bags stored in compartments, a literal moveable feast began and continued quite a long way to the Russian-Lithuanian border. Well after midnight, under the influence of jet lag, fatigue, and other causes, the small United Nations of Telecommunications fell into bunks for a few hours of rumbling sleep before the imperious train lady banged on our compartment doors with glasses of very hot Russian tea to announce an early morning arrival in Vilnius.

GARY HART

That day and the next, the sixty or so participants reached a general framework agreement on how an unprecedented consortium of this sort would allocate shares of financial responsibility and user access. This project was not a simple engineering challenge. The cable had to be laid undersea from London to Copenhagen, and then across the Baltic Sea to Leningrad, and then in a deep trench from Leningrad to Moscow, and on southeast for hundreds of kilometers before turning east south of the Ural Mountains, and all the way across historic Russia and its monumental steppes of Siberia, bypassing the southern shore of mighty Lake Baikal, on to the seaport of Nakhodka, then undersea to surface in Tokyo.

A man who had climbed telephone poles in the summer heat and strung lines in bitter winters across the upper Midwest, and who was a solidly built figure himself, Callahan wanted to meet the man who had the responsibility to engineer this project. At the close of one of the many negotiating sessions between the Americans and the Russians, Kudriavtsev gestured to the conference room door and announced the arrival of the chief project engineer. In the doorway appeared a very large, squarely built bulldozer of a man with a huge grin on his face. He had ginger hair, and he looked exactly like Callahan. This man looked as if he could dig the monumental trench all by himself. Any doubts Callahan might have had regarding feasibility were erased.

During the early years of the Cold War, the members of the North Atlantic Treaty Organization (NATO) had formed a subsidiary organization called the Coordinating Committee for Multilateral Export Controls (CoCom) to restrict the transfer of critical technology to the Soviet Union. This was meant to include all technology employed in commercial enterprises that might be converted to military use. Predictably, two members of CoCom had concerns about the project that had to do with the degree to which the Soviet military might use a new communications system to enhance its capabilities and communicate military commands. Over time these issues came to be openly discussed between US West and the Soviet ministry, and various options to overcome the problem were offered by the Soviets. Though highly technical, the solutions offered included bouncing communications signals off satellites or placing recording mechanisms at intervals along the cable, in both cases to permit the United States and its allies to monitor traffic to ensure that threatening military commands were not being transmitted.

Anyone even vaguely familiar with the tensions of the Cold War would have marveled at the novelty of an American company being given access to and actually modernizing the Soviet national communications systems. Still, a kind of rigid opposition to all things having to do with the Soviet Union was still dominant, and Gorbachev's reforms and thaws were still taken by Cold Warriors as some kind of trick on the West. Most of the European partners of NATO considered the Trans-Soviet project to be a huge commercial opportunity, but also profound evidence that the historically icy Soviet Union was thawing before their very eyes. After considerable deliberation, and even as the Soviet Union was fragmenting, two leaders of NATO and CoCom, Prime Minister Margaret Thatcher and President George H. W. Bush, vetoed the project on security grounds.

The secretary of defense, then Richard Cheney, later confirmed that he was the one within the first Bush administration who made the decision to veto the Trans-Siberian cable project. Nevertheless, after leaving office, he joined the US West board, whose major project he had spiked.

Despite US and UK opposition, other European nations broke ranks with CoCom and developed the cable linking London to Moscow. This was a lucrative communications opportunity, and commerce overcame Cold War politics. This cable link plus further US West projects laid the groundwork for modern communications networks crucial to the emergence of the Russian economy in the early twenty-first century. Though that economic boom was fueled by prodigious oil and natural gas production, it would have stalled had the Russians not already possessed the framework for a modern communications system.

Rejection of the trans-Soviet cable project by two CoCom members would not be the end of the US West activities in the Soviet Union, very soon to become traditional Russia, and my own work there. The measure of the friendship that continued to develop between President Gorbachev and myself was revealed by the fact that he had directed this massive new US-Soviet undertaking my way. But another proof offered itself a short time before. Just a month after I withdrew from the presidential race in 1987, our daughter, Andrea, was preparing to visit the Soviet Union as President Gorbachev's guest, an invitation initiated in our discussions the previous December. It seemed evident that previous December that Gorbachev believed I had a reasonably good chance to become president, an estimate confirmed by early polls, and that his invitation to Andrea was meant as a gesture of goodwill and relationship development.

Days after I ended the campaign in May 1987, I called Ambassador Dubinin in Washington to remind him of the invitation the previous December and to say that we assumed, under the circumstances, the invitation was no longer open. It was a way of letting Gorbachev off the hook as politely as possible. The ambassador insisted that he check with Moscow, meaning with Gorbachev himself. Within two days, Dubinin called back to say that President Gorbachev insisted that Andrea proceed to Russia for an extensive visit as his personal guest. Accompanied by our law school classmates and friends Doug and Anne Shrader of Connecticut, Andrea spent six weeks in Russia with the first woman cosmonaut, Valentina Tereshkova, an iconic national figure, as her hostess. She was given privileged access to space launch facilities and other parts of the western Soviet Union rarely visited by Americans, including Georgia, and red carpets magically appeared at every stop as they would have for an important foreign dignitary.

From the standpoint of a father, I found this to be one of the most generous, gentlemanly, and classy gestures of any world leader I had known, and it would cause me to respect Mikhail Gorbachev for his treatment of my daughter, as well as for the remarkable breaks with Soviet history that led to the end of the Cold War, for years to come.

Thereafter, in the midst of the efforts to construct the Trans-Soviet fiber-optic cable, the Soviet Union itself began to dissolve. By now US West had offices and development staffs in Moscow and Leningrad. A Western-based communications company led by a sophisticated Sioux Falls linemen had taken a bold step in dealing with our Cold War rival in the first place. Now its significant investment of time and money was suddenly jeopardized by a vast coalition of nations breaking apart. The instinctive, and conservative, choice would have been to liquidate the venture, pack up and leave, and look for opportunities elsewhere.

Somehow, the persistent and persuasive Callahan was able to convince his senior company colleagues that, despite the CoCom setbacks for the project now referred to as the Trans-Siberian Project, even greater opportunities now existed in Russia and its former Warsaw Pact allies in Eastern Europe. Among these opportunities were new cellular phone systems, in a nation whose antiquated landline phone systems were hopelessly outdated and inefficient, and the possibilities for cable telephony, the combining of cable television services with new fixed-line telephone systems operating over the same cable. Both these new sectors were exploding in other countries worldwide, and in a newly liberated Russian economy rushing headlong toward markets and entrepreneurship, both these systems offered the possibility of huge growth and profits for the first Western company on the ground. And, thanks to its early entry into the Soviet Union three years before, US West was that company.

Eighteen years thereafter, the collapse of the Soviet Union seems fated, even predetermined. But careful review of those fateful days between August 19 and December 31, 1991, particular for those who lived through missile crises and very cold days of the Cold War, these historic events can be described as nothing less than startling. From 1947 forward there was an assumption underlying US international policy that the competition between capitalism and communism, between the United States and the Soviet Union, was semipermanent. This assumption was based on the premise that Soviet communism did not contain the capability of internal reform. But this traditionalist premise discounted the impact of changing times, changing realities, and the rise of changing leadership. The new realities of technology—most vividly in the Soviet Union the introduction of the fax machine, which permitted private mass communications—eroding national borders, and rising economic integration all conspired to require new attitudes by new Soviet leaders. Gorbachev was not inevitable, but someone very like him was. However, he was faced with the impossible task of maintaining two empires, Soviet and traditional Russian, in the face of historic tides. But, as a few of us predicted in the early Gorbachev years, the Cold War was over.

The transition from Soviet Union to Russia, however, was not uneventful, even for an American telecommunications company. US West incorporated a subsidiary, with several financial investors, called the Russian Telecommunications Development Corporation (RTDC), to pursue these new opportunities in Russia. In relatively short order, US West constructed three "gateway switches," modern switching installations that facilitated movement of vast amounts of increased communications traffic between Russia and the West. Two other pioneering projects were new cellular systems, first in Moscow and then in the newly renamed St. Petersburg. These expanded eventually to eleven cellular phone systems in major Russian urban areas, which helped revolutionize the national economy.

In 1992, shortly after opening street-level storefront offices to market the new cell phone to mostly younger Russian customers, complications arose. Callahan called to say that there was trouble in St. Petersburg and, as the instigator of US West's ventures in Russia, I had to fix it. Additionally, in previous trips to Russia, including one hours after the Soviet flag came down and the Russian flag went up over the Kremlin, I had become acquainted with a number of younger democratic reformers in Russia, including the new mayor of St. Petersburg, Anatoly Sobchak.

The crisis involved visits to the St. Petersburg cell phone stores by men in long black leather coats informing the store manager that this was a dangerous neighborhood and that these men were available to provide protection—for a fee, of course. When payments were not forthcoming, serious harassment against the manager and sales staff began. Callahan asked me to go to St. Petersburg to make it stop, or US West would have no choice but to pack up and leave Russia.

Having made an appointment to see Mayor Sobchak two days later, I flew from Denver to St. Petersburg, checked in to the newly restored Hotel Europa, changed clothes, and proceeded to the mayor's office in the stately Smolny Institute, a former girl's academy that had been used as Communist Party headquarters under Lenin. Upon presenting myself at Sobchak's office, his staff apologetically informed me that he had been unexpectedly called to Moscow as a member of the new president Yeltsin's advisory council, and he had urged me to meet with his advisor on international affairs to solve any problems I might have. Disappointed after eighteen hours in the air, I had little alternative and was taken in to meet with the deputy, a quiet, modest-sized man, with whom I communicated through a translator. I explained who US West was, that its operations in St. Petersburg had been threatened, that US law prohibited protection payments, that in any case the company would not pay them regardless of legal prohibition, and that if US West closed down its now extensive operations in Russia, it would be sizable news in the United States and send a very negative signal to the entire US corporate world about the dangers of investing in Russia.

The advisor listened attentively and, when I finished, said simply, "We will look into it." I had traveled five thousand miles for that? I thanked him, took my leave, went to the hotel to collect my toothbrush, went to the airport, and flew home. I had been in Russia less than three hours. Thereafter, however, we had no more problems, and the cell phone business flourished. It turned out the advisor on international affairs was the former head of the KGB in Leningrad. His name was Vladimir Putin.

When the Russian constitutional crisis erupted in early October 1993, things became even more dangerous. The Moscow office of US West was on the corner of the Moscow World Trade Center, connected to the Mezhdunarodnaya Hotel on the Moskva River, and only two or three hundred yards from the Russian parliament building, called the White House. When the Russian parliament challenged Boris Yeltsin's constitutional authority, he surrounded the White House with armor, called on parliamentary leaders to surrender, then ordered the tanks to open fire. Ironically, this was the very site where Yeltsin had stood on an identical tank to protest the coup against Gorbachev. The Duma had its military supporters, including, it was rumored, one of the OMON battalions (Russia's most highly skilled—and feared—special forces) inside the White House and elsewhere, and intense exchange of fire ensued. In the process, as I saw only a day or two later, small-arms fire peppered the outside walls around the windows of the US West offices.

As dramatic as the vast project of restructuring the Russian telecommunications systems was, however, it was a great distance from the US White House. During the Senate years, I had given thought to what might happen after twelve years in elective office. Even before the decision to seek national office, it had become apparent that I was not a career politician and that holding elective office for life was not my desired destiny. Some former senators, mostly those who had lost elections, stayed in Washington and created new careers in lobbying. That was not an option. The senators whose behavior was most admired had simply retired and had never returned, except for rare, ceremonial Senate occasions. Even though there was life after politics, there was no way to know what it would be like or how it would feel.

There is an assumption that elected officials who leave office, one way or the other, leave their interest in issues and ideas behind with their ambitions. It has always been the subject for marvel that many who care enough to seek office quite often simply disappear from the public arena when office-holding ends. A few former officeholders seek to continue to be engaged, in my case more in the international arena than the domestic one, and must find a way to do so. That is not always easy. The opportunities that travel for Coudert Brothers, for US West, and for other clients provided to maintain friendships in various parts of the world were of great help in my case.

Maintaining international friendships was awkward, however, because as a private citizen, the only song I could sing for the supper of hospitality provided me was an update on current developments in American politics or direction of US companies toward important business opportunities. Efforts at continued engagement were further complicated by the never-questioned decision to return to Colorado. Basing one's home 1,500 miles from Washington's corridors of power and New York's salons of influence added to the challenge. Out of sight, at least for former senators, is out of mind.[33]

Ulysses on his rock did not fear death. He feared irrelevance. Irrelevance meant and means not being involved, not participating, not contributing, not trying. But age narrows our options and our opportunities, to a point so narrow that it gets down to staying alive. To breathing, "as tho' to breath were life."

For one whose purpose was to serve, and, for one whom service was the civic substitute for a "calling," and whose gospel became the social gospel—the search for justice, not to serve is not to live. The ancient Greeks thought the office of citizen to be the highest office in a republic. Simply because one no longer holds public office is no reprieve from the duties of citizenship: engagement, participation, contribution of time and ideas, the search for service.

The opportunity to serve for one who could not return to elective office came to depend on appointment to office, an office that might in some way match one's experience and qualifications. And those appointments largely depend in turn on one's party being in power. With the exception of the US Commission on National Security for the 21st Century, the opportunity to serve during the Clinton presidency did not arise.

Thereafter, so committed was I to service, and in retrospect so naive, that I offered to provide what small service I could in the early months of the George W. Bush years. That offer was made to three very senior figures in that administration whom I had known. It was naive because the offer to serve was based upon the obvious notion that this new administration would seek at least some limited form of bipartisanship and might want a few Democrats to occupy positions of value in policy or operations.

Given how things turned out, it was foolish in the extreme, and must have seemed laughable at the time to those Bush officials. In fact, it must have given them a very good laugh. For they had decided well before taking the oath of office that they would pursue policies at home and abroad that no one of my ilk would ever support. They saved themselves, and me, the embarrassment of a resignation in protest. But of course they were smarter than I was because they knew what lay ahead.

Tennyson's Ulysses becomes ever more powerful and poignant to a servant without a task. One does not have to have been the ruler over a small island kingdom off the western coast of ancient Greece to be a shipmate of Ulysses, to know the trials and triumphs of an odyssey, to feel in the depths of one's soul the satisfaction of service in a cause, to have cast votes for civil rights, to be in the phalanx for the liberation of women, to have been near the forefront of many of the great environmental debates, to have struggled for arms reductions and the end of the Cold War, to have fought for large causes in the company of great warriors.

To have known such service in so many causes and not to be able to provide it further can only leave a void and an ache in the soul. Better to set out to sea, to sail beyond the western stars, than to rust in disuse.

But foreign travel did help to maintain relevance. Passing through the Middle East in 1988, I took the occasion to pay my respects to Jordanian prime minister Zaid al-Rifai, who had been so kind to us a year or so before and who had handwritten a very warm and supportive letter of both friendship and dismay when I left politics. He insisted on a meeting with King Hussein, who raised the concern that so few American political figures were traveling through Arab portions of the Middle East. The king and prime minister took the trouble to organize contacts and invitations in the region and, though no longer a political figure, a short time later I visited both Baghdad and Damascus and then stopped in Amman once again. In Baghdad I met with Foreign Minister Tariq Aziz who, though the United States had provided both overt and covert support to Iraq in its decade-long war with Iran, took the occasion to lecture me on the poor state of US-Iraqi relations and to issue the standard complaint about US support for Israel. Aziz would appear as a very high card in the deck of infamy dealt by the US conquerors fifteen years later, and continues to serve his time in confinement.

While in Baghdad I had dinner with Deputy Chief of Mission Joseph Wilson, the senior American diplomat in Iraq until Ambassador April Glaspie was appointed sometime thereafter. Joe Wilson provided expert insights into Iraqi politics and ambitions, though I don't recall discussion of Iraqi claims on Kuwait at that stage. Wilson, later ambassador, would become famous both for his disclaimer of Iraqi efforts to acquire uranium in Niger, based on his on-site investigation, and for the retaliatory outing of his wife, Valerie Plame, a covert CIA operative, for her husband's disclosure of Bush White House perfidy.

This outing violated a federal statute, the Intelligence Identities Protection Act, and a man called Scooter Libby, one of Richard Cheney's key staff members, was convicted of perjury before federal investigators regarding the vice president's role. The other violators of the law were never prosecuted. Many arrows pointed to the office of the vice president. The irony, of course, was that Mr. Cheney had been instrumental in permitting Richard Welch, the victim of another outing, to be buried at Arlington thirty years earlier, and the Intelligence Identities Protection Act was enacted to prevent other such incidents.

Apparently the lessons of the Welch assassination were overridden by Cheney's desire to concentrate power in the White House, and jeopardizing the personal safety of a covert agent was not going to be a consideration in that quest.

The Damascus stop offered little new information, this being during the closed Hafez al-Assad regime, though senior foreign ministry officials were made available. They mostly demanded return of the disputed Golan Heights region, which Israel had taken during the 1967 war and continued to refuse to return. This, of course, was the same territory I had toured in an Israeli tank and had mock-bombed high and low in an Israeli F-4 two years before. Regardless, King Hussein's judgment was correct. More American members of Congress should have been visiting the wider Middle East and Arab world during the 1980s and beyond. This might not have prevented the first Gulf war in 1991 or the second one in 2003, but it might have provided broader and deeper context for those too casually voting for war resolutions.

It would take until 2009, more than twenty years later, for the new Obama administration to begin constructive outreach to the peaceful, vast majority of Arabs and Muslims.

Interesting and often surprising experiences continued. Early in 1991, a self-identified naval attaché from the Libyan Embassy in Greece, almost certainly a member of Libya's intelligence service, approached me at the Hotel Grande Bretagne during a business trip to Athens.[34] This contact with the Libyan "naval attaché" led to intensive contacts with the Libyan government over the next several months. The brief discussion with the Libyan had to do with my availability to act as intermediary between his government and the administration of George H. W. Bush. I discouraged the idea, pointing out that I belonged to the wrong political party and was no longer in public office. After arriving in Moscow from Athens the next day, I used a secure phone at our embassy to notify senior State Department officials of this contact. These officials discounted this contact on the grounds that it was one of several such approaches and none was being taken seriously. "We will have no discussions with the Libyans" was the policy response, "until they produce the Pan Am bombers."

I transmitted this response through Greek intermediaries back to the Libyan Embassy in Athens and thought nothing further of it. After passage of several weeks and further indirect contacts from the same Libyan officials, I was invited to meet with senior Libyan officials in Geneva—a neutral meeting place for such contacts over a number of decades—on the condition that the Libyans were prepared to consider the United States' demand. Once again I notified the State Department and indicated that, if I went to Geneva, I would do so only with the understanding that I would continue to deny any representation of the US government's views on the matter and would keep our government immediately informed of developments.

The Libyans were insistent, and within a few weeks, in March 1991, I met with the head of the Libyan foreign intelligence service, Colonel Yussef Dibri, and two other senior Libyan officials for the better part of three days in Geneva. The Libyan officials stayed at the Intercontinental Hotel, and our meetings were held at the Beau Rivage Hotel, where I stayed. Almost immediately, the Libyans said that they would release the two Pam Am bombing suspects, Abdel Basset Ali al-Megrahi and Lamen Khalifa Fhimah, in exchange for a firm commitment from the Bush administration that preliminary discussions would begin within a reasonable period of time regarding normalization of relations between our two nations. I questioned the bona fides of this proposal from every possible angle, then relayed it to Tom Miller, political advisor to Assistant Secretary of State Edward Djerejian, who in 2003, coincidentally, became US Ambassador to Greece. Miller had been my point of contact in the Department of State from the outset.

Within a few hours, Miller called back to say that State Department officials did not take this offer seriously and discouraged further contacts. After relaying this response to the Libyans, who in turn relayed it to Tripoli, they insisted on further discussions that would more specifically confirm their seriousness. The next series of discussion, all relayed to Washington, concerned specific legal and logistical matters.

By UN resolution, the Libyan government was required to submit the bombing suspects to criminal prosecution either in the United States or in Scotland (where the Pan Am plane had crashed).

We had lengthy discussions concerning the criminal justice systems in both countries (though I claimed no expertise in Scottish law), and I confirmed that under either system the suspects would have highly capable defense counsel and the full protection of traditional due process standards. The Libyans evidenced a great deal of skepticism on this score, but I explained that political necessity (apart from the integrity of our justice system) would require the trial process to be open and fair, and conviction could only occur on the presentation of persuasive evidence. In a word, the trials would not be fixed "show trials," the results of which were foreordained.

Finally, we got to logistics. I proposed that the suspects be flown to Geneva and then transferred to a United States or United Nations aircraft for travel either to New York or Glasgow. After consulting with Tripoli, the Libyans agreed. Late the second day of the discussions, I conveyed this fact to Tom Miller. Though still skeptical, he said higher administration officials would have to decide. Hours went by. Then the response came back very late that night: the Bush administration—Miller said a National Security Council meeting had been convened to debate the issue—rejected the offer. The explanation was lame (and I suspected Miller thought it lame): if the bomber suspects stepped onto Swiss soil, even for a few yards to transfer planes, they would be subject to Swiss jurisdiction and would be apprehended and confined, and perhaps never extradited to the United States or Scotland.

Several possibilities existed. Bush administration officials did not believe the Libyans were serious. Or they did believe, inexplicably, the legalistic argument about Swiss jurisdiction (though this still seems implausible). Or they did not trust me as intermediary. Or, perhaps most persuasively, they simply were not prepared to discuss normalization of relations—even in exchange for the bombers. In whatever case, any potential deal was off. My own view is that they did not want a Democrat involved in solving a thorny international conflict. To counter this, it was made clear to Bush administration officials throughout that I gave my word of honor never to disclose my involvement in the negotiations. That did not seem good enough.

But the Libyans would not take no for an answer. Several weeks went by, and my contact in Greece invited me to Tripoli for one more try. Using private Greek-registered aircraft and avoiding Libyan immigration, I spent almost three days in Tripoli that spring. Whereas I believed I would be in and out of Tripoli in less than a day, I ended up there, incognito and semicaptive, for three days. No one knew where I was, and I could not make telephone calls. Because this trip occurred during Ramadan, discussions occurred only after sunset, and because Colonel Qaddafi was observing the religious period in the desert, my principal discussions were with former prime minister Abdessalam Jalloud.

These elaborate dinner meetings started late and ended late—well into the middle of the night. The issues were essentially a repeat of Geneva. But the offer was confirmed: in exchange for releasing the Pan Am bombing suspects, the Libyans demanded opening negotiations on normalization of relations. In response to my insistence that these discussions must include cessation of any support for terrorism and abandonment of weapons of mass destruction programs, Jalloud stated that "everything will be on the table."

Jalloud had the reputation for being tough, and he lived up to the billing. During the day, I was taken on tours of the historic coastal city of Tripoli or I spent time debating the young deputy foreign minister in the massive presidential suite on the upper floor of the modern hotel along the water's edge. This man was tall, spoke excellent American English, and had a master's degree in engineering from Michigan State. He also demonstrated an excessive insistence on expressing his dislike for the United States and its leaders. Aware that the suite was bugged, I led him out on the balcony, more than twenty stories above the water. Our lengthy discussions were heated.

After almost three days, I was permitted to take the private aircraft to Venice to attend a major election event for my friend Italian foreign minister Gianni de Michaelis, whom I knew well from the New Leaders conferences a few years before. Once again, I relayed all my discussions with Libya to the State Department and was firmly told, once again, that there would be no discussions, even in exchange for the Pan Am bombers, with the government of Libya. Case closed.

The only plausible explanation for singling me out is that, based largely on my experience on the Church Committee, which revealed previous assassination plots, I publicly criticized President Reagan's attempt to assassinate Colonel Qaddafi by long-range bomber in 1983, bombings that killed a Qaddafi child but not Qaddafi himself. Nor was I really singled out; others had been approached. Do I believe the offer was rejected because the Swiss would demand jurisdiction in the fifty feet or so between airplanes? Not in the least. Was the offer rejected because the intermediary was a Democrat? The first Bush administration will have to respond to this question.

This account suggests, and strongly so, only one thing. We could have brought the Pan Am bombers to justice, and quite possibly have moved Libya out of its renegade status, a full decade or more sooner than it actually transpired. This series of episodes were finally revealed in a column in *The Washington Post* in 2003, because the George W. Bush administration was then claiming that Libya had abandoned weapons of mass destruction as a result of the United States' preemptive invasion of Iraq. The fact is, the Libyans were willing to turn over the Pan Am bombers and discuss an end of support for terrorism a full twelve years before, and the first Bush administration turned them down.

As proposed to me in early 1991, the two suspects were turned over to Scottish law enforcement officials in neutral Netherlands in April 1999, eight years later. The government of the Netherlands, needless to say, did not seek to detain them.

There was a coda. Following Gianni de Michaelis's very large rally in Venice on the way out of Tripoli, I related these events to him at dinner, and he confirmed, based on his own close contacts with the Libyan government, that the Libyans were serious. I particularly asked about the tall, westernized Libyan who had been my constant escort in Tripoli. Gianni leaned forward and whispered, "That is Mussa Kussa. He is the most dangerous man in the world."

Remembering our debates on the very high hotel balcony and his dislike of Americans, I suddenly saw myself doing an involuntary swan dive into the Mediterranean. Mussa Kussa was Libya's link to every terrorist organization they were supporting. He later became head of Libyan intelligence (and in 2009, foreign minister) and, ironically, was the principal contact between the Libyan government and the George W. Bush administration in 2003, when normalization negotiations finally took place. And, most intelligence services believe Mussa Kussa was the mastermind behind the Pan Am and French airline bombings.

On the way home I stopped in London for lunch with Pierre Salinger, former press secretary for President Kennedy and then head of the ABC bureau in London. I had first met Pierre in the 1972 McGovern campaign, and we had stayed in contact off and on over the years. On the condition of confidence, I told Pierre the whole Libyan story. He wanted to put it on the air immediately. If he did so, the Bush administration would quite probably be forced to denounce me and possibly charge me with negotiating with a foreign government, especially one with which we had no diplomatic relations, without authorization, and thus of having violated legal prohibitions. At the least I would be charged with political grandstanding. On the other hand, if someone in the administration did choose to denounce me, I wanted one trusted media source to have the whole story and to be prepared to counter administration attacks. The Bush administration knew I had this insurance policy, the charges were never leveled, and the full story was never published. A decade later I attended Pierre's funeral in Washington. He had kept his word.

In 1991, a book that resulted from a year and a half of research and interviews concerning the Gorbachev revolution was published. As a repeated visitor to Russia during the late 1980s and early '90s, I was continuously asked, What does it mean? Is this a serious change? Will it last? The only way to answer was to talk with as many of those involved in the glasnost and perestroika experiment as possible, and to use what access with senior Soviet officials I had to resolve whether this was a temporary digression on the long communist road or a permanent change of direction that would alter world history. In the process of researching the book, four or five dozen interviews, including with the last survivor of the signers of the revolutionary constitution in 1922 and four of the eight coup plotters who, in August 1991, tried to overthrow the Gorbachev government and reassert old Politburo control, were carried out.

One of those was Marshal Dmitry Yazov, minister of defense. Two brigadiers brought me to his office and marched me down what seemed a quarter of a mile of red carpet leading to his desk at the end of a basketball-court-sized office. Recovering from a severed Achilles tendon, I was still hobbling with the aid of a cane. At length, I presented myself to the medium-height but refrigerator-shaped marshal. Breaking his stony countenance with a grin that revealed several shiny silver teeth, he said, "In what conflict did you receive your wounds?" The brigadiers on either side thought this the most amusing thing they had ever heard.

The book concluded that the Gorbachev revolution was real, that there was a better-than-even chance traditional political forces would try to stop it, that any such effort would probably fail, and that the Cold War was ending if not over. It further offered the thought that the end of the Cold War provided a historic opportunity for the United States to address an unfinished national agenda, deferred by the Cold War.

I concluded the book with these words:

> Gorbachev's greatest gift to the United States has been the dawn of an era of peace and cooperation unimagined and unimaginable for three generations of Americans. But an even greater gift may be the opportunity for the United States to rediscover and rebuild itself for the first time in five decades. To do so will require a national agenda based on the national interest, the commonwealth. Our national agenda should describe both who we are today and who we want to be tomorrow.

Totally fortuitously the book was published on August 19, 1991, the day of the coup against Gorbachev and was titled *Russia Shakes the World: The Second Russian Revolution and Its Impact on the West.*[35]

What had triggered the internal counterrevolution against Gorbachev, as much as anything, was his decision to remove Soviet troops from one Eastern European country after another, and the consequent, and predictable, collapse of puppet communist governments from Poland to Hungary to Czechoslovakia and beyond that were totally dependent on Moscow to retain power. In late 1990 and early 1991, the message went out to Warsaw, East Berlin, Budapest, Prague, Sofia, and elsewhere: You are now on your own. Facing the political hangman, these governments packed their bags and headed for the exits, none more dramatically than in Prague.

In November 1988, I had the opportunity to visit Prague when the national playwright and conscience of the nation, Václav Havel, was yet again in jail for his brilliant literary critiques of the repressive regime. There were sessions with a visiting delegation from Human Rights Watch when we met with members of the dissident group Charta 77 and Havel's wife, Olga. Havel's letters to Olga while he was in jail were later compiled into one of his best of several books. A quiet but central figure in the Czech community in exile, whom I had met some years before, was instrumental in bringing outside financial support to the dissident patriots and, on the premise that I was least likely to be searched at customs on exiting the country the following day, at the request of this friend I smuggled a manuscript sharply critical of the repressive government out in my carry-on luggage to a source in London who saw to its publication.

When the barriers barring Czechoslovakia from the West came down in early December 1989, I was in Vienna, and with my Czech friend and two others took a taxi the three hundred kilometers from Vienna into Prague. This trip was a thrilling experience. The day before I watched the first Czechs cross the Austrian border and freely walk the streets of Vienna for the first time in four decades. Wearing old and dated work clothes, the women clutching pathetic plastic purses, they stared in wonder into the windows of the city shops at the luxurious goods and delicious pastries; at the well-dressed Austrians sitting at the coffeehouses reading their papers; at the magnificent opera house, cathedrals, and public buildings; and mostly at the brightly colored and chromed vehicles bustling up and down. They huddled to count their worthless Czech coins, make currency conversions, and I realized sadly there was nothing—nothing—they could afford. I wept openly then and, remembering, I weep openly now.

But in Prague the following day, the scene changed. At the top of Wenceslas Square, beneath the statue of St. Wenceslas on horseback and on the site of the young martyr Jan Palech's self-immolation, young Czechs gave stirring speeches on liberty and justice and democracy. Czech flags were everywhere. The young people packed and clung to the outsides of the trolley cars, making complete circuits of the city waving giant Czech flags. Shortly before, the national hero Václav Havel had addressed a vast throng of hundreds of thousands from a balcony several floors above Wenceslas Square. Remembering the end of World War II as a boy in Kansas, this is the closest I had since come to that explosion of human emotions of liberty and victory. Almost two decades later the memory of this scene and the emotions they inspired remain as vivid as they were experienced then, and they will remain so throughout my life.

Throughout the early 1990s other extraordinary projects emerged. During one of many trips to Russia, a Russian-American businessman who was constructing a bewildering array of partnerships between former Soviet countries and the United States introduced himself. One project was in Ukraine, where the government was looking for a Western partner to restore its cattle herd, which had been decimated by the Chernobyl nuclear disaster. I helped this man form a partnership with a highly reputable Colorado cattleman, Ben Houston, and after introductions and negotiations, a partnership with the Ukrainian agricultural ministry was formed for Houston to provide five hundred head of his best Colorado cattle to form a national breeding herd. Houston loaded the first eighty-five head of cattle on a DHL airplane at the Denver airport and flew them to Ukraine, and the remaining 415 head followed by boat. The last I heard, the transplanted Colorado cows had flourished as Ukrainians.

With the election of Bill Clinton in 1992, a new administration would inherit a post–Cold War world. The opportunities were enormous, the possibilities endless. Having no role to play in the new Democratic administration, I undertook to send a series of letters to President Clinton through friendly intermediaries. One of these, dated August 4, 1994, suggested that the new president seek to intervene in the seemingly endless dispute in Ireland between the Irish republicans and the British-dominated government in the north.[36]

By early 1995, Clinton took up the idea and appointed my former colleague George Mitchell to undertake the mission of reconciliation. The effort was highly effective, and the Ireland initiative was one of Clinton's unquestioned successes. Thereafter, I sent two or three letters urging Clinton to do more to move Russia into the West than merely strike up a friendship with Boris Yeltsin. The US-Russia Investment Fund was created to stimulate investment in new enterprises there, and I served on its first board. It did considerable good, but was substantially short of the all-out effort we should have made in the 1990s in institution-building, encouragement of private investment, incorporation of Russia into Western security and financial institutions, training of a generation of emerging democratic leaders, more extensive cultural and political exchanges, and consideration of mutual security alliances.[37]

During one of many trips to Russia, a young American involved with a political consultancy working for Yeltsin's election introduced himself at the bar of the Hotel Metropol and boasted about the amount of US government money then being covertly funneled into the Yeltsin campaign. There was plenty of precedence for this, but at that time we were busy lecturing the Russians on the importance of free, open, and honest elections, the need for transparency in politics, the need to root out corruption in government, and in short the need to adopt the ideal American political model.

Upon return I immediately fired off a letter to Clinton relating this experience and warning him that it would have explosive consequences if revealed. Within two days of the letter's receipt in Washington, Strobe Talbott, then deputy secretary of state and a former Rhodes scholar friend of Clinton's from Oxford, called. "You will not be surprised that gentlemen do read other gentlemen's letters," he said, and then proceeded to assure me that the conduct just called to the president's attention simply was not going on. After giving him chapter and verse, he checked with a staff member and then said, "I'll look into this." Whether the financial transfers to, and quiet subversion of, Russian politics were stopped or just made more discreet I never discovered.

One other letter was sent to the president on November 5, 1993, the end of his first full year in office. Citing the Truman experience in the 1945 to 1948 period following the end of World War II and the beginning of the Cold War, I urged him to quietly appoint a small panel of very experienced advisors to help lay out a new role for the United States in the post–Cold War years. The central organizing principle of our foreign and defense policies, containment of communism, now was redundant, and nothing had been put forward to take its place. The information and technology economy was preparing to take off, and relative peace prevailed. Clinton had the unique opportunity of defining our global role for decades to come. I suggested this commission draft a new, post–Cold War National Security Act for the twenty-first century to replace the almost fifty-year-old National Security Act of 1947.

For whatever reasons this idea was not pursued—that is, until 1998, when then Speaker of the House Newt Gingrich had a similar but somewhat smaller idea to appoint a group to propose a new national security policy for the twenty-first century and to make it available to the next administration, in 2001.

President Clinton saw this idea slipping away to a Republican Speaker and quickly proposed a joint bipartisan effort sponsored by both the administration and Congress that would carry out its work under the auspices of the secretary of defense and make its final recommendations to the next administration, of whichever party, no later than March 2001. Largely due to a long friendship with the Republican secretary of defense, Bill Cohen, I was one of the fourteen members, seven Democrats and seven Republicans, appointed to what eventually came to be called the US Commission on National Security for the 21st Century and was to become the most comprehensive review of US national security since 1947.

Project development with the expanding US West International spanned Eastern Europe from Poland to Hungary to Czechoslovakia, the Middle East, large parts of Asia, and a number of prospects in Latin America. In the late 1980s, an acquaintance introduced me to a provincial political leader in Argentina named Carlos Menem, and I visited him at his home in La Rioja province. Weeks thereafter Menem was inaugurated president of Argentina and opened the door to US companies interested in the privatization and modernization of the Argentinean infrastructure, much in need of help. Privatization of telephone systems was now under way worldwide, and Menem wanted a US or European partner to invest in and help operate his country's out-of-date system.

Dick Callahan indicated interest in the project, and we traveled to Buenos Aires to meet with government officials and national communications executives. To my amazement, Menem rolled out the red carpet, invited us to lunch at the presidential mansion, and organized a tennis match on his court between himself and his vice president, Eduardo Duhalde, who would later succeed him, and the two Americans. We politely managed to lose and drowned our sorrows in fine Argentinean wine. Menem led a merry national parade in the ten years he lasted, but a lifestyle flamboyant even by Argentinean standards and a sagging economy finally cost him the presidency. Whatever else he might have been, he was a congenial and generous host.

Retreating to the Colorado mountains during this period of intense travel offered decompression and the expected reunion with nature. Nature on our place takes the form not only of trees, steep slopes, small cactuses and wildflowers, but also deer, elk, foxes, an occasional bear or two, flocks of birds, and small creatures of every sort. Sometimes it takes more surprising forms. Early Easter Sunday morning 1995, I returned from picking up the Sunday papers and when I let my black chow Samson out of the car, he took off up the side of the steep seven-hundred-foot slope behind the house. His normal deep bark became a booming roar. He was after something. I trotted down the road, following the noise until it abruptly ended halfway up the slope. Climbing the steep slope and rounding a sharp rock, I saw Samson just ahead, circling the base of a tree. Approaching closer I heard a deep, rumbling growl. Looking up I encountered a full-grown male mountain lion about seven feet up on a stout tree limb and only fifteen or so feet away. His jumping range was thirty feet. He weighed about 150 pounds, was a glossy tawny color, and had a large head with startling yellow eyes fixed fully on me. It was at the moment the face of God. He was simply breathtaking and magnificent, a highly proficient predator free in his element. His expression was one of disdain and, I imagined, disgust that Samson and I had invaded his territory. He was vividly and stunningly beautiful.

It is conventional to say that time stands still but, in these circumstances, mere seconds seemed like minutes. Deciding, I imagined, that I was not worth the trouble, the cat turned his head and soared—there is no other word for it—off the tree limb and with huge strides loped down the steep slope with Samson, alas, in pursuit. The wonderful dog would surely never be seen alive again. As I climbed back down the steep hillside there was Samson, panting in the road, also not worth the lion's attention. The absolute wonder of that moment did not fade in memory for days and weeks to come, and the experience is as fresh today as it was startling then. This experience is not recommended to everyone, but when such an encounter with nature in its purest and most magnificent form occurs, you never forget it.

The "real" world quickly returned. A year or two later, in the 1990s, a powerful need for exile, for at least a short period, made itself felt. Something was amiss, and it couldn't be understood in close proximity. Work with Coudert Brothers and clients such as US West, participation in international conferences, and invitations to speak abroad all provided opportunities for maintaining contact with a rapidly changing world. But they involved too many airports and luggage packing and too little time for reflection. At the Heywood Hill bookstore in London one morning I encountered a former law professor, Robert Stevens, whom I had not seen in years. Did he have any ideas of a university in the British Isles or Europe where a sabbatical might be undertaken? I inquired. As it turned out, Professor Stevens had recently been named master of Pembroke College, Oxford, and after consultation with his fellows, extended an invitation to become a visiting fellow for a term or two. It was a timely and rewarding opportunity and led to residence during the Michaelmas, or fall, term at Pembroke in 1996.

It is very difficult, even for an American, to dislike Oxford, though it has been known to happen. For some it is the experience of being in a place one must have visited in a previous life. Pembroke offered a chance to work on a book on America's second constitutional army, the militia; to explore the rich history and culture of Oxford and its colleges; to attend lectures and concerts; and, come November, to spend a good deal of time commenting on the US presidential election with the British media. Additionally, Coudert had a lively London office and US West continued to broaden its international horizons, so professional travel continued. While I was at Oxford, Mikhail Gorbachev lectured at a packed Sheldonian Theatre and the great Roger Bannister, the first sub-four-minute miler in the world and a predecessor of Stevens as master of Pembroke College, visited. Thanks to the hospitality of the kindly and scholarly Robert Stevens and his fellows, *The Minuteman: Restoring an Army of the People*, which sought to make the argument for restoration of the republican ideal of the citizen-soldier, came to be completed.[38]

Beginning in the mid-1990s, the theory of the republic, its ancient roots and its modern relevance, became a preoccupation. The predecessor to *The Minuteman* was *The Patriot*, published in 1996, which was one of the first of a series of adaptations of Machiavelli's *The Prince* to modern times. These two books, followed by a doctoral thesis later, explored the nature of the republic, its use as a model by America's founding republicans, and its possible applicability to twenty-first-century America. We Americans, of course, consider our form of government as a democracy. But the founders routinely and consistently used the language and concepts of the republic, drawing on ancient Athenian and Roman texts for their ideals. Their training in the classics was not a matter of affectation. They sought to reach back two millennia for governing principles that transcended the intervening centuries of kingdoms, principalities, oligarchies, dictatorships, and chaotic revolutions.

The principles they found in Athens and republican Rome were popular sovereignty, civic virtue, resistance to corruption, and commitment to the commonwealth and the common good. Increasingly throughout the 1990s and before, Americans had insisted on their rights, and in the case of women, minorities, and others, rightly so. In the process, however, citizen duties, what the ancients called civic virtue, got lost. A reprise of the challenge to do something for our country, a direct echo from the Athenian republic 2,500 years before, was not heard in the land. Instead, a "court" had formed in Washington that had its counterpart in seventeenth-century England.

The founders understood that the "country" must challenge the "court," otherwise the nation would be ruled by wealth, privilege, and corruption. For them, as for their republican forebears, corruption did not have to sink to bribery to be corruption. It was, as it was for the Roman republic, placing personal and narrow interests ahead of the common good and the national interest (the commonwealth). Today, in early twenty-first-century America, what is needed is not just new leadership, a change of parties, and different policies. What is needed is a restoration of the republican ideal, an ideal that pits the "country" against the "court," that says that we must secure our rights by performance of our duties, and that places the national interest above the narrow interests of privilege and corruption.

Where the security of the republic was concerned, the ancients chose to rely on the citizen-soldier rather than a standing army, which they believed threatened republican liberty. That is why our constitutionalists insisted on the militia, later to become the National Guard, as the prime defender of the American homeland. That was the argument I made in 1997, in *The Minuteman*, and in 2001, in *Restoration of the Republic: The Jeffersonian Ideal in 21st-Century America*, and which was also made in *Road Map for National Security*, the final report of the US Commission on National Security in the 21st Century, presented to the George W. Bush administration in January 2001. All three of these publications preceded the terrorist attacks on the United States on September 11, 2001. Tragically, the "court" in Washington failed to heed warnings of terrorism's threat and, among other things, failed to train and equip the National Guard to help prevent and respond to such attacks.

Revisiting the ideal of the republic, with its insistence on duty and civic obligation, would offer American students and citizens alike a crucial understanding of the true nature of our nation. It could not come too soon.

Professional duties continued. During a brief stop in Spain in late 1997, I requested a meeting with former Spanish prime minister Felipe González. González had been prime minister for three terms, from 1982 to 1996, first elected at a ridiculously young age. Out of office he was vigorous and highly knowledgeable about world affairs generally and Europe and Latin America especially. In the course of the discussion, Castro and Cuba came up, and he politely derided the anachronistic US embargo and head-in-the-sand failure to deal diplomatically with the nonthreatening island so near the US shores.

Hearing my story about the Church Committee and my failed effort more than twenty years before to see Castro and interrogate him about the events of 1963, González asked if I still wanted to go and, if so, agreed to make arrangements. A few months thereafter, the first of three trips to Cuba in the late 1990s took place. After transiting through Cancun to Havana, Cuban foreign ministry officials escorted me around passport control and to the state guesthouse, used for visiting heads of state. A walking tour of downtown Havana, its historic sixteenth-century Old City, and the once spectacular Malecón, the seafront corniche, revealed what a few decades before must have been a spectacular city. An invitation to meet with Castro at his offices around 10:00 that evening came that afternoon. After waiting in a reception area in the presidential quarters, in El Jefe came. He is a tall man, and no attempt had been made to hide the gray in the beard and hair. He was cordial, polite, and congenial, though reserved. We spoke through his ever-present concurrent interpreter Juanita. After a few minutes he waved me into his office, where we were joined by Ricardo Alarcón, the perennial head of the Cuban assembly, and Felipe Pérez Roque, then chief of staff and later foreign minister.

Starting at the beginning, I reminded him of the 1975 context, the Church Committee, the CIA–Mafia connections, and the complications that presented regarding the Kennedy assassination. He remembered, or pretended to, that this effort had been made. He then began to talk and continued to do so for the better part of the next five or six hours, with very little interruption on my part. Instead of reviewing the history of the early 1960s or dwelling at length on the Kennedy assassination period, one for which a number of conservative groups believed him responsible, he merely said that he had opened all Cuban security files relating to the efforts to assassinate or overthrow him, the Mafia involvement, and the results of Cuban intelligence collections in Miami and elsewhere around the Caribbean to a Brazilian journalist, Claudia Furiati, who had used all this material to produce a book *ZR RIFLE: The Plot to Kill Kennedy and Castro* in 1994, a copy of which he presented.

The book concludes that the Mafia had serious motives for getting rid of Kennedy, especially after his administration had secretly forsworn any further effort to overthrow or assassinate Castro in exchange for the removal of Soviet missiles in Cuba. The Mafia's dreams of retaking Havana and reestablishing its casinos, hotels, prostitution, and drug networks had been dashed. The efforts of Santo Trafficante, Sam Giancana, and Johnny Roselli had come to naught. Left open is a role for Lee Harvey Oswald, but the arrows of culpability all pointed to the Mafia. Castro did not seem interested in pursuing the conversation further.[39]

Into the night and over his dinner table, we discussed, or rather his dinner companions listened to him discuss, world affairs. He brought out his daily briefing books, two-inch-or-more-thick compendia of extracts from the leading newspaper and magazines of the world. Prompted by occasional questions, Castro told stories of the multitude of world leaders he had met and the many convoluted experiences he had had. He registered disappointment at Bill Clinton, whom he had hoped would, at least after his reelection, take up the process of normalization of relations. "Instead," Castro said, "he thought he needed the Cubans [exiles] to carry Miami, and he needed Miami to carry Florida, and he needed Florida to win the election." Shaking his head sadly, he said, "And he was wrong on every level."

Sometime around 4 AM Castro noticed my eyelids sagging and, though bright and chipper himself, suggested he would drive me back to the guesthouse. Outside the presidential palace we entered a plain black sedan with black SUV battle wagons fore and aft and took off at speed through the mostly abandoned Havana streets. Passing early street sweepers here and there, each would routinely drop the broom, come to attention, and salute El Jefe racing by.

The next day a tour of a Cuban health facility that was both hospital and research center was organized. The Cubans had invested heavily in health care over the years, routinely sent doctors and medical personnel to poorer countries, and prided themselves on having the best health-care system in Latin America. After further exploration of Havana, a poor but historic city trying to make a comeback, an invitation to join Castro and his close advisors for dinner at one of a number of hideaways and private residences was provided.

While watching the seventh game of the all-Cuban baseball World Series, play that suffered little in comparison with the US World Series games, Castro reiterated complaints from the night before about continued terrorist harassment by exile groups in the form of offshore strafing of tourist hotels from swift boats and the recent bomb planted in a hotel corridor that killed a tourist. These attacks continue, he complained, and your government does nothing. The clear intent of these systematic attacks was to destroy the emerging tourist economy. In response to requests the previous evening to produce as much documentation of specific times, dates, and places of incidents, together with any intelligence he could provide about their origins, between innings Castro produced a detailed, single-spaced thirty-two-page document in English that was an incident-by-incident account of attacks on Cuba (many presumably originating in the United States) over a number of months. I promised that I would see that it got to President Clinton.

We dined well into the night on a six- or seven-pound native fish, much like a red snapper, caught that day in Cuban coastal waters. Afterward, after no more than two hours sleep, it was off to the airport and back to the States.

While in Washington a few days later, I went to the White House to deliver Castro's evidence. Something had come up with the president, so I was shown into the office of the national security advisor, Sandy Berger, a friend from the McGovern days. He and Clinton, in fact, had become friends those twenty years before. After briefing him on the trip and on Castro's accusations, he said, "I've talked about this to Janet (Reno, attorney general) and Louie (Freeh, director of the FBI), and they claim there's nothing to it." After handing him Castro's brief, he said he would talk to the president, share it with the FBI and Justice Department, and raise the issue again.

A few months later, while back to Cuba, I was anxious to find out the outcome. Assuming Castro wanted to complain that nothing had changed, when escorted once again into the presidential quarters, instead he immediately greeted me with a smile and thanked me. "Since you were here before," he said, "we have had no more attacks." By its crackdown, the Clinton administration was not simply doing Castro a favor. The issue of state-sponsored terrorism had begun to raise its ugly head around the world and, naturally, the United States took the lead in condemning it and committing to eliminating it. Under those circumstances it would not do for the United States to turn a blind eye to attacks on a neighboring sovereign nation that emanated from our shores or that were sponsored by Cuban-American citizens or residents.

On a third trip to Cuba, a bright and engaging woman who had been born in Cuba to a prominent family and who, for purposes of this narrative, we will call Nana, came along. Her family fled during the revolution, abandoning a very large sugar plantation in the southeast and a large home on Fifth Avenue, the Park Avenue of Havana. Her father then joined Brigade 2506, which took part at the Bay of Pigs Invasion in 1961. He was captured and imprisoned with 1,400 other Cuban invaders. After his ransom by the Kennedy administration, he told Nana and others in his family stories of being taunted by Castro through the prison bars and of refusing to denounce the United States or the attempted invasion when challenged by Castro. He was threatened with death in one of the gigantic trials carried out in a sports arena and was twice put before a firing squad without being shot. After spending two years in prison, mostly in solitary confinement, he returned to Florida, then moved his family to New York and made a living initially as a sugar trader. Only after his death could Nana even consider returning to Cuba.

When she learned of my planned trip, with some trepidation she accepted my invitation to go along. Arrangements were made, and her biography was forwarded to Cuban authorities. In the afternoon of the first day of our visit, the foreign ministry escort issued an invitation for dinner with Castro that night, and I asked whether Nana should attend as well. The escort checked and said yes, she was welcome. When we arrived later that evening at the presidential quarters, Nana was a bit of a wreck. She had listened all her life to her father denounce Castro as a demon and a maniac. Here she was, the daughter of one of his attackers, in the very lair of the legendary monster.

To complicate the picture even further, when the Castro brothers, Che Guevara, and the other revolutionaries on the rusty tub *Granma* landed on Cuba's southern shore in 1956 to make a revolution, they had landed on the estate of Nana's family and made their way into the Sierra Maestra mountains, *still* on their property. The coincidences, even forty years later, were eerie. After a couple of hours of political talk, Castro waved us to the adjoining dining room and he pointedly accompanied Nana to the table, quizzing her along the way.

In the wee hours Castro took the occasion to denounce at length the wealthy land owners who had mistreated the overworked peasants and had brought the revolution onto themselves. In what seemed to me mock curiosity, Castro turned to Nana and in Spanish asked whether her family might have been among those cruel oligarchs. Very politely she assured him that both her father's and her mother's families had gone out of their way to improve the lot of their workers.

It seemed to be playacting. Castro had her biography well in advance and knew exactly who she was. He could not resist, however, revisiting the revolutionary era and taking the occasion to pour scorn on all those who had, in his judgment, brought it on themselves. The next day we went to see Nana's family house on Fifth Avenue in Havana. Once a great house of a prosperous family on the capital's most elegant boulevard, the place was decrepit. We ventured inside and were met by a large number of curious but friendly residents. We clearly were not from Cuba, and when Nana told them she had lived in the house as a little girl, they understood the history immediately. Half ceilings and false walls had been constructed to accommodate more beds, and bath and cooking facilities seemed to have become dormitory-like. Nana summoned the courage to ask one of the residents politely how many families were living there. Thirty, she was told.

Nana's mother was certain that if Nana went back to Cuba and presented her passport showing her place of birth as Cuba, she would end up in prison and never return to the United States. There was a delay at passport control upon entry, and anxiety mounted. Her passport was confiscated on the grounds that the Cuban government did not recognize dual citizenship and that Cuban citizenship could not be renounced. Several days later, however, after visiting the old eastern capital, the colonial city of Santiago de Cuba, and Nana's family estate, Nana's passport was returned and we flew back to Cancun.

Along the way when asked whether she would tell her mother that she had dinner with Castro, Nana worried that her mother could not bear it. Nevertheless, we were not in the Cancun airport ten minutes when she called New York and began, "Mother, guess who I had dinner with?"

On the second two trips to Cuba other messages were transmitted back and forth. Eventually, perhaps they will do some good and US leaders motivated by the national interest and diplomacy will have the courage to overcome the temptations of narrow constituency politics and do what is both logical and right and in keeping with the principles of a great nation. This should require no one to die and no celebrations in the streets. Diplomatic relations, it must be repeatedly pointed out, are not signals of approval of any form of government. They are the way mature nations seek to resolve their differences peacefully. The emergence of a new generation of Cuban-Americans publicly willing to seek diplomatic openings, unlike their parents, is a signal that maturity might finally have arrived.

The new Obama administration is undertaking steps that should have occurred years ago toward normalization of relations, but now younger Cuban-Americans are finally demanding it.

It is difficult to spend time in Cuba, particularly given its central role in the Cold War drama, and not have the imagination stirred. That stirring in my case led to two fictional works, written under the pseudonym John Blackthorn, both in the late 1990s. The resort to the pseudonym was less to conceal my visits there and more to focus the attention of the reader and reviewer on the stories, not the author. The first story, *Sins of the Fathers*, had to do with an attempt by a small group of extremist Cuban exiles who, thinking to carry out the lifelong mission of their fathers to kill Castro, conspire to detonate a small nuclear device left over from the Cuban Missile Crisis in the José Martí tower in central Havana on the occasion of Castro's speech marking the fortieth anniversary of the revolution. The fact that it might also kill two or three hundred thousand others does not deter them. The warhead itself they obtained from a Russian arms dealer who had received the warhead, or at least the location where it was still hidden, from his dying father, who had supervised the storage of the device during the missile crisis, in 1962. The plot was based at least in part on the fact that the Soviets had introduced upward of a hundred such missile warheads, known as FRGs to the Soviets and Frogs to us, onto Cuban soil, in addition to the intermediate range missiles we discovered and that were our principle concern. The story was full of action, centered on interesting American, Russian, and Cuban figures, and cinematic, though no one in Hollywood seemed to believe so.

The second story, *I, Che Guevara*, had to do with Castro stepping aside and Cuban politics dividing between a socialist party composed of Castro leftovers and a neoconservative party composed of Cuban exiles with a little assist from the Mafia, still anxious to reclaim Havana. The former party mirrored those that emerged in Eastern Europe when the wall came down, and the latter party, heavy-handedly managed by imported pollsters and media advisors, mirrored the worst of current American politics. Both parties are corrupt and corrupting. Into the mix arrives an elderly man holding forth in coffee shops in small villages, first in the Sierra Maestras and then across the country, preaching an idea he calls the new republic. As the first national election approaches, word starts to circulate that the old man is Che Guevara, mysteriously back from the dead and converted to a new radical politics free of taint. As cinematic as the first story, and as equally neglected by Hollywood, the author outed himself during a television interview to prevent further obfuscation and denials. Alas, it mattered only a little to sales.

The earlier term at Oxford had, meanwhile, stimulated the idea of a return to academia. A hoped-for PhD program in philosophy and religion had been abandoned in 1961 in favor of law school. Now, four decades later, in a fit of whimsy I applied for graduate admission and, surprisingly, was accepted as a DPhil (PhD) candidate at Oxford. Triggered by citizen discontent since the 1970s having to do with their loss of control over their government and their lives, I had been preoccupied with discovering whether some avenue might exist for direct citizen participation in government in a mass democracy of 300 million people. The inquiry repeatedly returned to the ideal of the republic with its demands on civic virtue, citizen assembly, and popular sovereignty.

My search as a lifelong student of Jefferson through his voluminous writings, almost all in the form of tens of thousands of letters, revealed that he had anticipated concerns about citizen participation. Writing to John Adams and others after his presidency and his return to Monticello, Jefferson acknowledged that his fellow founders had left out of the constitutional structure a place for direct and immediate citizen participation. How could sovereignty be asserted and virtue demonstrated when the only citizen task was to vote for candidates?

Short of major overhaul of the Constitution, Jefferson thought, there must be a forum available in which everyday Americans could participate in government. The ward, or elementary, republic, modeled on the Athenian assembly and the Roman forum, was his answer. In this forum, citizens collecting regularly could solve community concerns involving education, law enforcement, security, and all other matters important to the local commonwealth.

The notion was overlooked or dismissed as the impractical ruminations of an aging but restless mind and another of Jefferson's quirky and impractically radical notions. The most radical of the founders by far, Jefferson was accustomed to being dismissed. Very little of the voluminous Jefferson scholarship thereafter focused on the elementary republic notion, especially as the greater American republic expanded and eventually emerged on the international stage. But, as one millennium ended and another began, it seemed timely to explore the notion as it had occurred to Jefferson and to seek to apply it to twenty-first-century America in an effort both to restore ancient republican ideals and to solve the practical problem of citizen disengagement and disenchantment.

Besides which, with an overpoweringly curious mind encompassing multiple scientific and humanistic facets, Jefferson was as close as the American founding came to producing a Ulysses. Restless, seeking, absorbing, exploratory, up to his last days Jefferson sought knowledge beyond the sinking stars and never yielded in his search for a newer world. For anyone seeking knowledge concerning roots to which his nation might recur, Jefferson was a natural focus.

At the end of January 2000, in a flat near St. Antony's College, my assigned college at Oxford, I began to write. Having done months of research and note-taking before, and having outlined the project in considerable detail, draft chapters formed quickly. Composition has always come easily, but this was not a standard work of public policy or government programs. An aspect of the decision to go to Oxford was to test the soundness of these ideas against world-class scholarship and, honestly, to see if an aging student seeking knowledge could pass muster at the intellectual Mt.

Everest. The standard practice was to submit chapters to the thesis advisor, in this case Professor Gerald "Jerry" Cohen, Chichele Professor of Social and Political Theory at All Souls College, and have him critique the submission and suggest ways of making it more intellectually respectable.

On a previous warm-up visit to Oxford, Professor Cohen had given me lunch at All Souls and, though imminently likeable, he was an intellectual force of nature. The product of a working-class socialist family in Montreal, Jerry had the finest analytical mind one could ever hope to encounter. Not by accident was he awarded perhaps the most prestigious chair in political thought in the world, one whose previous occupant was Isaiah Berlin. He let it be known immediately that the only things he knew about Jefferson was that he was a racist and a slave owner. One of the most prominent Marxist scholars in the world would find little in common with Jefferson. Nevertheless, Professor Cohen was more than up to finding gaping holes in logic and theories and was not shy about pointing them out. But he did so with a flair.

He was fascinated by musical comedy and, with less than the drop of a hat, in personal discussion or public lectures, was known to break into spontaneous song, whether to emphasize a profound point or simply because it amused him at the moment. At the close of a term's lectures on complex political theory, and finding (not accidentally) an hour left over, Cohen asked his graduate seminar class whether they wished to leave early or have him sing and tell stories. Some had heard legends regarding this performance, but others seemed stunned. Jerry then proceeded to sing, render impressions of the philosophers of the ages from Plato to Wittgenstein, tell humorous anecdotes, and pose imponderable conundra. It was a hoot. In 1995–96, he was asked to deliver the highly prestigious Gifford Lecture series at the University of Glasgow and, halfway through, at lecture seven, he invited the audience to join him in an evening of sing-along. The printed versions of the lectures contained this notation: "Lecture Seven: Professor Cohen invited the audience to join him in an evening of song." Period.[40]

After producing almost half my thesis manuscript and revising it according to trenchant recommendations by Cohen, he went on sabbatical and Professor Alan Ryan, warden of New College, former lecturer at Princeton and a renowned political scholar and critic in his own right, became my thesis advisor. Given his years teaching in the States, Professor Ryan had greater familiarity with Jefferson and the founding era, was slightly less put off by the slavery question, and helped guide the thesis to completion. Regular meetings with Ryan produced enormous benefits. Like Cohen, he could spot gaps in logic and theory before his questing student walked through his door, and he politely steered this advisee away from embarrassing intellectual flaws. Needless to say, a former American political figure now in his early sixties was not a conventional graduate student. But Oxford being Oxford, and among other things having been the seat of government during the English Civil War, it was up for anything and could absorb oddball, would-be scholars of peculiar dimensions.

Oxford is on a three-term system, Michaelmas (fall), Hilary (winter), and Trinity (spring), with each term approximately eight weeks long. Between terms, other obligations had to be fulfilled. Responsible for assisting US West, now largely reconstructed as Callahan Associates International, worldwide, as well as other clients, and helping Coudert Brothers develop new clients continued throughout. And in October 1998, President Clinton and Speaker Newt Gingrich had collaborated to form the US Commission on National Security for the 21st Century, a variation on my recommendation some years before.

An original member of the commission, I then was appointed cochair with a former Republican Senate colleague

Warren Rudman of New Hampshire. The commission met monthly and was in the process of producing its final, very comprehensive report containing dozens of recommendations for protecting national security and repositioning the United States in the world. When in residence in Oxford, I returned to Washington to share commission duties with Warren. Given these triple duties, these early twenty-first-century years turned out to be among the busiest, if not also among the most productive and interesting, periods of my life. Juggling was not an adequate metaphor for this complex multitasking.

But the duties were not disparate. The national security commission, under the influence of testimony from White House counterterrorism expert Richard Clarke, other senior Clinton administration officials, and noted terrorism experts, had concluded as early as 1999 that "America will be attacked by terrorists using weapons of mass destruction and Americans will die, possibly in large numbers, on American soil." This led us to recommend in our final report in January 2001 that the new Bush administration consolidate federal border protection and emergency response capabilities—Coast Guard, Customs, Border Patrol, and the Federal Emergency Management Agency—under one cabinet-level officer responsible to the president, Congress, and the American people. We also recommended that the National Guard of the various states become the backbone of homeland security in preventing and, if necessary, responding to a terrorist attack.

Concurrently, I was identifying ways in which twenty-first-century Jeffersonian elementary or local republics could engage citizens and become vital parts of the federal system; local public education, public assistance or welfare, and homeland security were designated in my Jeffersonian thesis as illustrations of areas of citizen involvement. With regard to homeland security, the argument was that terrorist attacks were not only plausible but increasingly probable (citing the earlier reports of the US Commission on National

Security) and that, under the US Constitution, the second army, the militia composed of citizen-soldiers, not the standing regular army, should have the duty of frontline prevention and response. Our founders, based on ancient republican principles, did not want a standing army to enforce the laws of the United States. The original militia, acknowledged in three places in the US Constitution, had become the modern-day National Guard, and its first responsibility remained to defend the homeland.

Citing the final reports of the US Commission on National Security as authority for the proposition that terrorism was a plausible threat and that citizen-soldiers were better prepared and constitutionally obligated to respond, my thesis included local security as an instance of how adoption of the Jefferson ward republic might work in twenty-first-century America. Professor Ryan as advisor took it all with a degree of amusement. This was, after all, a work of political *theory* not political science. After Ryan gave his final approval, the thesis, *Restoration of the Republic: The Jeffersonian Ideal in 21st-Century America*, was submitted in May 2001.[41]

Then, in June, came an examination in which successful defense of the thesis was required. On a sunny Saturday morning, in Schools, the brick pile on High Street where seminar rooms are set aside for such purposes, the apprehensive student appeared in "subfusc," dinner jacket (tuxedo), white tie, and academic gown, before two examiners, Professor John Lewis Gaddis, then George Eastman Visiting Professor, and Professor Mark Philp, head of the politics faculty.

A surprisingly high number of Oxford DPhil theses, all the result of years of work, are "referred," a polite term for rejection, for further revision. Once referred, they must then be rewritten, resubmitted, and reexamined. As a mature, or late-in-life, student who had not done serious academic work in decades, the defense was undertaken with considerable trepidation. How embarrassing to tell friends and family that your thesis had been referred and you had at least partly to begin again. Further, by tradition thesis defenses had to be announced, notice given in the *Oxford University Gazette* so that the public could attend and assure itself that degrees were not being handed out by the ancient university willy-nilly. Happily, the examination of a long-retired American politician on an early Saturday morning had gone without public attention. I faced my interrogators, also in subfusc, and Professor Philp waved me to my table and said, "We are going to recommend you for your degree. Now, let's have an interesting discussion." Deep exhalation, it was hoped, would not be heard across the room.

On July 28, 2001, the doctorate degree was awarded at a graduation ceremony in the Sheldonian, roughly forty years after its pursuit had been abandoned, and Lee and I immediately caught the chunnel train through London to Paris, where we joined General Charles Boyd and company for a long-weekend tour and celebration. General Boyd had been the executive director of the US Commission on National Security, successfully organizing seventy-five staff members and advisors, three major reports, and a complex series of hearings and travel. A native of Iowa, educated in Kansas, Boyd had been shot down over North Vietnam in an air force combat aircraft and had spent seven years in prison during much of the same period as John McCain. He was the only POW to return and receive four stars in his service, and had ended his military career as deputy commander-in-chief of the US European Command. In the course of our work, he, Warren Rudman, and I had formed strong ties, an honor for those of us who know him.[42]

Almost a year thereafter, when returning to Oxford to speak at a conference, my examiner Mark Philp came across the room at the opening reception. He pushed his way toward me and said, "I want you to know that I have dined out for the past many months on the story that I examined a DPhil candidate who predicted the terrorist attacks on America *in his thesis*." It may have been a first among the tens of thousands of doctoral theses lodged over the centuries in Oxford's ancient Bodleian Library archives.

Sometime after completing my work at Oxford, Arthur Schlesinger Jr. invited me to contribute a brief history of the James Monroe presidency to the series on the presidency he was supervising. He apparently thought knowledge of Jefferson presumed knowing something about Monroe. That was a dubious assumption, but in the course of research I learned a great deal about Monroe and, as is often the case with those considered minor historical figures, I discovered that he and his presidency were more interesting than American students are normally taught. Monroe was not only the last of the Virginia dynasty begun with Washington (and including Jefferson and Madison) and the author of the eponymous doctrine, he also presided over the Era of Good Feelings, which was characterized by economic recovery, relative peace, and the absence of partisanship, produced by the disappearance of the Federalists as an organized entity.

The project's greatest benefit was to provide an opportunity to know Professor Schlesinger better, an opportunity that could only increase my respect and admiration for him. His theory of cycles in American political history provided a more than plausible account for the pendulum swings in our politics. From his posthumously published diaries, he purportedly considered me some kind of Gatsby-like figure in the 1980s, but he managed to keep that impression to himself when we became better acquainted later. He attended a lunch sponsored by the Century Foundation in New York at which I was invited to summarize *The Shield and the Cloak*, a book outlining a US security policy for the twenty-first century, and my remarks included a quotation from Monroe's secretary of state and presidential successor, John Quincy Adams, in reference to our invasion of Iraq: "We go not abroad seeking monsters to destroy." Sitting immediately to my left with his chin on his chest, and I assumed deep in sleep, Arthur said: "July 4th, 1821."

When the US Commission on National Security finished its work in January 2001, ahead of time and under budget, we were mandated to report to the next president, whoever that might be. It turned out to be George W. Bush, and he would not make himself available. Nor would the new vice president, Richard Cheney. This was a matter of curiosity, let alone a matter for concern. Ours was the most comprehensive study of US national security since 1947. We had prepared fifty specific recommendations for reorganizing our security, agreed to by all fourteen commission members unanimously. Among our commission members we represented more than 250 person-years of experience in defense and security matters. We were warning of a serious terrorist threat and attacks to come. Yet neither of the two national leaders was available to meet with us.

Only one conclusion seems to account for this. One of our original commission members was insistent early on that China represented the next international threat, that we should consider it the next Soviet Union and major superpower competitor, and that we had no choice but to begin a major military buildup to confront China and thwart its global ambitions. Though a prominent Republican, she could not get concurrence from her Republican colleagues Newt Gingrich and former defense secretary James Schlesinger, among others. After a few months she resigned from the commission, in early 1999. The assumption was that she thought our efforts of little consequence because we had not adopted her central thesis. Two years later, her husband would be the new vice president. Perhaps it was that Lynne Cheney had forewarned her husband against paying attention to a historic commission that sought to warn the president and the nation that terrorists were on their way.

The public and press never held the new Bush administration accountable for ignoring this and other warnings. Its standard defense when confronted was that a specific date, place, and time were never given by those of us issuing the warnings. But that is a poor excuse for not immediately insisting on tighter border controls and passport inspections, on identification of those who might carry out threats by training to fly airplanes, for example, or on mobilization and training of security forces and emergency health workers for any eventuality. Besides, the CIA warning of August 2001 did mention al Qaeda, airplanes, and tall buildings, and it was insistent that the threat was elevated.

Years before, a University of Denver graduate student named Condoleezza Rice had helped in my presidential campaign. She also was on the board of advisors of the Center for a New Democracy, a policy center I created after 1984. After a speech in New York in the late spring of 2001, she invited me to visit her in the White House. Our commission had gone out of existence that spring after urging Congress to create a federal homeland security department, and we had no further public mission or authority. Nevertheless, continuing to warn of the impending terrorist threat, I gave a speech in Montreal, to the International Air Transportation Association, ironically, and the Montreal papers carried the headline "Hart Warns of Terrorist Attacks on the U.S." the next morning. That day in Washington I went directly to National Security Advisor Rice's office in the White House. During our brief discussion I urged her and the administration to move more aggressively on homeland security. Though little or no effort had been made by the administration to that point, she promised to take it up with the vice president. That date was September 6, 2001, five days before 9/11.

In 2004, a third pilgrimage to Oxford, this time as a visiting fellow at All Souls College, took place. This was a remarkable experience. All Souls has no students, but instead has perhaps four or five dozen fellows, scholars in residence performing immensely creative study and research from theoretical physics to scholastic philosophy and fields of study in between. Built on two quadrangles with a facade on High Street, the original quad, begun in the fifteenth century, was later influenced by Christopher Wren, and the "modern" quad by his successor Nicholas Hawksmoor. Its towering twin spires glimpsed through imposing wrought-iron gates facing the Radcliffe Camera give the viewer a sense of an ethereal world of learning remote from the turmoil of the outside world. It is set apart even in the midst of a historic university set apart. Additionally, its Codrington Library, with forty-foot ceilings, approximates a cathedral more than any library in the world.

Visiting fellows shared the fellows' dining room with its massive fireplace and looming portraits of ancient fellows and wardens, its stunning but human-scale chapel, and the common-room discourse among men and women of great learning and wisdom. If knowledge was to be had anywhere, it most surely was to be had at All Souls.[43] Ulysses' last voyage in search of knowledge could have landed there happily.

Years earlier, while I was still in office, a respected Washington columnist had written a curious piece that seemed meant to be a character study of sorts, and its theme was that I had a pattern of not finishing things. As I recall, he enumerated several ideas or projects or legislative proposals that I had initiated then abandoned unfinished. This was briefly confusing to me. I had and have an eclectic nature and found many things, including policy areas, of interest and even fascination. But the writer knew, as well as anyone else who studied the subject, that one parliamentarian cannot pass a law and that after making best efforts and failing in forming a majority, perhaps it is best to try another approach or another crusade with a better chance of success.

Thinking back over the years, it occurred to me to try to assess whether a kind of adolescent pattern of leaving things unfinished really did characterize my life. I tried to summarize the evidence. There was the matter of going back to school to finish a doctoral program forty years after it was left uncompleted. The military reform effort and national security projects begun in the 1970s continued throughout my life as the subject of attention and concern in a wide variety of arenas and culminated in the sweeping reports of the US Commission on National Security. My efforts to build bridges to the Soviet Union and then to Russia over thirty years, including a twenty-year friendship with Mikhail Gorbachev, offered evidence of consistency. In 1980, and even before, I wrote articles and gave speeches warning that dependence on Persian Gulf oil would lead us into war in the region and unnecessarily cost American lives, and that cause continues. A lifelong concern for the environment has led me to help organize both national and international projects on climate change since joining the University of Colorado in 2006. One of these is the Presidential Climate Action Project involving the nation's leading experts producing a climate action plan for the president elected in 2008, and the other is a University of Colorado partnership with the Aspen Institute to consider new international institutions to administer a Kyoto II treaty in the hope that one will be negotiated. The theme of republican duty has preoccupied me and my writings for close to twenty years. Education for a technology-based economy has been a continuing theme since the 1970s.

Unlike other officeholders I have also sought, principally through writing, lecturing, and teaching, to promote themes of a lifetime. Then, in 2008, Lee and I celebrated our fiftieth wedding anniversary, a completion of sorts. I am too far along to feel the need to mount personal defenses, but this recitation is undertaken as much as anything to illustrate how wrong some of the country's most respected political observers and analysts can be when they take it upon themselves to peer inside the soul of another human, even a political one. Plus, isn't it a little premature to judge a public figure's stick-to-itiveness while barely in midlife?

Those in the journalistic world often justify their ventures into human psychology on the grounds that "character matters." It does indeed. But qualifications to judge character are not given out with a journalism degree or even the award of a regular column or television panel appearance. There was a suggestion in that very early commentary that it is better to focus on one or two subjects in public office than try to encompass everything. But national leaders do not have the luxury of specialization and should be judged rather on the breadth and scope of their interests, their curiosity and inquisitiveness, and their ability to hold more than one thought at a time. We recently tried the other approach, and it did not work out very well.

A combination of adventurousness and fortune may provide an interesting life. But for that life to become more than a series of anecdotes, an odyssey requires a purpose. Our Ulysses wishes to return to life's troubled seas to seek knowledge in that newer world. It is a question less of whether life's experiences have been interesting, or even unique, and more a question of what lessons those experiences offer and whether one has taken the time and trouble to sort them out and seek some meaning, some knowledge, some wisdom.

An odyssey that has largely taken place in the broad political arena would yield different sets of lessons, one having to do with our system, one having to do with who we are, and one having to do with who we ought to become.

My own odyssey has led to a central conclusion that the United States Constitution is a document of genius and should be amended, if at all, only to expand its reach. Argument continues well into its third century over how literally it should be interpreted and how it should be adapted to new realities. Its core principles, including its basic distribution of powers among three branches, with checks and balances built in, and its bill of rights establishing the basic relationship of the individual to the state, are not and must not be contested.

In this context, the recent political fascination with "values," a code word for doctrinaire religious and social agendas, misses the point. Values are temporal. Principles, especially those embodied in our Constitution, are eternal. In recent years, values language has been used divisively to suggest that some, Republicans, have values, and everyone else presumably does not. Thus, if you have values, you must necessarily vote Republican. But some of those elected under the banner of values have been the most eager to violate the principles embodied in the Constitution of the United States.

We are a republic, which simply means we secure our democratic rights by performance of our civic duties. In our continued struggle to expand and perfect our rights as democrats, we—being both political parties and the nation at large—have neglected our responsibilities as republicans. Thus, the Democratic Republican Party was the closest Jefferson would come to a title for a project he didn't particularly believe in, the formation of a political party. A republic is not self-perpetuating. It requires civic virtue, the duty to participate in the public forum, popular sovereignty, resistance to corruption of the republic by special interests, and a sense of the common good or commonwealth.

We are a commonwealth. There is a quantifiable and definable national interest greater than the fragmented plethora of special interests. We leave a public legacy as well as individual private legacies. It does little good to leave private wealth to our children if we also bequeath to them a hazardous environment, a fragmented society, and a more dangerous world.

Though progress is far from inevitable, it does sometimes occur. After struggling for the better part of a lifetime to control and reduce nuclear arsenals wherever they are found, it is gratifying now to see zero-option projects that would totally eliminate nuclear weapons springing up and even more gratifying to see them endorsed by public figures who were dedicated to the expansion of those arsenals only a few short years ago.

There are social goods and social obligations. Any civilized society, including capitalistic ones, requires attention to those unable to care for themselves. Ideals of individual independence, private resourcefulness, and personal responsibility do not account for those too young, too old, or too infirm to care for themselves. Social concern in a civilized nation is not the enemy of private initiative, and the use of political and economic ideology as a shield from social responsibility is morally unworthy. Blather about "a thousand points of light" and "faith-based initiatives" is merely an excuse to escape a civilized society's obligations to its citizens. Private charity alone, as necessary and worthy as it is, will never suffice to account for the demands of social justice and the requirement for responsibility by a civilized government.

Well into our third century of national existence we must finally arrive at the conclusion that the nation, and the state that governs it, are not the enemies of liberty. Thumping our collective chests and declaring our freedom may make us feel better, but these are not mature responses to the necessities of governance and fulfillment of our national purpose. American citizens are not more or less free under either conservative or liberal governments. Neither socialist nor fascist tendencies have found root in the American character or its political systems, nor will they.

Care must be taken to prevent the perversion of language, the first step toward totalitarianism and the surest refuge of political scoundrels. Success may have been found in recent years in the demonization of liberalism, to the extent few if any political figures would admit to this legitimate and often productive approach to governance, but it was obtained at the cost of serious discourse. Polemic is one thing. Destruction of language is a good deal more dangerous and is the province of scoundrels of every stripe.

For to be liberal is to be tolerant of difference, to be experimental, to avoid judgmentalism, to seek new knowledge and new solutions, to accept the necessity of adapting to change, to be inquisitive, to be enlightened, and to give due credence to the opinions of others, even when they disagree with us. No wonder liberalism frightens some on the Right for whom these qualities are unknown.

We are people of paradox. This is a matter for concern only when we permit our paradoxes to prevent progress, impede our ability to address challenges, or excuse us from mature behavior. Adolescence is characterized by the inability to resolve conflict. For grown-ups, choices must be made. Life is full of contradictions. An individual or a society may be judged by his, her, or its ability to make decisions and stick with them. As vast and productive as our God-given nation is, it cannot do everything and it cannot have everything.

Whether social, political, economic, or otherwise, issues that divide society must be resolved if America is to move on. The callous and cynical political effort to use social division—appropriately called "wedge" issues—to obtain and manipulate political power harms our nation. Sooner or later every American must decide whether he or she is a member of a narrow interest group or a citizen in the nation of America first and foremost.

Beyond care for the structure of our system and the occasional damage we do to it by our behavior, there are lessons in these paradoxes regarding who we might become. Some means must be found to incorporate intergenerational thinking into our public policies. We legislate for the near term. What we decide, or refuse to decide, resonates into the lives of our children and beyond. Yet the political system has little room for or acknowledgment of our moral obligation to future generations.

The preamble to our Constitution declares that we seek a more perfect union, justice, domestic tranquility, common defense, the general welfare, and the blessings of liberty for ourselves "and our posterity."

This is true of our economy, our environment, our relations with the world, the weapons we produce, and the pollution we emit. In fact, there are few matters we attend to in our public arena that affect only ourselves and our generation. The composite of all of our actions, public as well as private, represents our legacy to the future. To neglect the responsibilities this truth represents is to diminish our standing as parents, as citizens, as Americans, and as human beings.

However, our Ulysses is a seeker not a preacher. He has learned many lessons about man and nature, heaven and earth. He wishes to learn more, to seek knowledge, to discover revelations in that newer world. Until he reaches it, if he ever does, his lessons are for him to ponder, to test, and to constantly revise. There is no stopping, no discovery of any one true way. There is only the halting, imperfect, and unending search.

Whether a blessing or a curse, he is forever restless. He must move on. He must inquire. He must search. He must learn.

Though our Ulysses is now old, his mind will be forever young and restless until he dies, until he sails beyond the sunset seeking his newer world.

CONCLUSION
ULYSSES' LAST VOYAGE

The poet is right. Life is an arch through which gleams a newer world that recedes and recedes as we journey toward it. This life seems to me linear and cyclical but not circular, though there have been a surprising number of recurring events. We have had leaders of every kind, some unreflective, like a Washington, and some reflective, like a Lincoln. We tend to trust the unreflective ones as more prone to action in our interest and less likely to take the time for a second guess. But as a young president showed when confronted with the prospect of national if not also global annihilation, the lessons in the history of flawed judgments are instructive.

Humility requires us to accept our destiny, especially when it falls beneath our aspirations. Character is destiny, and my own life is offered as evidence. But not the way that others may assume. Like Ulysses and countless others, what destiny I had was to follow knowledge like a fading star—and in my undoubtedly stubborn way not to yield.

Once in the arena of politics, the farthest star of power had to be sought. Laden with more than a share of ambition, an idealist's improbable efforts have to be justified on grounds of the good uses to which that power might be put. In the process, a searcher may become a name, not a very large name nor the kind of name he might have hoped for, but a name nonetheless, a name that led him to be the guest of kings and governments and notable people of his age and be honored of them all. And, as a name, a flawed idealist, always within the bounds of many human frailties, must seek to bring honor to those dearest to him, to those who honor him with their friendship, and to the nation he is forever bound to serve.

None of us can truly know why we are here, in this place, at this time, and in this life. An early pursuit of philosophy yielded few persuasive answers. Early roots planted deeply in religion provided a faith in things unseen, but no explanation (an *apologia pro vita sua*) for a presence in this life. The closest answer rests in service, service to one's country and to those particularly on whom Fortune has not smiled.

The most concrete version of that abstraction of service is found in the profound and elemental human hope that we might leave a better world for our children than we have found. In that cause, as an idealistic odyssean views the harbor of eternity from a rocky vantage point, a claim to have succeeded cannot be made.

A favorite Gospel parable regards the prosperous man who went on a journey and left differing amounts of money, "talents" they are appropriately called, with three servants, "according to his several ability," with instructions to invest them wisely. Upon his return he settled accounts with his servants, praising the two for having wisely invested their talents and condemning the servant with a single talent for hiding his talent for fear of losing it.[44]

For one who has been given even a modest talent and did not, in the ultimate test, invest it wisely, the prospect of this judgment is harsh. Leaving divine judgment aside, this has remained a heavy burden for many long years and an unknown number yet to come. This burden may also account for the odyssey, the yearning to travel, the rallying of the faithful crew, the search for knowledge, the hope of a newer world before the light fades. How can we know? The human heart has many chambers.

On a plane from New Hampshire to Colorado in May 1987, on a journey home to retire from the turbulence of politics, Tolstoy's book *Resurrection*, the story of a haughty, self-regarding man who wronged others and, in search of redemption, humbled himself, offered instruction. Can the talent given by the Master once lost ever be redeemed?

Ulysses' talent and compulsion—for isn't talent a form of compulsion?—was to seek knowledge and to seek—and perhaps never find—a newer world. To see over the horizon, to look a little farther ahead than most, to anticipate outcomes, including unpleasant ones if patterns of behavior do not change, does not qualify as a talent, but it is a kind of clairvoyance in a minor key.[45]

It has always been a cause for wonder that a nation that sees itself so often as on the forefront of change is yet so deeply conservative at heart. We are powerful in reaction yet resistant to anticipatory action. Much of this has to do with our strong strain of individualism and resistance to collective preparation, meaning government.

Perhaps it will always be thus. In one of the best books ever written on the American character and its duality, *People of Paradox* (for which he received the Pulitzer Prize), Michael Kammen cites Henry Adams's various descriptions of himself as a "conservative anarchist" or a "Unitarian mystic" as illustration of a kind of national schizophrenia or what he calls "biformity."[46] The theologian Reinhold Niebuhr commented on the same confusion: "Our idealists are divided between those who would renounce the responsibilities of power for the sake of preserving the purity of our soul and those who are ready to cover every ambiguity of good and evil in our actions by the frantic insistence that any measure taken in a good cause must be unequivocally virtuous." How could he have so anticipated George W. Bush and the neoconservative agenda, and Guantanamo and Abu Ghraib, unless he saw a paradox in the American character left perennially unresolved?

Our paradoxes are most evident to foreign visitors. The Frenchman Alexis de Tocqueville took note of "the mutability of the greater part of human [American] actions, and the singular stability of certain principles" in America, and the Englishman James Bryce later observed, "They [Americans] have what chemists call low specific heat; they grow warm suddenly and cool as suddenly." John Quincy Adams saw the contradiction as accounting for parties: "Freedom and order were also the elementary principles of the parties in the American Union and...each party sympathized with one or the other of the combatants." "There is both integrity and intrigue in American politics," concludes Professor Kammen. "That is why we believe that our government is weak, stupid, overbearing, dishonest, and inefficient, and also believe it to be the best in the world and would like to offer it to others." He did not anticipate it being offered at the point of a bayonet.

If paradox is endemic to the American character, then it probably precludes resolving underlying contradictions and moving beyond adolescence, where *adolescence* is understood as the inability to resolve conflicting opposites. We could simply shrug and laugh off our paradoxes, except that on occasion they have deadly consequences. One may distrust and disdain government all one wants, except when one has taken an oath to be responsible for it.

Taking terrorist attacks on 9/11 for example, why would our leadership not pay heed to warnings and take steps that might have protected us? After the attacks we rallied with great force against the Taliban and al Qaeda in Afghanistan before wandering off into the Iraqi deserts. But would much leadership have been required to compel the FBI to vitalize its watch lists, or Customs and Border Patrol to tighten their screening of emigrants, or local security forces to report any strange doings at flight training schools? Is not the deeper reason that those elected to govern did not believe in the government of which they had asked to be placed in charge?

A great deal of leadership is common sense combined with a higher degree of alertness and intensity. But if one's political credo is that government does not work very well, one has little motivation to prove otherwise. It is another cause for wonder that those who disparage government try

236

so hard to run it. Perhaps it is that they wish to prove their theory. That was certainly the case in the government's reaction to Hurricane Katrina. A 230-year-old nation is by now old enough to resolve certain contradictions and decide pretty clearly how much government it wishes to have.

It is well known that the size of the national government, both in terms of budgets and numbers of employees, does not diminish under conservative administrations. Taxes may go down, but deficits, predictably, go up. And, of course, the same government that manages the Pentagon also manages the Department of Health and Human Services. It is odd, to say the least, that this government does so well, at least in the minds of many, at the former and so poorly at the latter.

Ideology reduced to dogma is a dangerous thing. It causes people to twist themselves into illogical pretzels and to reduce complex matters to simple blacks and whites in an effort to shape reality to belief. Years of thought and observation have led to the conclusion that adherence to rigid political doctrine is an almost surefire guarantee of suppression of intelligence. No better recent example exists than the early twenty-first century's witness to a return to pre-Enlightenment thinking in American politics and to the rejection of reason and science. Metaphorically at least, witches were being burned and we were asked to choose between presidential diktat and our lying eyes. Regression became the order of the day, and truth had little meaning. "We make our own reality" was the watchword of the George W. Bush administration. By comparison, the Cold War was crystal clear, and Dr. Strangelove was born years too soon.

The greatest casualty of these years was the United States Constitution. The highest officials in the land surrounded themselves with lawyers who were given the mandate not only of avoiding the laws but of bypassing the very Constitution upon which those laws were based. Overnight the first article of the Constitution, giving Congress the responsibility of making the laws and seeing to their faithful execution, was rendered null and void. The third article, bracketing the other side of the presidency, was bypassed by the systematic appointment of ideological judges who were selected according to their willingness to suspend independent judgment and to routinely approve any action taken by the executive, at least so long as the executive was of the right ideological persuasion. Career attorneys for the chief law enforcement agency of the US government were screened by foolish young people for their partisan and ideological purity. Torture was legally defined as rendering permanent bodily or mental harm or death, and everything up to that was permitted. And, to cap it all, the most sacred principle in the law since medieval times, the Great Writ of habeas corpus, was suspended, and an acquiescent, even supine, Congress—including many Democrats—by statute authorized the president by himself to decide when, where, and as to whom the writ was to be suspended, without question or review.

Laypersons, that is, all those not steeped in the law, must understand that this action gives the president or anyone operating under his direction the authority to apprehend anyone he chooses and to place that individual in custody without charges and without access to legal counsel for as long as the executive chooses. If this can happen to one person, it can happen to all of us. This is why the writ is so sacred.

Never in American history has such a systematic suspension of the United States Constitution taken place. And, to compound this historic felony, the American people and the press, the only organized institution in American society given specific constitutional protection, let it happen virtually without a whimper. Even if the ever-vital Constitution regains its health, generations yet unborn will look upon this period with wonder and, one hopes, with outrage and disgust.

We are a conservative nation. Our picture of ourselves is of ragtag fife, drum, and flag bearers marching to the revolution. In reality, once sufficiently frightened, we plead with authority to take our freedom in exchange for protecting us. Patriots, yes. But mostly when the sun is shining and little service or sacrifice is required. One of our remaining glories is the number of young men and women who will willingly march off to war if told by their commander in chief that the nation is threatened. They have been as brave, in Afghanistan and Iraq, as any troops in a long-embattled American history. Their cause is just, even if the president's cause was not. But even if their loyalty is unquestioning, their parents' loyalty to them and to their nation should have demanded thoughtful and penetrating challenges to authority.

Congress so long ago surrendered its constitutional responsibility to declare war that scarcely a senator is alive who last voted for a war declaration. Throughout the conversion of an Iraq invasion to a decade-long Iraq occupation, members of Congress, largely but not exclusively of the president's party, repeated with robotic inanity, "I support the president." No member of Congress ever takes an oath to support the president. Every member of Congress takes an oath to "support and defend the Constitution of the United States." And that Constitution demands that Congress oversee the operations of the executive branch with a skeptical and critical eye. Somehow, in a mere decade, every branch of our constitutional government has let us down and has abandoned its responsibilities.

The issue before the country now is what we are prepared to do about it. Will we insist that the new president, Barack Obama, and those he appoints swear to tell us the truth, the whole truth, and nothing but the truth, and swear to enforce the laws of the land whether they like them or not? Will we demand that those we elect to Congress hold the executive branch to account for the faithful execution of the laws and for putting the national interest before party interests? Will we insist that judges be those most qualified

by judgment and experience to fairly and impartially inter-
pret the laws without ideological biases?

America's best hope is to restore our republican heritage.
Our founders consciously created a republic on a scale never
before attempted, from Athens through the Scottish Enlight-
enment. Our founding was based on principles of federation
and representation, but it also, like all republics before it,
recognized a central truth: the republican ideal is based on
civic virtue, or what we today would call duty, and that duty
is the best, perhaps the only, protection against corruption,
that destroyer of all republics.

A British scholar, Quentin Skinner, has offered the prescription that "we must earn our rights by performance of
our duties." That formula might be amended only to say that
we must protect our rights by performance of our duties. Our
duties are to the preservation and promotion of the commonwealth, all we hold in trust for future generations. This is not
only a political duty, it is also a moral duty. When citizen duty
fails, corruption overtakes and ultimately destroys the republic.

Anger at corruption of our Constitution alone offers no
platform from which a searching odyssean might lecture
fellow citizens. Years of minor prophecy and limited reform
are all that remains of his years in early twenty-first-century
Ithaca. It is rather now to study the harbor, the wind bil-
lowing the sails of the ship, the setting sun, and the arch
wherethro' gleams that ever-retreating world. We do the best
we can, and then we must sail on. But out there, somewhere,
beyond the wine-dark sea, is knowledge, knowledge like a
sinking star, but knowledge nonetheless.

Is there life after politics? is a question surprisingly
often heard. Of course, is the obvious answer, an answer
particularly given by those for whom political office was neither a career nor an obsession. Politics is merely one world
through which to seek knowledge and perhaps in which to
point directions. But it is only one of several such worlds.

In a long essay, *God and Caesar in America*, written in protest against the systematic violation of the First Amendment prohibition against intermingling church and state, a kind of valedictory is offered:

> I have been so greatly privileged that sometimes it almost makes me weep. My story is not all that much different from other Americans born into humble circumstances to upright parents and blessed by fortune. I have experienced economic depression and I have been blessed with a comfortable living. I have attended small-town public schools and I have graduated from great universities of the world. I started without political advantage and I have approached the gates of the American presidency. I have driven spikes into countless railroad ties and I have been the guest of kings.[47]

EPILOGUE

Looking out to sea from his barren rock, our king does not have in mind to return to the land of the Lotus Eaters or even to Calypso. His thoughts and his compass are set on a newer world. There is no redemption in the past, in the effort to repeat old formulas or even old victories.

For Ulysses exhausted nostalgia years ago. He is eternal because he does not look back, he does not worship his past, as extraordinary as it was; he only wishes to see that world toward which the setting sun is headed. He has become a name, and been honored of kings and governments, not for what he has done but because those kings and governments know he will never rest or rust unburnished, he will always strive for knowledge, he will never give up. He will always manage, against whatever odds and at whatever cost, to be a name.

For our age that worships youth, it is notable that Ulysses has no interest in recapturing his youth. He has no jealousy, no envy of the young. He does not long for his youth; he distinctly prefers to seek new experience and new knowledge over repeating old triumphs and previous adventures. He inhabited an age that did not mistake image for wisdom. Long ago he discovered a central truth of human life: we stay young by venturing forth and actively engaging in an ever-changing world, even in life's closing chapters.

After his soliloquy, what happens to our aging restless warrior?

He rises from his barren rock and carefully, with the aid of his staff, picks his way down the steep and rocky slope toward the dimming harbor below. A few of his shipmates, the regulars, sit sipping ouzo as they do every evening at this hour. They rise, bow, and greet their captain and their king.

Where is Your Excellency off to so late? they inquire.

I'm off to resume our voyage, he says, and you, my friends, I challenge to join me once again. You may choose to rust here unburnished, or you may yet again be those whom I know you to be. Man the lines as we sail beyond the sunset. See, the sails are filling even now. The mighty Poseidon, our ancient foe, waits to test us yet again. He mocks us and wonders where we've been all these years. He thunders that we are not up to it.

I say we are! Ulysses shouts. I say no better crew of voyagers has ever lived. For you have proved yourself in every respect to be among those the great Pericles called "men worthy of their city."

Stepping lighter now, Ulysses strides toward the ship. His comrades look at one another, and first one, then another, then all but one or two start after him. They chuckle like schoolboys, they elbow each other, and then the chuckles of their boyhood turn to large-throated laughter of daring men. Echoing the voices of their youth when they first launched for Troy, they say: Why not? What the hell? What do we have to lose? I'm for the king! I'm with Ulysses!

And so, the heavy stone anchor is weighed, the sail fills and is set, Ulysses takes the helm, and they slip steadily out of the harbor, to sail toward the setting sun, but a sun that for them will never set. They may fail again. They surely must. But in the words of the modern poet, this time they will fail better. For, from this, their last voyage, they will not return home again. The great Ulysses and his crew intend to seek, to strive, to find…and never, ever to yield.

APPENDIX

ULYSSES
ALFRED, LORD TENNYSON

IT little profits that an idle king,
By this still hearth, among these barren crags,
Match'd with an aged wife, I mete and dole
Unequal laws unto a savage race,
That hoard, and sleep, and feed, and know not me.
I cannot rest from travel: I will drink
Life to the lees: all times I have enjoy'd
Greatly, have suffer'd greatly, both with those
That lov'd me, and alone; on shore, and when
Thro' scudding drifts the rainy Hyades
Vex'd the dim sea. I am become a name;
For always roaming with a hungry heart
Much have I seen and known: cities of men
And manners, climates, councils, governments,
Myself not least, but honor'd of them all;
And drunk delight of battle with my peers,
Far on the ringing plains of windy Troy.
I am a part of all that I have met;
Yet all experience is an arch wherethro'
Gleams that untravell'd world, whose margin fades
For ever and for ever when I move.
How dull it is to pause, to make an end,
To rust unburnish'd, not to shine in use!
As tho' to breathe were life. Life pil'd on life
Were all too little, and of one to me
Little remains: but every hour is sav'd
From that eternal silence, something more,
A bringer of new things; and vile it were
For some three suns to store and hoard myself,
And this gray spirit yearning in desire
To follow knowledge like a sinking star,

Beyond the utmost bound of human thought.
This is my son, mine own Telemachus,
To whom I leave the sceptre and the isle—
Well-lov'd of me, discerning to fulfil
This labor, by slow prudence to make mild
A rugged people, and thro' soft degrees
Subdue them to the useful and the good.
Most blameless is he, centred in the sphere
Of common duties, decent not to fail
In offices of tenderness, and pay
Meet adoration to my household gods,
When I am gone. He works his work, I mine.
There lies the port; the vessel puffs her sail:
There gloom the dark broad seas. My mariners,
Souls' that have toil'd, and wrought, and thought with me—
That ever with a frolic welcome took
The thunder and the sunshine, and oppos'd
Free hearts, free foreheads—you and I are old;
Old age hath yet his honor and his toil;
Death closes all; but something ere the end,
Some work of noble note, may yet be done,
Not unbecoming men that strove with Gods.
The lights begin to twinkle from the rocks:
The long day wanes: the slow moon climbs: the deep
Moans round with many voices. Come, my friends,
'Tis not too late to seek a newer world.
Push off, and sitting well in order smite
The sounding furrows; for my purpose holds
To sail beyond the sunset, and the baths
Of all the western stars, until I die.
It may be that the gulfs will wash us down:
It may be we shall touch the Happy Isles,
And see the great Achilles, whom we knew.
Tho' much is taken, much abides; and tho'
We are not now that strength which in old days
Mov'd earth and heaven, that which we are, we are:
One equal temper of heroic hearts,
Made weak by time and fate, but strong in will
To strive, to seek, to find, and not to yield.

NOTES

1. Sir Walter Scott, "Patriotism," lines 1–3.
2. "The Death of the Hired Hand," *North of Boston*, lines 122–23.
3. All quotes are from Alfred Lord Tennyson's "Ulysses."
4. That is, until Iraq. And even then, the war in Iraq, more a colonial occupation than a traditional war, would not begin to match Vietnam in its political repercussions, largely because of the absence of a draft.
5. See the author's *Right From the Start: A Chronicle of the McGovern Campaign* (Chicago: Quadrangle Books, 1973). Shortly after this book, my first, came out, Governor Jimmy Carter came through Denver on a political exploration and, at his request, I gave him an early copy. I was later told that it went directly back to Georgia and became a handbook of sorts for key Carter organizers.
6. Already known to cult readers of *Hell's Angels*, Hunter would show up during the Florida primary in 1972 and proceed, according to him, to lend his press credentials to a figure he chose to call the "Boo Hoo," who would then spend a day plaguing the previously front-running campaign of Senator Edmund Muskie by pulling on the candidate's pants leg at every stop of a campaign trip down the length of Florida while loudly demanding that Muskie start telling the truth. Amazingly, few journalists could be found who would verify that the mysterious Boo Hoo was in fact Hunter himself. By then, most of them had become mesmerized by Hunter to the degree that, eventually, they would want to *become* Hunter.
7. Organizing performances by Neil Diamond, Simon and Garfunkel, Nichols and May, and an emerging "kid act" called the Jackson Five.
8. Willie Brown became Speaker of the California State Assembly and then mayor of San Francisco. Ms. Steinem and Ms. Abzug cornered a bewildered campaign manager in the lobby of the Doral Hotel at 4 AM, demanding justification for an intricate parliamentary maneuver they mistakenly felt was gender biased.
9. Segretti's other great invention was to park prostitutes in boats on the canal in front of the campaign hotel and let it be known to one and all that they were available to McGovern delegates, who had merely to show their credentials to move to the head of the line.
10. Possibly fewer, because three were Frank Mankiewicz, Rick Stearns, and Congressman James O'Hara, the convention parliamentarian, and the fourth, myself, lost track of this intricate house of cards on the few occasions when sleep intervened. One of the few coherent accounts of

what happened is contained in Part III of *Right From the Start*, but it would be of interest only to intellectual puzzle fanatics.

11. It must also be said with regard to George McGovern that the ultimate passing to which we are all subject should not become the occasion for critics, who manage still to blame "McGovernites" for the nation's recurring ills, to heap hypocritical praises on the man they have so casually loathed. To them I state, If you have anything good to say, say it now or keep silent thereafter.
12. *Right From the Start*, p. 329.
13. Ibid.
14. US Constitution, article 1.
15. This lesson fell disproportionately on a more or less amateur political figure, myself, who beat the odds twice, not a common occurrence and not one to go without its penalties.
16. In 2005, Margaret Atwood wrote such a story and called it *The Penelopiad* (Edinburgh: Canongate).
17. Many years later I was in conversation with one of my law partners, Ed Matthews, about his pro bono work against the death penalty, and he remarked that he was representing a long-term death row inmate, Don Paradis, in Idaho. I asked him if he had ever heard of Creech, and he said he was in a nearby cell to his client. The last I heard, Creech was still on death row, though the heroic Matthews helped the wrongfully convicted Paradis walk out of the Idaho State Penitentiary a free man after twenty-one years.
18. Though the company still exists, now producing gaming software exclusively.
19. "Where's the Beef?," *Denver Post* column, January 6, 2008, citing an article I wrote in *The Futurist*, December 1981, in which I predicted that we would have to go to war in the Persian Gulf if we continued to increase our reliance on oil from that region, one of many Cassandra-like prophecies from the late 1970s on. We are still involved in our second war in the region, though unwilling to admit to ourselves or others that oil has anything to do with it.
20. A variation of this plan appeared a few years later in *The Double Man*, a spy novel I coauthored with Bill Cohen, a Senate colleague and future secretary of defense.
21. Although I was one of a few votes against the Intelligence Identities Protection Act on final passage, for what seem now to be fairly obscure freedom of speech grounds, its principal purpose had my full support.
22. This newspaper would reemerge in highly questionable context later in my life.
23. It was one of Newman's best roles, though not recognized as such. Once asked why he made a movie so different from most of his others, he said

that he wanted those who thought Gary Hart was bad to know what a
real scoundrel looked like. Mr. Newman and I were acquaintances and,
I like to believe, friends. I recollect, I hope accurately, that he was a con-
tributor to one or more of my campaigns.

24. Editorial, "America's Next Chapter," *The New York Times*, June 26, 2008,
www.nytimes.com/2008/06/25/opinion/25hart.html.

25. "Just Another Word," *The New York Times*, March 19, 2009, www.nytimes
.com/2009/03/22/books/review/Hart-t.html.

26. A week later I followed Barry out of a meeting of the Armed Services
Committee and thanked him for his very generous comments in my
home state. He, of course, knew exactly what he was doing when he
made those remarks. He snorted a laugh and said, "Those damn Republicans. My phone has been ringing off the hook." They wanted him to
retract his statement, and he refused. The father of modern conservatism no longer identified with the protoconservatives who had followed
him through the door.

27. A version of this account appeared for the first time in a *New York
Times* collection of convention stories, August 28, 2008. www.nytimes
.com/2008/08/29/opinion/29hart.html.

28. Most Americans are unaware of how closely our politics are followed by
people around the world. Following the 1984 campaign I was astounded
to be recognized on the streets of Moscow, Paris, and Rome. Emergence
on the national scene had other rewards. In 1985 Lee and I were invited
to dinner at the British Embassy in Washington in honor of Prince
Charles and Lady Diana on their first trip to the United States following
their wedding. Passing through the formal receiving line, I introduced
myself: "Your Highness, I'm Gary Hart from Colorado." Prince Charles
smiled and said, "We know who you are."

29. John's long legs extended beneath President Mitterand's ornate desk.
During the discussion I had a terrible thought. Looking down I saw that
John was not wearing socks.

30. This came in 2009 in the form of a very important book by a career
diplomat and former US ambassador to Russia, Jack Matlock Jr., who
published *Superpower Illusions*, a powerful and persuasive case that
the conventional understanding of the end of the Cold War was almost
totally wrong and thus misled us into tragic imperial ventures such as
the invasion of Iraq.

31. We all, one way or the other, give cause for disappointment. I have taken
to national television to apologize for mine. But disappointment is a
two-way street. It is disconcerting, to say the least, to see nationally
respected journalists say on television and write in papers things about
oneself that you know they know not to be true.

32. If ever remembrance there may be, I hope that Martin O'Malley will sing

in his clear tenor voice the lyrics of Thomas Moore's "The Minstrel Boy."

33. It never occurred to me to stay in Washington. As a place to live, Colorado suffers no comparison. As small-town Kansans, my sister, Nancy, and I had taken the train to Denver toward the end of World War II to spend a week or two with our father's brother. He showed us the glories of the mountains, and thereafter, from the age of seven, I never doubted that this would be my home.

34. I was in and out of Athens a number of times on business in the early and mid-1990s. On one occasion friends insisted that I meet the actress Melina Mercouri. We went to her home, where her husband, the director Jules Dassin, met us, and presently the great actress, elegantly turned out, made a theatrical entrance down the stairway. After being properly introduced, Ms. Mercouri presented a decorative cigarette case. "Do you smoke?"she asked in her idiosyncratic husky voice. I said, "No, I'm afraid I don't." "Coward," she responded, and proceeded to light up. Sadly, within a year she died of lung cancer.

35. *Russia Shakes the World: The Second Russian Revolution and Its Impact on the West,* (New York: HarperCollins, 1991).

36. The letter read, in part, "After consultation with all parties, you should appoint a 'personal representative' to observe, monitor, and report to you on the progress of further peace negotiations, with an emphasis on seeking new formulas to facilitate progress."

37. I also called to Clinton's attention that almost a half century after the end of World War II, Russia and Japan were still technically in a state of war, never having resolved the lingering dispute over what the Japanese call the Northern Territories and the Russians call the Kuril Islands. Japan needed Russian raw materials, and Russia needed Japanese finished products. Peace and trade would benefit both. Unfortunately, I was apparently less persuasive in this case than in the case of Ireland.

38. During this period of the 1990s, I continued to write books, both fiction and nonfiction. One of these, *The Good Fight*, a semiautobiographical effort recounting the travails of a political reformer in a nation plagued with assassinations and with more conservative resistance to change than that nation understood, made a *New York Times* Notable Books list in 1995. Much influenced by the classic *The Education of Henry Adams*, this book was largely written in the third person. This "voice" drove my publisher at Random House, Harry Evans, to near distraction. The reform efforts included military reform, campaign finance reform, and economic, energy, and intelligence reform efforts over a number of years.

39. Claudia Furiati, *ZR Rifle: The Plot to Kill Kennedy and Castro,* (New York: Ocean Press, 1994). ZR Rifle was the CIA code name for an "executive capability," or assassination assets. Based on the files made available by the Cuban security services, Furiati concludes that the same cabal of

Mafia, exile Cubans, and more or less renegade CIA personnel carried out the assassination of John Kennedy more successfully than it had the plots to kill Castro. She accords a larger role for the colorful William Harvey in all this than the Church Committee did.

40. Professor Cohen passed away at much too young an age in August 2009.
41. This thesis was later published by Oxford University Press, 2002.
42. Thanks to General Boyd's friendship with Lance Armstrong, we watched Armstrong win his third Tour de France from near finish line seats on the Champs-Elysées.
43. While at All Souls, I completed the draft of *The Shield and the Cloak: The Security of the Commons* (Oxford University Press, 2006) and edited the manuscript on the Monroe presidency.
44. Matthew 25:14–30.
45. As evidence, the epilogue to my first book recognized, perhaps before others, the end of the New Deal era and called for the Democratic Party to adapt its policies to a new and changing world in order to produce the social outcomes the party stood for. Earlier than most, in the mid-1970s, I tried to call attention to the twin tidal waves of globalization and information beginning to sweep across the country. I predicted wars in the Persian Gulf brought on by our oil dependency during this same period. Along with other new leaders, we urged attention to environmental safety to prevent destruction of the planet. Following my initial meeting with Michael Gorbachev, in 1986, I predicted the end of the Cold War. Earlier I helped found a military reform movement to adapt to the changing nature of warfare. I warned of campaign finance scandals and was the first to reject special interest money in a national campaign. In 1979, I warned that a taxpayer bailout of Chrysler would set a precedent for failed corporations for decades to come. Most recently and most sadly, our warnings of terrorist attacks were to no avail.
46. Michael Kammen, *People of Paradox* (New York: Knopf, 1972).
47. *God and Caesar in America: An Essay on Religion and Politics* (Golden, CO: Fulcrum Publishing, 2005).

INDEX